CHINA TODAY

HOW POPULATION CONTROL,

HUMAN RIGHTS, GOVERNMENT

REPRESSION, HONG KONG,

CHINA TODAY

AND DEMOCRATIC REFORM

AFFECT LIFE IN CHINA AND

WILL SHAPE WORLD EVENTS

INTO THE NEW CENTURY

DONALD SHANOR &
CONSTANCE SHANOR

ST. MARTIN'S PRESS
NEW YORK

For Rebecca, Lisa, and Zoë

Design: Junie Lee

Photographs: Donald and Constance Shanor

Library of Congress Cataloging-in-Publication Data

Shanor, Donald R.
    China today : How population control, human rights, government
    repression, Hong Kong, and democratic reform affect life in China and will
    shape world events into the new century / Donald Shanor and Constance
    Shanor.
        p.   cm.
    ISBN 0-312-11759-0
    1. China—Economic policy—1976–   2. China—Social
conditions—1976–   3. China—Social life and customs—1976–
I. Shanor, Constance. II. Title.
HC427.92.S498   1995
338.951—dc20   94–46637
                                                       CIP

First Edition: March 1995
10 9 8 7 6 5 4 3 2 1

After Five Dynasties' turmoil and strife
The clouds dispersed and revealed the sky
Refreshing rain brought old trees new life
Culture and learning once again were high
Ordinary folk in the lanes wore silk
Music drifted from mansions and towers
Under the heavens all was serene
Men dozed off at noon midst gay birds and flowers

—TANG DYNASTY (618–907) POEM
TRANSLATED BY SIDNEY SHAPIRO

CONTENTS

FOREWORD

The authors lived in China for the 1984–1985 academic year and returned twice for four months of reporting and travel in 1987 and 1993. Donald, a professor at the Columbia University Graduate School of Journalism, was asked by the Chinese government to teach journalism to graduate students enrolled in the Chinese Academy of Social Sciences; Constance joined the international division of the Xinhua News Agency in Beijing as an editor or "polisher," the Chinese term.

The mid-1980s were a good time to be in China. The economic reforms had begun to take effect and ferment; new openness and optimism were readily apparent, even to foreigners. During that year we met Chinese from all walks of life and traveled throughout the country, sometimes as guests of our Chinese hosts, sometimes on our own, braving rowdy, rambunctious ticket lines to get on overcrowded trains, coastal steamers, canal boats, and peasant buses.

We bought our groceries in the Chinese markets and cycled to work with the streams of Beijing commuters or into the countryside on excursions to villages and farms, temples and palaces. We studied the Chinese language, puzzled over the newspapers, and watched the nightly television news, historical dramas, and operas.

As we saw the results of China's new policies and realized what it meant for the everyday lives of the Chinese we had come to admire for their warmth and kindness, their patience and ingenuity, we developed a deep interest in and concern for China's future. That twice pulled us back for visits: for three months in 1987 and again for a month in 1993.

During our stays in China, we traveled to at least twenty of the thirty provinces and autonomous regions as far north as Inner Mongolia, and as far west as Xinjiang and Tibet. We sailed down the Yangtze from Chongqing to Shanghai, through the Three Gorges, and hiked along the Yellow River. We watched factories rise in the four original special economic zones and markets blossom in our old Beijing neighborhood. We also had the opportunity to conduct scores of interviews with officials in party and government in villages and cities. We were guests in peasant homes and visitors to quarries and factories. We attended dozens of briefings by academic and official sources. Best of all, we got to talk to a range of ordinary people in the cities and countryside.

On each subsequent visit to China, we saw the amazing changes in city skylines and farming landscapes, and learned of the problems that keep turning up to impede even more rapid progress.

This book is about China as we saw it and understood it. With a country so vast, so varied, with political and economic scenarios unrolling so rapidly, we approached the task with some humility. We made the fullest possible use of the views of observers more expert than we, in China, in Europe, and in the United States. Many of them cannot be given credit by name, for obvious reasons.

As for the statistics and numbers we have written here, it seems impossible to quantify anything about China without citing millions, tens of millions, even hundreds of millions. But even the Chinese confess to inaccurate statistics and numbers.

Deng Xiaoping himself cast doubt on the accuracy of government statistics in a 1974 conversation with the Massachusetts Institute of Technology sinologist Lucien Pye. Deng explained that "local authorities report all kinds of numbers, some thinking it good to have a high number because it might give them more rations and benefits, while others would deflate their numbers because they were worried that they would be assigned higher quotas and made to pay more to the state." In any case, all Chinese movements, projects, or reforms involve enormous numbers. We have sought to use them carefully and accurately.

We respect the work of sinologists, as some of our interviews and acknowledgments show, but we approached the task of examining and explaining China as journalists, not specialists.

What we have written is intended for the general reader, in the hope that it may help to explain what has gone before in China, what life is like there now, and what may happen in the future.

In addition to the many Chinese men and women who cannot be identified, we are grateful for the help of Rick and Fritzi Shanor, James Aronson, Jim Anderson, Sheila Carney, Bridie Cooke, Derek Davies, Robert Delfs, William Eaton, Ulli Franz, Alex Frere, Amos Gelb, Carl Goldstein, Diane Goon, Jeff Greene, Kelly Haggart, Simon Johnstone, Robert Korengold, Julia Leung, David Lindorff, Bryan May, Bill Middleton, Andrew Nathan, Katy and Chester Peake, Robert Petretti, Lucien Pye, Linda Rogers, Louise do Rosario, Steven Ross, Jay Sapsford, James Seymour, Stephen Toth, and Sophia Woodman. Our editor, Barbara Anderson, deserves special thanks for another job of long-distance guidance.

None of the individuals or institutions that helped in the preparation of the book can be held responsible for its imperfections, content, or findings, which remain solely our responsibility.

Donald and Constance Shanor

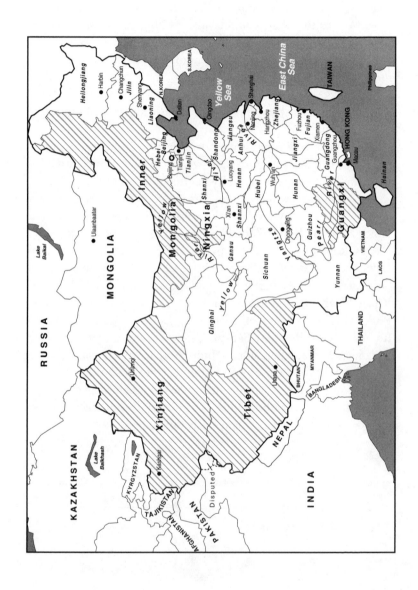

PART ONE

CHINA'S PRIORITIES
AND PROBLEMS

China must come to terms with new conditions in international relations and the pressures for political and social change at home. Its old adversary, the United States, has emerged as the world's sole superpower and appears determined to use its economic position to encourage political liberalization. But China is already trying to adjust to a domestic problem greater than that of human rights, the pressures of population growth that resist all government measures to contain them. This part addresses those issues, along with the history that may help explain them.

ONE

REFORM: THE ACHIEVEMENTS TO DATE AND OBSTACLES TO FUTURE GROWTH

Just inside the gates of a new factory in Shanghai, drummers with sweaty headbands beat on red lacquered drums the size of wine vats to the accompaniment of the clanging gongs of other musicians. Young women in tan hostess uniforms pass out literature, stepping around the strings of snapping and popping firecrackers. The noise, the festivities, and the bilingual information packets announce the opening of another enterprise in the belt of suburban land along Shanghai's ring road. Bicyclists stop to watch the black Japanese sedans enter with officials and businesspeople, and the men and women wedged standing in the city buses that pass by look on with pleasure and perhaps anticipation of job opportunities.

With greater or lesser fanfare, 350 of these business openings or expansions take place across China on an average day. They are a main factor in the average annual growth rates of nearly 10 percent that have been recorded since Deng Xiaoping's team of economic reformers started opening up the marketplace, little more than two years after the death of Mao Zedong, at the end of 1978.

Hundreds of millions of Chinese enjoy a better standard of living; the Chinese Communist Party's grand plan to loosen economic controls and reward individual effort has changed how much of China looks and how much of its population lives. Workers have left their secure but low-wage jobs at state enterprises for the much better paying ones in free-market businesses and factories. Chinese men and women who have struck out on their own sell everything from building materials to socks, home-grown vegetables to smuggled CDs, from stalls in village markets and along city sidewalks. Private restaurants, some no larger than four oil-clothed tables, compete for sidewalk and commercial space with shoemakers, candied-apple sellers, and barbers. Carpenters and other skilled workers stand on busy intersections to advertise their availability with hand-lettered signs. Consumer goods are everywhere. They're stylishly displayed in the new boutiques of the cities and piled high on bicycle carts in the farm markets.

The loosening of party and state control that was pervasive in every aspect of economic life for so long is creating a new China by reviving the traditional, lively talent for business and trade of old China. The Chinese were renowned throughout Asia as merchants and controllers of wealth and commerce. Prerevolutionary China swarmed with private businessmen and -women, moneylenders, artisans, small manufacturers, and hawkers. After decades of near-complete state control, the initiative that had been virtually wiped out burst forth again with astonishing speed, enthusiasm, high hopes, and energy.

China's economy is booming. There is no shortage of optimistic predictions that China is only at the beginning of its economic growth and will inevitably surpass Japan, Europe, and the United States in a matter of decades or even years. But China also faces myriad problems—some exacerbated by liberalization and reform, others left over from four decades of Communist rule. These economic, political, social, and infrastructure obstacles must be overcome if China is to achieve real prosperity, let alone overtake its rivals.

First, the achievements. The first was the bold decision taken by the Communist Party in the early 1980s to return the nation's farmland to its 950 million rural residents, in fact if not in title. This sweeping step was the largest single privatization undertaking in history. In contrast to the delays and half-measures in the former Soviet Union, it gave peasants instant incentives to work harder and produce more. As important, it put them on the side of the party and reform. Soon the farmers were organizing factories and trucking companies, hotels, and restaurants.

This largely unplanned burst of free enterprise, in the cities as well as the countryside, was the second achievement. Instead of a system where working for oneself was penalized, as it had been under Mao, China got slogans that called on one and all to get rich. Starting with peddlers and artisans, the system grew to include investors and financiers. Ordinary citizens won a direct stake in prosperity, whether at the basic level of trading in the free markets or the more sophisticated buying and selling on stock and property markets.

The third achievement of the reforms was to attract foreign investment and participation in the Chinese economy, with promises of tax breaks and high profits in an emerging market. U.S., European, and Japanese investors led the way, but drew back after the repression of the democracy movement in 1989. At that point, the Chinese abroad—in Hong Kong, Taiwan, and other parts of Asia—stepped in. Their success and the receding images of the bloody crushing of the demonstrators at Tiananmen Square drew the West and Japan back in. But none or very little of this investment, joint ventures, and foreign-owned banks and factories would have been likely had the Chinese people themselves not taken the lead.

In permitting the reforms, the Chinese Communist Party was helping to compensate for the lost decades when its social experiments caused millions to starve to death and impoverished the rest of the nation. Now the party owes even more to the Chinese people. They made the reforms work and made the party look good. There are signs, however, that this unspoken social contract is beginning to come apart.

Despite a decade and a half of nearly unbroken economic successes, it is apparent that all is not well in China. The economy is subject to recurrent overheating; inflation and the national deficit have soared to uncomfortable heights. Shortages of raw materials and energy, inadequate telecommunications, and transport bottlenecks hamper production. And although the Communist Party has discovered it can macro- and micromanage the economy, it also has come to realize that liberalization and reform pose serious threats to its power and control.

In many parts of the country, peasants incensed over being paid for their grain in IOUs and over their growing tax burdens have rebelled against the party officials they hold responsible. Nervous officials have had to deal leniently with peasant leaders.

Factory and construction workers have joined the protest movement. Chinese officials confirmed that 10,000 strikes and other incidents of labor unrest took place in 1993. In 1994 thousands of workers staged a two-week wildcat strike at the Ertan Dam in Sichuan, China's largest construction project. The strikers won 30 percent wage increases, matching rural inflation rates. "There is clearly widespread, spontaneous industrial unrest emerging," Robin Munro of Human Rights Watch/Asia said.

With a population of 1.2 billion, the largest in the world, the Chinese government has the Sisyphean task of providing more housing, more education, more jobs, more of everything for many years to come. The state-imposed policy of one child per family to control population growth has encountered stiff resistance domestically; reports of infanticide as well as government-enforced abortion and sterilization have drawn harsh criticism from abroad.

A fast-growing population raises the specter of unemployment in the tens of millions. Liberalization policies that relaxed the restrictions of residence permits and ration cards precipitated a population shift from countryside to cities. More than 100 million underemployed men and women from rural areas have gravitated to cities seeking work. An equal number of laborers in the countryside are considered surplus. Neither group is counted in the official estimates of 4 to 5 million urban unemployed.

There is worse to come. The planners have ordered a 25 percent personnel reduction in the overstaffed, money-losing state-run enterprises that employ 110 million workers. As China pares down its 3-million-member army, it sends at least another half million more young, often unskilled workers into the labor market. Foreign and private firms may be required to hire ex-soldiers. And the labor contract system that is gradually being implemented, allowing managers to hire and fire, eventually will apply to all labor.

Some of the small cooperative enterprises that sprang up in the 1980s in towns and villages are failing. With few competitors, they did well in their first years, but now foreign and joint venture rivals are appearing to cut into their market. Some have responded to the challenge with modernization and productivity gains, but others are lagging: ill-conceived, impractical, and undercapitalized. Consumers who once bought anything they produced have become more selective, and the rural industries have little expertise in marketing or advertising.

In spite of early triumphant reports in the media of millionaire farmers, many people in the countryside have fallen farther behind as their brethren working in the cities, joint venture industries, and the booming special economic zones with their tax and customs concessions, have become richer.

Corruption and crime, petty and major, perhaps inevitable in a period of such flamboyant expansion, have flourished along with the opportunities to make deals, reap unheard of sums of money, and get rich. Party officials and bureaucrats, as well as ordinary citizens, have been tempted by illegal opportunities to make money. In Anhui, a province in eastern China that is one of the nation's poorest, one in five provincial officials, a total of 300,000, were caught in an anticorruption sweep that found they had embezzled or misspent more than $100 million in public funds for private homes, gambling, or prostitution. Nationwide, there have been hundreds of executions of government or party workers, most of them lower ranking, for corruption.

The People's Liberation Army (PLA) has become a major factor in the Chinese economy, dealing in arms, trading in currencies, and running a variety of businesses, from small hotels to TV game shows that simulate warfare. Although the military has published a list of the "ten nos" of forbidden business transactions, including smuggling, PLA units account for much of the piracy in Hong Kong waters, and at least one general was dismissed for smuggling in 1,000 cars from Korea. One PLA subsidiary supplies some of the assault weapons sold in U.S. inner cities.

So far, China's new prosperity has not been distributed uniformly throughout the country and among its citizens, creating wide areas of resentment and dissatisfaction. Urban workers make at least four times the pay of rural workers. Development and investment and rising incomes have grown largely along China's coast and in the Special Economic Zones, leaving huge inland provinces as undeveloped and poor as ever.

Inflation that regularly tops 20 percent and is as high as 30 percent in some regions has led to widespread fears and grumbling against government policies. Chinese who were accustomed to state-subsidized groceries, utilities, transportation, and rents, particularly the elderly, the poor, and the retired, are frightened and angry. Measures to rein in credit to lessen inflation and to reintroduce price controls create a fitful stop-and-go pattern for the economy and financial planning.

Statistics are apparently used as much to deceive as to inform. Chen Muhua, a leader of the National People's Congress, reports that China will reform its statistics law to curb deception. "The accuracy and timeliness of figures has been severely affected" by fabrications and exaggerations, the *People's Daily* said. Currently officials at the provincial or village levels can find loopholes to report income inaccurately in order to qualify for more government money, or conversely to overreport some figures to receive promotions or awards.

Electricity shortages are endemic. The demand for electric power created by continually increasing industrial and consumer consumption has caused a 20 percent shortfall. Power cuts regularly black out offices and factories in major cities. Only the sparsely populated and little-industrialized Northwest has sufficient supplies of electricity. More than 120 million people in eight provinces and regions have no electricity at all.

Freight terminals are so crowded and rail lines so overloaded that Shanghai businesses must reckon on a forty-five-day wait for freight to arrive from Xian—only 800 miles distant. On passenger trains, travelers help each other in and out of windows because the aisles are so packed.

Catching up with supply to meet demand will be like the task of the Sorcerer's Apprentice.

Unrest and dissatisfaction also has surfaced more openly and even violently among some of China's fifty-five minorities, particularly the Muslims and Tibetans. The rise of new, independent states along the Chinese border since the breakup of the Soviet Union has aroused and fired nationalistic desires within China.

Two chronic deficiencies, poorly educated workers and inadequate infrastructure, may slow China's breathtaking growth. An official of the Education Ministry says the worst damage of the Cultural Revolution was to education: "We lost two generations." China will eventually catch up with enough engineers, physicians, and skilled personnel to compete in the modern world. But in a country that built roads, dams, and railways with barefooted workers equipped only with shovels and baskets, acquiring enough capital and equipment to rapidly modernize the overburdened transport and telecommunications systems is a major concern.

The greatest risk to the Chinese Communist Party leadership in pursuing the nascent free-enterprise system it has labeled the socialist market system is the loss of its own power and control. China's leaders have wholeheartedly embraced Western technology and welcomed the foreign investment that has been crucial for industrial modernization, but the reforms and the opening to the world have led inevitably to a relaxation of the total government control that once permeated daily life in China.

The result are moves inside and outside party ranks to assume some of the power. Increasingly independent party officials and provincial leaders are defying directives from Beijing and seeking their own paths to prosperity. Dissidents, regrouping after the 1989 crushing of the democracy movement at Tiananmen Square, are demanding more political freedom. The party's central authority seems incapable of coping with either kind of rebellion.

Many Chinese blame an inflexible, aged leadership for this political paralysis, but other, more perceptive critics point to the failure of the system itself, not the men who lead it. A single-party state, whether run by one leader or a handful of men, may have been equal to the challenges of revolution and civil war, but finds it increasingly difficult to manage the flexibility and openness needed to compete in today's world.

A country with unbounded economic potential thus remains burdened with a political system that seems almost designed to thwart great power status, whether economic or political.

At the heart of the system are three flaws that history shows have crippled the most powerful Chinese rulers, ancient and modern, and defeated those with the most potential. First, there is no mechanism to bring about a peaceful, logical, generally acceptable change of leadership. Like the ancient medieval guilds, the Chinese leaders choose their own successors in a secret cabal and then hope the nation accepts them. If not, military force stands behind their choice until the next conclave produces an alternative. Second, the electorate has no way to control the leadership through provincial and national legislatures. Although the huge representative bodies that the party permits have begun to show a few slight sparks of initiative or opposition, people and leaders alike still dismiss them as powerless. Third, an independent legal system is needed to make sure that laws the legislature passes have validity, that elections are held regularly, and that power is not usurped.

These institutional shortcomings have been noted by commentators on China for at least a century, whether the nation was ruled by emperors, warlords, or Communists. China's potential to become a world power has been chronicled much longer. Anyone "traveling from the mud and disease of Tudor London via the tepee settlements of North America to the Ming mandarinate of sixteenth-century Beijing would have guessed without a millisecond's hesitation that China would lead the world for centuries to come," Christopher Patten, British governor of Hong Kong, has written. China's past superiority in technology, civilization, military and naval power, and industrial might have seemed too great for any other nation to compete against. But, as it turned out, China's governments were not able to adapt to change; Britain, Europe, the United States, and eventually the rest of Asia caught up with China and then passed it.

Now the predictions of a Chinese Century are proliferating again. The time spans vary, but a common theme is that before very long, China, the most populous nation on earth, will become the richest as well. Every optimistic projection of China's power in the world—as a vast market for imports, as an equally great source of exports, as a diplomatic or military ally or adversary—fails to consider the political weakness and instability that has kept giant China a sleeping giant for half a millennium.

Chinese officials, however, equate change with chaos. Hundreds of millions of citizens cannot simply be given the ballot, they say. Representative bodies such as the National People's Congress must work within limits; decades of education must come before fuller democracy can be attempted.

Some ordinary citizens agree that the alternative to strong leadership is chaos. Given their limited experience with democracy and China's recent history, this isn't surprising.

War and civil disorder is something most Chinese, even the young, know quite a bit about. The Civil War in the United States is a century and a quarter distant, but China's ended less than half a century ago, and its cost was greater: twice the number of battlefield deaths, around 1.2 million, compared to America's 650,000. More important, the defeated forces are still intact, on Taiwan, with a record of economic and political success that makes the winners and their people envious and nervous. Nothing outside China compares with the 1958 Great Leap Forward, when at least 20 million Chinese died of starvation, or the Great Proletarian Cultural Revolution of 1966 to 1976, when government, economic growth, and education all but stopped, but their cost is known to every Chinese family.

The potential for chaos continues, and here the parallels with the

United States are closer. Ethnic tension and incipient violence held down by superior armed force are bigger problems among the Muslims in the Xinjiang Autonomous Region and the Tibetans than they are in America's inner cities.

But there is also great potential for democratic reform. China need look only to its immediate borders for examples. South Korea has ended military rule and replaced it with a functioning democracy. Japan has broken the power of the Liberal Democratic Party for the first time since the end of World War II, and Taiwan has produced a viable opposition to the ruling Kuomintang. Russia is also an example, although not an entirely reassuring one. Russian difficulties with democracy notwithstanding, Chinese do understand how political inflexibility not unlike their own caused the Soviet Union, China's one-time model, to collapse.

But in contrast to the talk of political reform we heard at every interview and briefing ten years ago, even Chinese officials who consider themselves liberal say that democracy, as the West or even Taiwan and Japan understands it, is no longer on the agenda. Their argument, buttressed by the ever-upward growth charts on office walls, is that a healthy economy that benefits all or most of the nation's millions is the *Chinese version* of democracy.

They further argue that this growth can continue only if the current leadership is undisturbed by challenges and distractions such as elections and parliaments. Some add quietly that these leaders, a mixture of ancient warriors, younger careerists, and skeptical modernizers, are the likeliest force to rid the nation of communism in every way except perhaps the statues, the forms, and the label.

Whether the traditionalists or the modernizers take over in the vacuum following the death of Deng Xiaoping is the question of the hour in China, in the same way that succession has dominated so many other crucial periods in the nation's history.

No one can accurately predict which individual or group of men will succeed Deng, but it can be safely said that a power struggle rather than an orderly transfer of power is likely. Chinese history is replete with examples of these struggles. In the most recent, it took many years for the succession to Mao to work itself out. Even the popularity of the reforms is no guarantee of their permanence. Deng has had to defend them constantly from opponents within the party.

If the traditionalists win, China would survive as a museum of communism, perhaps at the risk of a South-North division, with the commercially oriented states south of the Yangtze joining forces with returned Hong Kong while in Beijing, leaders and the military split ideological hairs over the various forms of "commodity socialism." Under these circumstances, the economic modernizers could still send gross domestic product (GDP) growth lines upward, but China's prospects for real prosperity and leadership would be limited by party cronyism and corruption.

The most favorable course is one derided by both the conservatives and the current liberals, which is to accept the plea the dissident Wei Jingsheng made in 1979 and paid for with fourteen years of political prison: Modernize the political system as you modernize the economy. Rule through sharing power, not dictatorship.

Wei's cry was taken up by the democracy movement's demonstrators in 1989. It is fiercely opposed because in the fifth decade of Communist rule, no Communist leader is likely to want to bet his job on voter approval. ("In a free election, would we have chosen Li Peng?" student democracy marchers asked on a banner.)

But elections are only one facet of democracy. The real target of the political reformers is the infrastructure of democracy, something that most people take for granted in an established democratic state. Before there can be meaningful elections, there must be a reasonable and universally accepted legal system, to guarantee not only the elections but also the executive and legislative processes that will follow them. To interpret this law, an independent judiciary is needed. To guarantee its independence, a real legislature must be able to pass laws rather than rubber-stamp directives from the leadership. Independent regulators must be able to police industry, the environment, the stock exchanges and marketplaces, the accounting and the statistical reports.

Since Deng's opening of China to the West in 1978, legal and constitutional experts have been crisscrossing between China and Europe, China and America, perfecting plans that, as every new nation or regime hopes, would adopt the best of the existing systems and avoid the worst. What is lacking, however, is the political will to introduce even the most modest of these plans to the public. The party has no stake in sharing power; acceptance of free elections or independent regulators would mean an end to the system in which the word or gesture of a party functionary is final.

And yet, unless these steps are taken, China will not be able to take its place in the modern industrial and commercial world, to compete with entrepreneurs and traders largely unfettered by their governments. Without democracy at the grassroots level, China's enterprises will continue to be allowed to pollute; to permit horrendously unsafe practices in the workplace; to buy, trade, and stockpile scarce materials as if they were independent principalities. Without relaxation of central control on economic policy, China's banks will continue to make decisions with political dimensions, not purely business ones. Without a system of credible laws and a credible judiciary to enforce them, few of the 30,000 Chinese who have studied abroad, the cream of the nation's intellectuals, will hazard a return home, and foreign businesses and traders will look to other markets where the labor is equally cheap but the guarantees of being able to operate are more solid.

Replacing party power with a growing measure of people power is a third and viable course for China. The alternatives are a continuation of the artificial combination of economic freedom and political repression or a step back to the failed egalitarian programs that the Old Guard wants to see revived. After thirty years of communism, China borrowed from the capitalist market system to invigorate its economy. Now it could safely borrow from the world's democracies to invigorate its politics.

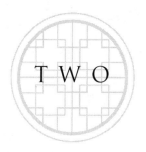

T W O

CHINA AND THE UNITED STATES:
THE QUESTIONS OF HUMAN RIGHTS
AND MOST FAVORED NATION

Most Americans don't really understand China, just as most Chinese don't understand America. This leads the two governments to make numerous miscalculations in their relations and leads the two peoples toward numerous misunderstandings of the opposing regime's conduct.

—THE OPENING WORDS IN THE FIRST ESSAY WRITTEN
BY CHINA'S BEST-KNOWN DISSIDENT, WEI
JINGSHENG, AFTER HIS RELEASE FROM FOURTEEN
AND ONE-HALF YEARS IN POLITICAL PRISONS

China's relationship to the United States has become the most important element of its foreign policy and a leading factor in its domestic policy. The United States also gives its relations with China high priority, although with superpower status and a network of alliances elsewhere in the world, it is less dependent on smooth ties with China than China is with it. Despite these mutual needs, however, American-Chinese relations are uncertain and subject to sudden crises. Unlike the United States' relations with older partners in Europe and Asia, there are frequent confrontations and charges. Both sides emerge from these sharp exchanges puzzled by the other's behavior.

If Americans and Chinese don't understand one another, it is because the societies are so different from each other—a 200-year-old multicultural democracy and a 4,000- or 5,000-year-old absolutist system resistant to adapting to the modern world.

But more than ever before, each society now possesses something that the other wants. With more than $40 billion a year in two-way trade, both see the real and projected increases in business and investment across the Pacific as a guarantee of jobs and prosperity at home. In trade as well as politics, each seeks to influence the other's course. The Chinese want the Americans to accept them as equals in foreign policy and ask no questions about domestic policy. The Americans worry that the arms and technology China sells to the Third World cause instability, and charge it with human rights abuses at home.

Despite President Clinton's decision to stop using China's human rights performance as a criterion for granting Most Favored Nation (MFN) trading status, the issue continues to overshadow all others in American-Chinese relations. The Clinton decision ended the annual duels between the Americans who want more freedom for the people of China and the Chinese leaders who fear that such freedom would imperil their rule. But it did not end the concerns of the United States and other Western democracies, nor those of the democracy advocates in China. The human rights controversy seems unlikely to go away as long as it is argued only on terms of freedom versus stability. Real change may come only as China continues to modernize and begins to see the extension of the rule of law not as a threat but as an advantage to its development, as many other Third World nations have.

Until then, Chinese leaders and officials will maintain a tough public posture on human rights, detaining and harassing Wei Jingsheng and other dissidents when it serves their purpose, and rounding up or harassing hundreds of others on a regular basis in nationwide actions that never get reported abroad. Chinese officials insist the leaders need to act tough against political opposition, since they equate the free expression of other viewpoints with the chaos that all Chinese fear. The United States can, if it chooses, strike a balance to assure both human rights and trade advantages, and even to ignore bombast and diplomatic slights to the secretary of state and his aides. But if such an agreement is to work, China's steps to open the political process must be genuine. If they are not, an array of critics in Congress and the media are waiting to point out the difference between token improvements in human rights and real progress, with or without the MFN leverage.

Since isolated China opened itself to the United States and the rest of the world at the beginning of the 1980s, the parallel process of modernization at home has meant that its differences with America have moderated. But they have not gone away, despite growing indications that Chinese society, followed by a reluctant government, has become more like the rest of the world.

Eating McDonald's hamburgers does not make the Chinese any more American than eating Chinese food transforms Americans into Chinese. But other American ideas have more power to affect the people of China. Freedom is the main one, whether the Chinese think of it as personal or political. China has no such strong idea to export; the days when communes and egalitarian living caught the West's fancy are over, and, in any case, those ideas have been rejected by most of the Chinese themselves.

The relations between the two countries, then, could lead to a process in which China becomes more like the United States, rather than the other way around. This is not to say that the Americans have nothing to learn from the Chinese. Chinese and other Asians have a way of life that has much to teach Americans, from the strengths of traditional religions and beliefs to the support and obligations of the family structure.

But now traditionalist China has rediscovered the compelling power of freedom—not as an American product but as a universal striving. It is shaking off the ideas of both Communists and ancient philosophers, who taught that subservience to the rulers was the natural order of things, incapable of being changed. Not until a century ago was this seriously questioned, when the first Chinese intellectuals began living and studying in Tokyo, and noted with admiration how Japanese reformers were modernizing their traditional society. China still awaits the flowering of the democracy so ardently advocated by those early liberalizers.

As China grows more like the United States, it will be easier both for the Americans to understand it and for the Chinese to understand America. If there is a leavening of ancient Chinese wisdom in American life, that too should aid understanding. But this is unlikely to happen very soon, despite the reports of growing hamburger consumption. Century-old differences are not done away with in decades. In the meantime, both countries must try harder to minimize them.

For China, this means accepting that human rights is fundamental to civilization, that trade agreements should not be skirted, that the men who run its aggressive military-industrial complex should not be permitted to violate international nonproliferation agreements with technology and arms sales abroad. For the United States, it means understanding that too much public pressure on human rights or these other issues could cause a conservative backlash in the Communist leadership and imperil a transition to more liberal rulers in China, but that quiet pressure could help such a change. For both, it means that there are other ways to present arguments than in the glare of television lights, and that agreement on the issues that divide them should not be seen as victory for one side and defeat for the other.

The United States must recognize that Chinese pride and sensitivity to outside interference is as strong among ordinary people as it is among government officials. It must take into account that the language of bombast and threat can conceal weakness, as China's aggressive talk during Cold War days showed. It must realize that even if there are no real voters, there is a constituency that Chinese leaders are answerable to—old men in the corridors of power in Beijing—and that until voter power grows, their word can be as effective as election results.

Wei Jingsheng believes that China's leaders won their civil war in the 1940s by promising the nation human rights, which in those days meant freedom from starvation. Now that they rule the land, they see no need to expand human rights to include the freedom to speak out and disagree with their policies. Far worse, from their viewpoint, such concessions could create a strong political opposition and cost them their power.

But human rights remains the touchstone of the American relationship with China, whether the Chinese leaders want it to be or not.

AMERICANS LOOK AT CHINA

Economic issues are bound up closely with human rights because of the years that the United States used Most Favored Nation status to try to pressure China's leaders to grant more freedom to their people.

MFN gives each trading partner tariff concessions equal to the best they accord other nations. The provision was introduced in the first U.S.-China trade agreement in 1980. But economic relations between the United States and China were important long before either government thought of linking them to human rights performance. Those relations began more than 200 years ago with the first voyage of an American ship, the *Empress of China,* to Chinese ports, which was followed in a few decades by the first Chinese immigrant laborers to reach the United States.

Security issues matter as much as the economic. The United States and China fought an undeclared war in Korea in the 1950s and a Cold War as intense as that with the Soviet Union for another two decades. Although Americans worry about losing jobs to the cheap labor force of China and about being flooded with Chinese imports, they are also uneasy with China's armed strength and proliferation policies in the Third World. Their concerns are heightened when visiting senators such as Larry Pressler, a Republican from South Dakota, warns that China's nuclear arsenal still presents a threat far greater to the United States than does North Korea's.

In both the United States and China, ordinary people and their governments sometimes disagree on how to deal with the other country. China has few public opinion polls to sample such views, and their effect on leadership decisions is probably slight. In the United States, on the other hand, the views of the man and woman on the street are being measured constantly, then expressed strongly when Congress and the administration take decisions on China.

Seen from the United States, the Chinese alternate between good, industrious people and threats to the American way of life. Images from the missionary days are still strong, and for a long time the Chinese were admired for qualities Americans didn't want to bother to acquire but thought it nice that others had: working for low but equal wages, putting the community before self.

China also has alternated between victim and aggressor in the view of Americans, although its leaders generally are blamed for the aggression. Under the emperors as under the Communists, the Chinese people have been considered ill-used and long-suffering. For a few years, particularly during World War II, Chiang Kai-shek's Nationalists were admired in the United States as a good government, but they lost their standing as they lost the civil war. The people of China became enemies briefly in the 1950s, when large numbers of them were fighting U.S. troops in Korea, but before and since generally have been pitied.

The Chinese Communists were admired by some Americans, particularly in the 1960s, when they seemed to be achieving, through communes and shared poverty, what U.S. radicals were preaching. A typical view was that of the American teacher Ruth Gamberg in 1974: "The wretchedness of the past is dead, and the Chinese are fashioning a new society, to be inhabited by a new breed of human beings."

But now the Chinese are viewed largely in market terms: Either they are going to swamp American markets with cheap goods, costing Americans their jobs, or they are going to open up their own vast markets to Americans, creating wealth and jobs.

In congressional debates about MFN status, the representatives' views on the subject are strongly influenced by whether their districts gain or lose through trade with China.

"China has invaded our shores big time," Representative Douglas

Applegate, a Democrat from Ohio, said in a 1993 debate. "The American people are mad as hell about it. They have invaded big time with slave-labor-made products, child-labor-made products, 37-cents-an-hour-made products. All you have to do is go to any department store . . . and find all this Chinese crap lying all over the counters. Opening our doors? And then Americans are losing their jobs?"

Republican Senator James Inhofe of Oklahoma takes the other side. In the China trade, he said, "I have seen the boat that we are about to miss. In Guangdong Province, [there are] 7,000 factories where a few years ago there was none." Technology and equipment for the factories, he said, "are coming from Oklahoma and New York and from the United States, and it is a growing market."

To the U.S. government, this trade magnet has replaced China's role as a counterbalance to the Soviet Union in international affairs. After the Soviet Union crumbled in 1991, China lost much of its value as a power that could be played off against it. Russia, although remaining a danger through its instability, was seen as a threat greatly lessened.

But just about that time, a new threat emerged in the United States. Recession put unemployment, jobs leaving for Third World countries, and the need for growth in American exports on the national agenda.

Wei, the dissident, says many Chinese believe that the American people really do care more about money than they do about freedom, at least the freedom of others. Giving in on human rights as they think the Clinton administration has done, he says, leads Chinese people to believe that "the party was right all these years in saying that the American government is controlled by rich capitalists [and] all you have to do is offer them a chance to make money and anything goes. Their consciences never stopped them from making money."

Tiananmen cannot simply be forgotten. The massacre of hundreds of Chinese democracy demonstrators, including scores of students, and the wounding or imprisonment of thousands of others is a political crime whose resolution must await the change of leadership in China. The toll of dead, wounded, and imprisoned alone makes the Tiananmen tragedy stand out from the sectarian violence of recent years in other nations. The fact that the violent suppression of peaceful demonstrations was deliberate, not an accident of war or a riot out of control, and was ordered by China's leaders and carried out by China's People's Liberation Army compounds the crime. It is a real impediment to better U.S.-Chinese relations, not an excuse. No ally or adversary could ignore such an egregious violation of human and civil rights, and this applies particularly to the United States, where such issues are so much a part of political and journalistic discourse.

But the Chinese argue that the United States has greatly overreacted to disputes since then. They cite the American intervention against Beijing's hosting the 2000 Olympic games; the tracking down of a Chinese cargo ship on accusations it was carrying chemical weapons ingredients to Iran; the sanctions imposed when Beijing shipped missile components to Pakistan; congressional interference in the British-Chinese negotiations on Hong Kong; the controversy over textile quotas, false labeling, and trade balances; and the disproportionate publicity China says the United States affords dissidents. And, although Americans often forget this, Beijing considers the worst kind of offense the U.S. military aid offered Taiwan and support for Taiwan's return to the United Nations. Americans, the Taiwanese, and the world may think of that island as an independent nation; China's officials, at least, consider it a province that sooner or later will be united with the mainland.

Many of the points of dispute are indeed a matter of interpretation, a State Department China specialist concedes: "The Chinese could well say 'Your human rights is our right to control our populace. Your concern about our military outlays is our right to defend ourselves in a world made more uncertain by the collapse of the Soviet empire on our border. Your protests about our balance of trade ignore our striving to develop to your level and that of the other industrial economies.' "

Governmental relations between China and the United States seem to be following the same course that America's relations with the Soviet Union did in the 1970s and 1980s. In both cases, the trouble came from trying to blend two systems of such great differences into a partnership. The United States considered Mikhail Gorbachev a democrat and pretended that Leonid Brezhnev was one; it sponsored exchanges of academics and visits by officials, staged television roundtables, and made available limited Western technology transfer.

But something kept getting in the way of a cordial and trusting relationship. The Soviets let tourists pay with credit cards, but kept acting like Communists. They arrested their own dissidents and Western journalists. They behaved in rude and unexpected ways in joint political or diplomatic ventures.

The U.S.-Chinese relationship has been relatively smoother. Moscow never achieved the military cooperation with the United States that China enjoyed in the years when it served as a counter to Soviet influence in Afghanistan and when its army was fighting Vietnam, then a firm Soviet ally. Moscow never would have permitted anything like the flood of Americans who went as teachers to China's cities and remote provinces, or the flood of Chinese students who left the country for American colleges.

Despite these closer relations, Washington and Beijing frequently had the same kind of bumps and jolts the Americans had experienced with the former Soviet Union. If Americans were overzealous in pursuing the Chinese ship in search of chemical weapons, perhaps it was because China had been found to be lying when it denied that it had supplied Silkworm missiles to Iran in the 1980s, or because it ignored U.S. protests and continued to ship missiles to Syria. Both incidents, which occurred at the height of the military cooperation and technology transfers between the United States and China, made it clear that the U.S.-China relationship was far from partnership.

The end of the Cold War slowed down the arms race and made it less important for Washington to nudge China's military-industrial complex toward partnership. It also abruptly changed the definition and consequences of fleeing across the Iron Curtain. A few years ago a shipload of refugees from the Soviet Union would have been welcomed as heroes. A shipload of Chinese is seen as trouble—on one level as a threat to American jobs, on another as a possible Chinese plan to unload excess population on the United States. Instead of a welcome, the smuggled passengers on the *Golden Venture,* which grounded off Long Island in 1993, were greeted with jail, deportation, and jail again in China.

Americans were unsympathetic. "Two hundred twenty-seven Chinese . . . getting medical treatment furnished by citizens of the U.S.," a reader wrote to the editors of Long Island's *Newsday.* "Fine and dandy for these people. Aliens can get medical care, but when the problem comes up for OUR citizens, it's a big debate." Democratic Representative Charles Schumer, whose district is near where the *Golden Venture* was stranded, attacked the "snakeheads," the smuggling ring members who were paid as much as $35,000 each for transporting the illegal immigrants to the United States, often under inhumane conditions: "It's time to clamp down on these thugs much in the same way we've been battling the mob."

In dealing with the United States, China faces new and often tough conditions that resulted from the drastic lessening of the threat of the Soviet Union.

HUMAN RIGHTS

Human rights advocates inside and outside China were dismayed at President Clinton's 1994 decision to uncouple the human rights and trade issues, calling it a betrayal both of China's political prisoners and America's democratic values.

Because the American business community and its Chinese counterparts were overwhelmingly in favor of MFN without conditions, Washington seemed to be living up to Wei's scornful assessment that Americans put moneymaking before principles.

U.S. officials concede that concern about loss of trade was a large factor in the decision, but not the only factor, and perhaps not even the most important. A larger concern was isolating China at a time when its cooperation was needed in international crises, above all North Korea's reckless nuclear maneuvering.

"China has an atomic arsenal and a vote and a veto in the U.N. Security Council," Clinton said in his statement renewing MFN for China. "It is a major factor in Asian and global security. We share important interests, such as in a nuclear-free Korean peninsula and in sustaining the global environment."

Other factors include the belief or hope that encouraging trade will help political liberalization in China, while restricting trade would set it back, and the plans to apply quieter pressure on human rights using methods other than trade.

Trade, however, has not been ruled out entirely as a means of pressure for democracy in China—only the institution of MFN. Rather than the bilateral MFN bargaining, where the United States emerges as the only villain in Chinese official eyes, the administration plans to use the negotiations for China's membership in the World Trade Organization, successor to the General Agreement on Tariffs and Trade (GATT), to force concessions in the way China treats its workers. Freedom to organize and other workplace rights are among the main demands of Chinese human rights activists. China won its quarrel with the United States on human rights and trade but will find it hard to buck the majority of GATT members on workers' rights won decades ago in other nations.

But in whatever form the attempt is made, with all the societal and cultural differences between China and America, is it right that the United States still tries to impose its standards of human rights on China? And, as many Chinese and Americans ask in elaborating the first question, does the United States, with all its own shortcomings, have the right to do so to China or any other country?

A veteran U.S. diplomat in China responded that the United States and other Western countries are not seeking to impose any particular rules of behavior on China, as long as China does not wish to have trade and other relations with the outside world. But if it does, then the outside world *can* impose conditions. The United States wants to encourage China to adopt generally accepted standards of freedoms and protection for citizens as well as respect for international arms accords. Washington concluded many agreements with dictatorships (including China) when the Cold War seemed to make them necessary, but now that concerns about Russia have abated, closer cooperation with China can be made contingent on Beijing's behavior at home and abroad.

Another argument for keeping the issue of human rights alive—although not necessarily in the public spotlight—is that China has made progress, if not the "overall significant progress" the Americans wanted. Political prisoners have been freed, plans are under way to permit the International Committee of the Red Cross to monitor prisons, and Chinese officials say they have banned the export of prison-made goods and are looking into ceasing the jamming of foreign broadcasts.

These officials say China took these actions as part of its general domestic liberalization, not to please the Americans or anyone else. They deny, in fact, that there are any human rights violations, insist that the issues the Americans have brought up are internal matters of no proper concern to the outside world, and proclaim that China's economic reforms constitute true guarantees of human rights through better living standards, now and in the future. The Americans, Chinese officials say, are endangering these living standards and social stability by listening to the demands of a few dissidents.

Despite these claims, however, the Chinese also display some willingness to make concessions under pressure. "We think they pay attention to what the world, including the United States, thinks of them," the diplomat said. "They can no longer live in Maoist isolation—their opening to the world changed that, along with the ties of trade, not only with the Americans but with the Europeans, who also complain about human rights violations and weapons proliferation."

China insists, and its supporters agree, that the Communists have provided for a billion plus people the most basic human right of all, freedom from need. "Where are our homeless? Where are our starving children?" a Chinese diplomat at the United Nations asked, contrasting his nation to other Third World countries. "How do you measure these achievements against an unfortunate incident in Tiananmen Square? A growing economy is the best guarantee for the Chinese people that these conditions will remain."

Human rights advocates, however, say that every nation's responsibilities go beyond the standard of living. Just as basic, they say, is that citizens must be able to live and work under the guarantee of laws. People must be able to associate and speak out freely.

China's government agrees to this proposition, at least in the paper promises of its constitution, which provide freedoms of speech, press, and opposition. Anyone seeking to make use of these freedoms, however, quickly realizes how hollow they are.

Wu Shishen, a Chinese editor, is serving a life sentence for leaking an advance copy of a speech by President Jiang Zemin to the Hong Kong press. The charge was "selling state secrets overseas," even though Jiang delivered the speech the following week to a nationwide television audience.

Bai Weiji, a former Chinese Foreign Ministry employee, was imprisoned for ten years for providing "national secrets" to Lena Sun, Beijing correspondent of the *Washington Post.* Those secrets were copies of the internal newsletters that party officials receive. Sun herself was detained twice, apparently because of her contacts with dissidents.

Sophia Woodman, editor of *China Rights Forum,* concedes that the scope of individual freedoms has expanded substantially since the reforms began, with people able to say what they like in private. "But as soon as the dissenting viewpoints are shared, even in the setting of an informal discussion group, such tolerance ends," she adds. "Some of the Chinese dissidents serving the longest prison terms were convicted of belonging to 'counterrevolutionary organizations.' People continue to be sent to prison for little more than talking about setting up a political organization."

China has thousands of cases of violations of basic human rights every year, so many that monitoring organizations cannot keep track of more than a few of them. But some cases can be described in detail—by the victims themselves.

What follows is one account of these thousands, told to illustrate the point that in China, anyone courageous enough to call for a course that deviates from that of the leaders is deprived of multiple human rights, not just a single one. As the victim is the first to stress, it is by no means the most serious human rights violation China has perpetrated—no torture, as in the case of student leader Liu Gang, no long sentence, as with Wei Jingsheng, no execution, as with countless thousands of unnamed prisoners in the past.

The case involves a journalist, now outside the country, but still wishing for anonymity. In his two-year ordeal, the Public Security Bureau inflicted enough human rights violations on a single person to keep an entire investigative commission busy. He was imprisoned for his opinions, not for an overt act against the government. He was held without trial or charge, with murderers and other criminals, in inhumanely crowded conditions. His family was never told of his arrest. He was denied counsel and denied access to the laws he thought he might be accused of violating. He was accused by his interrogators of nonexistent crimes and plots and beaten when his answers didn't suit them. He was denied employment, spied on, and harassed after his release. Perhaps most damning of all, he considers himself lucky compared to others.

Journalist X, who was arrested in the first days after the Tiananmen crackdown in Beijing, said that the worst of it was not knowing what he was being charged with and not knowing what the situation in the country outside the walls of the prison was so that he could judge how serious his situation was.

"My interrogators told me about a 'white terror' that had followed Tiananmen," he said. "For all I knew, the nation was in chaos and the Communists were about to be overthrown. I knew that if that were true, I should probably be prepared for execution."

He was put in a fourteen-by-fourteen-foot cell with sixteen other prisoners, and used a quick motion of the hands close to his body to show how tiny each person's space was. His cellmates were criminals. When a new prisoner would enter, everyone would ask what he'd done. If the prisoner said he had killed a man, the response would often be "Only one? I did two," or, in one case, five. Journalist X was a puzzle to the other prisoners. "You're in here for *thinking?*" one of them asked.

He would explain to both prisoners and interrogators that he had written stories supporting the government's economic reforms but also had criticized corruption and other shortcomings. Many of the prisoners became his friends. Those about to leave for sentencing—and often for execution immediately afterward—would ask him to write farewell letters to their families or simple wills, since most were illiterate.

"At least they knew what they had done and what awaited them," Journalist X said. "Those facing execution could tell from the language of the charges against them. Others thought they'd get off with five or eight years in prison. But I wasn't even charged or arrested."

He was held under a loophole in Chinese law permitting almost indefinite detention pending the outcome of an investigation. One fellow inmate held the record of eight years without trial.

Journalist X was questioned daily for most of the first six months, although there were also periods during which he was purposely left alone because his interrogators knew that he would be more likely to talk after some days without contact with anyone but his cellmates.

His interrogators were skilled and intelligent men who knew what they wanted—for him to confess to being part of a movement that had tried to overthrow the government. If his newspaper's role in exposing corruption and trying to push along reform was good for the country and the Communist Party, this was lost on the interrogators, the journalist said: "All they wanted to know was what I had been attempting to do to overthrow the government and, above all, who I might implicate as part of the plot that they took as a given."

As the months dragged on, the journalist's wife and family had no idea where he was or even if he was still alive. Since he hadn't been arrested, there was no record of his whereabouts.

Seeking to argue his way out, he asked for copies of relevant laws and the constitution, but the interrogators told him they were secret. An appeal for a lawyer had been rejected from the start. Journalist X still won't talk about certain painful parts of this detention. But friends say that he was beaten when he refused to supply details of the nonexistent conspiracy against the government or name names in the nonexistent circle of plotters.

Journalist X was released after more than a year in the crowded cell, never having been charged. He thinks he got out because the political climate changed, but his interrogators were no more forthcoming about his release than they had been about his charges. As a free man, back in his Beijing neighborhood, he found he had become a criminal. He was ordered to report regularly to the local police command for questioning, and the police often came to call. They were clearly still looking for the plot—and the other plotters, since he was asked again and again about his friends and contacts. Barred from working as a journalist, he finally managed to go abroad.

The journalist sums up the experience in two ways: first, there were many cases worse than his; not only do hundreds of men and women remain wrongfully imprisoned, but more are being arrested and harassed every day. And second, the United States and other countries must keep up the pressure to force China to end such violations of human rights, if not through the leverage of Most Favored Nation status, then by other means.

Human rights in China touches a whole series of raw points in the Sino-American relationship, beginning, as always, with history. To the Chinese, American members of Congress or human rights activists speaking on the subject bring back memories of the American missionaries preaching about salvation early in the century. As with their predecessors, it is not that what they say is bad for the Chinese. It may be the way that they say it. Chinese old enough to remember the missionary era, as well as those who learned about them in history books, agree that although missionaries and other foreigners helped them, they also intruded into China's affairs— establishing foreign concessions, where Chinese law didn't apply; seizing territory such as Hong Kong, and, in the case of the Japanese, occupying the country. China is an old and proud country, but also one that has been very weak. Any perception of interference in China's internal affairs brings out not only understandable nationalistic reactions but also fears rooted in history.

Most Americans have never heard of the Treaty of Wangxia, but not a few Chinese can cite it. Signed in 1844, it granted the United States the same rights Britain had won in the Opium War—including Most Favored Nation status in trade and exemption from local courts in five Chinese ports.

Chinese also see the contradictions in the way Americans look at human rights in different countries, not objecting enough about abuses in some places and being quite public about less serious situations in others. They wonder whether the fact that Cuba and China are among the few nations in the world still ruled by Communists has anything to do with the attention human rights gets in those places.

Another topic is relativism, whether human rights are indeed universal or whether Asian societies have a different standard that the West should not consider in violation of the acceptable. That point was stressed by Asians, not only Chinese, at the Vienna conference on human rights held by the United Nations in 1993. China's delegates argued that Asian governments work for the benefit of society as a whole and place less stress on the individual's rights. The position was vigorously rejected by the Americans and Europeans.

"Even those Asians hostile to America's heavy hand nonetheless want to see China adhere to minimal standards of behavior," Jusuf Wanandi of Indonesia's Centre for Strategic and International Studies says. "China needs direct criticism when its policies fly in the face of established international conventions."

But how should that criticism be conveyed? In the struggle for human rights in the Soviet Union, Western Europeans called for quiet diplomacy and criticized the Americans' open confrontations. Which side was right may never be determined; the human rights cause ultimately benefited from both approaches.

The Clinton administration's human rights dealings with China were confrontational from the start, when Candidate Clinton made clear he would not emulate the Bush administration in "coddling" the Chinese dictators who had perpetrated the Tiananmen Square massacre. The Chinese confronted Clinton too: When the president held his first meeting with Chinese president Jiang at the 1993 Seattle summit of Asia Pacific nations, he was told that China "does not approve of the concept of linking human rights issues with the issue of trade." But Clinton had a letter from more than 270 members of the House of Representatives urging him to get tough with the Chinese as well as appeals from Asia Watch, Human Rights in China, and other human rights groups urging the use of economic leverage.

The annual State Department review of human rights that came out a few months later showed no sign of a softening of tone, whatever the economic consequences. Propaganda barrages from both Washington and Beijing were reminiscent of the Cold War.

Secretary of State Christopher's meeting with Jiang and other leaders in Beijing showed that confrontation had become belligerence. The Chinese detained Wei Jingsheng and many other dissidents to prevent their meeting with Christopher, and imposed house arrest on seventy-four-year-old Beijing University professor Xu Liangying, who had publicly warned the government that modernization would fail without concern for human rights. They resorted to the diplomatic pettiness of refusing a banquet for the American officials, thus inflicting loss of face on the visitors. The Chinese seemed to need to show the world they do not accept interference from outside and do not countenance even mild dissent.

China dug in on the human rights issue for two related reasons. First, with Great Power aspirations of its own, it cannot afford to be seen subordinating its policies to the demands of other nations. And more important, its leaders see those policies of tough police and security measures against any form of dissent or opposition as essential to their survival.

But even this recalcitrance would not have worked had the Americans stuck to the original human rights/MFN linkage adopted during the Clinton campaign as a popular and liberal alternative to the Reagan-Bush accommodation of dictators whose cooperation benefited U.S. security or trade.

The Americans did not. With President Clinton's approval ratings weakened by scandal, human rights became a politically expensive luxury when measured against the American jobs that backers of granting MFN warned were at stake. A lot of those backers were in his own Treasury and Commerce departments, publicly disputing the human rights positions of the Department of State. Chinese government officials, aware of the pressure and discord, refused any significant concessions. In the end, the president gave in. "Over $8 billion of United States exports to China last year supported over 150,000 American jobs," the president said in his MFN statement, immediately after mentioning China's importance to U.S. security concerns in Asia. Both trade and security were placed well ahead of his remarks criticizing continued human rights violations.

With the main lever of trade abandoned, few expected much progress on human rights through the voluntary code of conduct U.S. businesses are supposed to adopt in China. But human rights advocates see some hope in the president's promise to "stay engaged with those in China who suffer from human rights abuses" through diplomatic channels rather than the annual publicity splashes of MFN renewal debates.

One of those advocates who still has hopes for progress is Journalist X. He says human rights and trade are indeed linked, but his views differ from those of most Western commentators, the result of his professional work in covering and analyzing the Chinese economy before his imprisonment, in his experience in coming up against the hard side of the Chinese government in his cell and interrogations, and in his reflections since then.

In his view, the pressure is on the Chinese, not the Americans, to maintain good relations, and quiet progress on human rights will be one important component of improving these relations. Even without MFN as a lever, he says, China needs a friendly United States, providing technology and markets, for its continued prosperity.

"Chinese officials know exactly that their behavior in suppressing dissent and punishing dissenters is unacceptable to the democratic part of the international community," he said. "They do it because it is their way. They understand power, and they apply repression as the easiest way of retaining power. Calling the world's attention to these misuses of power is the only way to rein them in. They would understand that too and accept it, even if they didn't like it.

"Why? Because China's leadership also depends on a rising standard of living, relative prosperity, to stay in power. It is more than raw police force and power, in other words—people must believe that their leaders are making them better off."

CHINESE LOOK AT THE UNITED STATES

Chinese officials look on the United States as a place that threatens their grip on power, by subversion or by example. And yet it's a love-hate relationship, since the United States plays such a key role in China's modernization and exports.

The Chinese people, however, look on the United States in quite another way. The American threat to their government's abuse of power is an attraction to those who care about civil liberties. For others, generations of immigration have provided family links across the Pacific and knowledge and appreciation of American society.

To the Chinese leaders, human rights and any other American policy that they consider interference in their internal affairs is anathema. They do not find it contradictory that China is a signatory of UN agreements that make human rights a concern of the world community. Conversations with Chinese officials and diplomats have brought out two reasons for their strong stand, one historical and one based on their interpretation of current political reality.

The historical reason is that from the first contact with the East, Westerners were trying to interfere in China's affairs and, because of the East's weakness, were stunningly successful. The mid-nineteenth century is not remote history to Chinese, whether pro- or antigovernment. People still have strong feelings about the way the West, with the British leading, humiliated the proud Chinese empire.

The contemporary political reason is the belief that having "won the Cold War," the United States still has plans to mop up the remnants of communism and make victory complete. Chinese officials are painfully aware of how the United States supported and aided first Gorbachev and then Boris Yeltsin, the successively more radical advocates of dismantling communism. Why would they not do the same in China, if they could find a Chinese Gorbachev (a title now held, at least abroad, and probably to his great discomfort, by Deputy Prime Minister Zhu Rongji)?

That's what Deng Liqun, former propaganda chief and leading hard-liner, would like to know. The man Chinese call Little Deng, to distinguish him from their leader, had this to say in an internal party speech: "Lessons from the disintegration of the Soviet Union and the removal of the Communist Party of the Soviet Union from power are profound. If we don't study such a problem now, we'll fare worse when we come up against the same fate as the CPSU did."

Another extremist, former *People's Daily* editor Gao Di, blames the threat to the party on the West. "The bourgeoisie are looking for agents in the party," he said.

It isn't hard to imagine their reaction to statements easily flung around in Congress during human rights debates, such as this one of Republican representative Gerald B. Solomon of New York:

"We denied Most Favored Nation status to the Soviet Union and the Soviet Empire is gone. There is no more communism in Central and Eastern Europe, and we, as Americans, can be proud because we helped bring it down. . . . If we had been smart and never given MFN to China fourteen years ago, its people could well be free today."

Old Deng, or Deng Xiaoping, and his successor, President and party chief Jiang, take strong exception to this line of argument. Deng called the angry American reaction to the Tiananmen Square massacre "a new Cold War" and in the years since repeatedly has warned that outsiders should not tell the Chinese what to do: "America should understand that since Liberation in 1949, the Chinese people have never cowered before or curried favor with" outside powers.

President Jiang says the United States has "never given up its peaceful-evolution tactics against China . . . to confuse the thoughts of our people and wreak havoc on our socialist economic construction."

The standing of the U.S. government has always been higher with the Chinese people than that of the Chinese government with Americans, mainly because it generally is successful in practicing democracy and working for higher living standards, something the Chinese would like their own government to be more successful at. The Chinese people rate Americans even higher, in part as exotic creatures seen from a nation that is still largely isolated and in part because they represent a country the Chinese admire.

Chinese are coming to the United States in greater numbers, not as missionaries but as people with no higher aim than improving their economic lot. In the process, however, they're having some of the same affects on American society that American missionaries had on the Chinese a century earlier. The Americans who came to save souls also improved health and education standards. The Chinese who come to get rich are saving many inner-city businesses, reviving urban schools, and swelling enrollments at state universities.

In the unofficial Chinese view, at least, getting to the United States is a perfectly logical extension of the human rights the Americans are always advocating. About 200,000 have done so illegally, Chinese officials estimate, part of the 700,000 illegal Chinese scattered in other Asian nations and the West. The right to better oneself, if only to exchange a kitchen job in Shanghai for one in San Francisco, certainly seems reasonable to these Chinese.

Chinese restaurants may seem to be ethnic clichés, but they are an important link for success in foreign societies for immigrants, legal or not. Just as the propagandists on the mainland proclaim, everybody gets rich, comparatively speaking, although, again as in China, not all at the same time. Opening a small restaurant requires little capital and can start bringing in $10,000 a month if the managers all work hard enough. The help earns $2 an hour, but tips, long hours, and working off the books to avoid taxes convert that into a reasonable pay scale. In the view of one intellectual who had to support himself as a waiter when he first reached the United States, a restaurant is a real Chinese community, offering jobs, a warm place where one can speak Chinese but also learn English, with a multiplier effect for many people, families, and friends.

The first thing that Chinese discover when they arrive in the United States, unless they come as boat people, is freedom. The exchange scholar finds out that her academic advisor gives her complete freedom in choosing courses, instructors, and thesis topic; the midlevel diplomat who used to bicycle to work with Beijing's other 3 million cyclists now drives a car and parks it in blissful ignorance at fire hydrants; the engineer is given his own project and apparently limitless time to work on it.

Some Chinese find little time to enjoy these freedoms, if they're working to get a university degree or as laborers, indentured or not, to provide hard currency for families in China. But even these immigrants learn that the police, the bureaucrats, and the politicians have far less to do with their daily lives than they did at home.

Other Chinese learn quickly to take advantage of this freedom the way Americans do. Some leap into the free-market economy, which seems to them to offer opportunities and a lack of restrictions that far eclipse the attractions of the special economic zones at home. Some embark with equal enthusiasm in crime, bringing to America's shores the protection rackets, smuggling, drugs, and prostitution so long established in China (and in America).

Law-abiding Chinese, however, are quick to criticize what they consider the United States' foolishness in coddling criminals and in general having loose standards of enforcing public behavior. Many urban Chinese look down on their African-American and Hispanic neighbors as less admiring of the work ethic; many others worry constantly about criminals victimizing their small businesses and the violence of American city streets. The homeless, in whose ranks few Asians can be found, also draw the ire of many Chinese.

Immigrants say the United States could learn from the way China deals with criminals and social outcasts. The evening news on China's local television regularly shows accused criminals paraded before tough judges, then taken away quickly for sentencing or even execution. When questioned closely about which system they prefer,

Chinese in the United States concede that American justice is probably fairer but should be more strictly enforced.

Their experiences feed the imaginations of those left at home. We did not meet any relatives of Chinese criminals who made good in the United States, but we had many conversations with the families of successful business- and professional people, scholars, and artists. The underlying theme was this: In China, they had no chance. In the United States, they can become what they want.

This is a powerful incentive to the talented as well as the restless to be on their way to the United States, and it helps explain why young Chinese will spend weeks in the hold of a ship and years in paying back the "snakehead" smugglers to get abroad.

Most of the smuggling originates in Fujian Province, a mountainous slice of territory about the size of England along China's southeast coast. It sent the first immigrants abroad centuries ago and continues to be the main embarkation point for the most recent waves of boat and airplane people. Fujian is hard to get to but easy to leave from. Its railroads crawl up and down the coastal mountain ranges, which makes train traffic no match in speed for the coastal steamers. The crowded two-lane roads are no faster. But there is speed aplenty in Fujian's coastal waters, where smugglers' boats, powered by as many as four U.S.-made Mercury outboards, criss-cross to Taiwan with cases of cigarettes and other contraband. The military and the police also have introduced Mercury outboards but, apparently limited to one or two per boat, can't keep up with the smugglers.

Fujian has hundreds of miles of virtually deserted shoreline, with plenty of rocks, islets, and bigger islands to hide in. It also has a legitimate fishing industry that keeps thousands of boats in coastal waters day and night. So the smugglers prosper, fitting out better and faster boats.

The profit on a boatload of cigarettes has been calculated in the Chinese press as $500. But the profit on just one peasant leaving Fujian for Taiwan or perhaps directly for the United States is many times that.

Americans began to take note of this refugee trade only recently, when freighters and planeloads of Chinese, guided more or less expertly by professional smugglers of human cargo, began to land on U.S. shores. The figures ranged wildly from 10,000 to 100,000 boat and plane illegals every year. (China's annual legal immigration total is 20,000.) Immigration officials spoke of twenty to fifty ships either preparing to leave or, more ominously, already on the high seas, as if they were an invasion fleet, each with up to 300 smuggled aliens aboard. Congress was flooded with demands for new laws to combat the threat. Officials promised to provide satellite tracking for refugee ships and intelligence agency cooperation.

Americans were puzzled. On the one hand, the media were reporting the risks that the Chinese were taking in dramatic adventures like that of the *Golden Venture,* which ran aground with the loss of ten refugee lives, while hundreds of others scrambled to safety. Who could be so desperate as to endure such conditions and risk such dangers? The public was particularly puzzled because everything it had been reading about China spoke of boom and prosperity.

In Fujian, this conundrum can be explained easily. It is precisely the reforms of the past fifteen years that have opened up China to smuggling as well as other forms of criminal activity. As local Chinese explain it, the controls have been relaxed. Freedom to make money also means freedom of movement. A taste of money causes an appetite for more. As long as everyone was bound to his or her work unit, with housing restrictions and grain coupons, freedom of movement was impossible. But now these restrictions are gone.

A young man in a certain neighborhood of Fuzhou, Fujian's capital, has become a kind of local hero through his decision to contact a professional smuggler and make his way to the United States. Friends didn't want to identify the man, who is in his midtwenties, except to call him "the Wrestler" because of his skills in that sport. With the help of relatives abroad, the Wrestler paid $15,000 to a local specialist in alien smuggling. When he wrote friends, he included few details of his trip to the United States, but he was proud to say that he was not only a bona fide (although of course illegal) resident of New York but lived in Flushing, Queens, a better neighborhood than Manhattan's crowded Chinatown. Friends in China have figured out that it wouldn't take long to pay back the snakeheads for passage, even at the low wages the Wrestler is earning as kitchen help. They are well aware of working conditions in the United States, because of the large number of Fujian emigrants there, legally and illegally, and there is much correspondence and not a few visits from those emigrants who have made it.

These visitors are easy to spot in banks and stores in Fuzhou, with new blue passports and shiny American credit cards that attract attention in what is still largely a cash economy. Locals say some of these passports are as false as the visitors' claims to be legal U.S. residents. But these are matters the Chinese police state does not concern itself with.

No one we talked to about the smuggling situation in China views it with very much alarm. But the situation has become yet another issue in the up-and-down relations between the United States and China. The United States is displeased with China's laxity in enforcing its otherwise stringent police controls. China is singled out as both a facilitating country (helping refugees from other nations, such as Vietnam, move on toward the West) and an originating country for illegal aliens.

There is also widespread blame of the Chinese authorities, in the general sense of not making living and working conditions better, so that people want to stay in China, but also in the specifics of permitting virtual free rein to the smugglers in Fujian and other coastal areas. Smuggled cigarettes are as common in Chinese street markets as locally produced ones. As one smoker who enjoys this situation notes, everyone assumes that there is a mutually beneficial arrangement between the smugglers and those who are supposed to catch them, both on the mainland and in Taiwan, source of most of the contraband.

If officials can look the other way when the Mercury-powered boats show up with cases of Marlboros from the Taiwanese coast, only one hundred miles from Fujian, it is to be expected that they also turn a blind eye to the boats taking refugees out to rendezvous with Taiwanese, Indonesian, or other oceangoing ships for the trip to the United States.

Asians are the fastest-growing group of legal immigrants in the United States. China, as Asia's largest country, is bound to play a big role in any future immigration, legal or illegal. The Fujian coast and any other means will be used to get to the United States, but if both governments work to control smuggling and other abuses, Chinese immigration will bring the two nations closer, as every previous wave has done for other countries whose emigrants have helped build the United States.

These family and societal links between China and the United States will be supplemented by those of commerce. For the first time in two centuries, there is a real chance that the relations between the two countries will become more equal and mutually beneficial, as the great strands of trade and investment, so long promised but never fulfilled, begin to span the Pacific. If this happens, China will no longer be the supplicant in need of shoes and rice, and the United States no longer the imperial power but the partner.

To lift Chinese-American relations to this level of equality, however, might involve many more strains between the two nations, and a great effort by the United States to insist that these relations be based on shared respect for human rights and the rule of law. When the Communists or their successors accept this basis, China will not become Americanized but democratized. But the obstacles to democracy in Chinese society are so great that such changes will not happen quickly.

THREE

CHINA'S BABY BOOM

In the mid-1980s, a gigantic billboard thermometer in the heart of Beijing reminded citizens that the Chinese population should not reach the 1.2 billion mark until the year 2000. The red mercury that measured population figures rather than temperatures was comfortably below the century limit. Provincial, local, and neighborhood officials all over China were expected to relay that message and enforce it.

A decade later the thermometer was gone; the goal was unrealistic. China was already perilously close to the year 2000 limit. According to its own statistics, by 1993 population had soared to 1.17 billion.

Statisticians in China's State Family Planning Commission were estimating by 1990 that unless stricter controls were observed, the population could reach 1.3 billion by the turn of the century and 1.6 billion by 2050. The baby boom had a ripple effect that could set back the other goals planned for the year 2000: average annual per-capita income, $300; average per-capita living space, 86 square feet; an inventory of 13 to 15 million cars, buses, and trucks.

Worst of all, from the Communist Party's point of view, the failure of the population program is another sign of its decreasing control and discipline over its members and officials as well as the general population.

In spite of spectacular economic growth since the introduction of economic reforms, the Chinese population still threatens constantly to outgrow the country's ability to provide enough housing, schools, jobs, power, infrastructure, even food, for all of its citizens.

Alarmed by the surging population figures and the disturbing predictions, the minister of the State Family Planning Commission, Peng Peiyun, called for new tactics to overcome resistance to the one-child policy at home and criticism of it from abroad. Government efforts to limit the growth of population, an obvious failure domestically, also had attracted censure from the United States and other Western countries.

The Chinese government has strongly objected to any international criticism or interference in matters which it considers are strictly internal affairs such as the treatment of dissidents or population control. Nevertheless, central planners have gone out of their way to earnestly defend and explain their birth control policy which is a high priority on the national agenda. Their response to criticism of the program is simple: Western reports of government-approved forced abortions and sterilization are unfair or untrue. They insist that involuntary abortion or sterilization has never been their official policy. They rely instead, they say, on family planning education, free contraceptives, and voluntary sterilization.

The official rebuttal concedes only that any coercion should be blamed on a few overzealous local officials. Any cases of forced abortions or sterilization were the work of misguided village personnel who are responsible for the carrying out the official family planning program, Chinese spokesmen explain. In some cases, grass roots officials may have taken such extreme and unauthorized measures, seeking approval from provincial or national authorities for maintaining quotas or fearing penalties for not doing so.

However, when reports leaked out that the Ministry of Health was drafting legislation for the National People's Congress to enforce sterilization of physically or mentally handicapped people, the Family Planning Commission moved quickly to have it withdrawn. A national survey estimated that more than half of China's 50 million handicapped citizens have congenital diseases. The Ministry of Health prediction that 13 out of every 1,000 newborns would have such diseases is alarmingly high, if accurate. Western infant mortality and morbidity rates for congenital anomalies are much lower, which may be due to more sophisticated prenatal detection and postnatal care. In any event, the Commission wished to avoid further Western criticism about family planning and decided the law should be reworded to remove the word "eugenics" and to be "less confrontational."

The U.S. government has long criticized the Chinese birth control policy and tried to force changes on it. The Reagan and Bush administrations withdrew American financial support from the UN Population Fund and the International Planned Parenthood Federation, asserting that the aid would be used to subsidize abortions in China. This policy was reversed by the Clinton administration, a move applauded by groups such as the Worldwatch Institute, which warns of the worldwide adverse effects of uncontrolled population increases on limited natural resources and food supplies in developing countries.

The renewed American financial support for international family planning programs may work at cross purposes with the pressure the State Department has exerted on China's human rights record. Some of the international family planning funds may well subsidize China's policy of abortion and sterilization (whether it is voluntary or involuntary) as well as family planning education. American courts have granted political asylum to Chinese immigrants who claim that the one-child policy has violated their human rights.

The apparent failure of population control has created a host of new problems. Larger rural families, as well as inflation and low rural earnings, have increased income gaps between peasants and urban citizens. Overpopulation, underemployment and poverty in rural areas has encouraged peasants to migrate from the countryside to already overburdened cities. Bribery and corruption, a major concern for the government, taints even the population control program.

The latest birth control program is targeted particularly at the rural population, 80 percent of the Chinese total. Surveys show that the largest number of multiple births occur to peasant couples, the least educated, the poorest, and the most traditional or "backward-looking" segment of the population in the eyes of policymakers.

Now they are to receive "special priority and care" and a wide range of social benefits. As incentives, the government offers a list of services and goods in short supply in the countryside: increased allocations of medical care and education, tools, and fertilizers. Although there is no indication that universal social security is high on the agenda of the central government, the Family Planning Commission has even proposed old-age pensions for elderly peasants, a benefit only a very few enjoy in rural China, where children are expected to support their aged parents.

The State Council commission charged with aid to the poor estimates that 80 million citizens, chiefly those who live in the deep mountains, steep hills, or desert areas of rural China, do not have enough to eat or wear. Planning officials expect that the benefits-oriented program that links antipoverty work with birth control propaganda will persuade rural couples that they will enjoy a higher standard of living if they have small families.

BOYS VERSUS GIRLS

Attitudes toward both large families and female offspring have changed, at least in more prosperous communities, rural and urban. Jinming, a twenty-nine-year-old peasant and the father of a seven-year-old daughter, said in a conversation in his village that his mother persuaded him that one daughter was as satisfactory as several sons. "She reminded me that we were a family of five boys and we never had enough to eat in the old days. She's right. We have plenty to eat now. A nice house. A television set and a washing machine."

Since childhood, he had worked on the terraced hills planted with tea that surround his small village of 600 inhabitants. Now he and his wife work in the five-year-old village factory that manufactures bales of brilliant red, green, purple, and blue velveteen, earning almost $400 a year, a princely sum by rural standards. The villagers who agreed to continue to plant and pick tea, used to working sunup to sundown, were given the shorter hours of the factory workers, eight hours a day, six days a week, with two-hour lunch breaks, and guaranteed the same wages as the factory paid.

The factory has been so successful that the manager had to recruit 300 more workers from other villages. The trucks that deliver the bales over a two-lane road to a nearby city bring back new televisions, washing machines, and electric fans. A new school, a new clinic, rows of whitewashed new houses, each with its own small vegetable plot, and hangarlike factory all encroach on the terraces of tea bushes. The loss of farmland to the new houses and factory buildings worries the central government, but it remains convinced that the rise of rural industry will not only reduce poverty but also create enough economic security to lessen the desire for large families.

Without a son to support him and his wife in their old age, Jinmin is counting on an old folks' home the village says it will build. Family planners criticize peasants who desperately desire at least one son to carry on the family name and to make sacrifice for ancestor worship as tradition bound and superstitious, but the need for old-age support is critical for the peasants.

Traditional attitudes among peasants toward girls are just as persistent. Peasant girls, as they have from Confucian times, work alongside their parents and brothers in the fields or paddies. Household incomes in rural China are a joint endeavor with everybody contributing and sharing. The opportunity to earn money by farming their own plots under the household responsibility system or to send members of the family to work in the rural factories is a powerful incentive to have families of two or more children. An old Chinese adage, "one pair of hands to work, only one mouth to feed," is a common peasant rationale for a large family.

Once she marries, a daughter and her pair of hands is no longer an asset for her parents. Many peasant girls, some of them only fifteen or sixteen years old, leave their villages to earn their dowries by working in the enormous silk, embroidery, or carpet factories, which employ thousands. They work long hours, live in cheerless dormitories, and save their wages. As soon as they earn enough for a dowry for a prospective husband, they will return to their villages to marry. The young bride, typically, moves to her husband's village, taking with her the dowry and her labor and earning power.

Better educated, less traditional in many ways, urban couples are discouraged from having second babies for many reasons other than the one-child policy. Until the introduction of the economic reforms, every Chinese urban worker was completely dependent on the government for all the necessities of life. A central authority assigned jobs in work units. And the work unit—a state enterprise, factory, or office—provided everything for its workers, housing as well as medical care, child care, ration cards, and old-age pensions. The size and type of housing, the quality of medical care, the availability of day-care for working mothers, the amount of pensions and bonuses depends on the size, status, and financial success of the work unit.

Unlike the state-employed workers, workers who have "broken the iron rice bowl" and are working for a private employer or are self-employed are not deterred by penalties such as the withholding of subsidized medical and child care or bonuses. In spite of a constant bombardment of propaganda, speeches, posters, and stories in the press explaining the urgent need to limit the population, the most compelling reason for urban couples to have only one child is insufficient, cramped, and inadequate housing.

Blocks and blocks of walk-up apartments, four and five stories high, and, more recently, taller apartment buildings have sprung up in every major city, but the housing supply is still insufficient. Many city dwellers are living in prewar, even turn-of-the-century one-story houses, often without indoor running water. Residents in the neighborhood share a public toilet, and heating is provided by small stoves stoked with polluting pressed coal briquets.

China's most modern housing, with all the indoor amenities, allots minimal space, roughly twenty-one square feet per person, not much more than the average American bathroom, and three to four rooms to the apartment. The traditional extended Chinese family still exists, if only for a lack of sufficient housing. A couple sharing their small apartment with one or more grandparents are hardly tempted to have more than one child.

The cramped and close living conditions enable the delegated neighborhood committees, usually older retired women, to keep close track of the young women in their areas and to monitor pregnancy rates and births, exhorting, pressuring, and reporting them to their work units, which hand out penalties if they don't heed the family planning policy.

The Chinese working mothers (and most women under fifty-five years work) cannot take for granted disposable diapers, prepared baby food, even the possibility of fitting a washing machine into a tiny city kitchen. If the work unit cannot afford a day care center, urban mothers must rely on elderly relatives or friends to care for preschool children. The parks are filled with gray-haired retired grandparents pushing babies and toddlers in bamboo carriages, which are rapidly being replaced with spanking-new chrome-and-plastic strollers.

One-child policy propaganda is also supported by ideology, impressed on men and women during the regular, required political study sessions. A well-educated couple—a laboratory technician and his wife, a librarian—who live in a tiny two-room apartment in a large city are perfectly satisfied with their only child, a little girl. "Girls are just as important as boys," says the father. He is citing sound socialist doctrine that insists that there are no tensions or differences between the sexes, only between classes. That means, in theory at least, that a girl will have equal opportunities for education, employment, and pay.

That is not universally true in China today, particularly in the countryside, where boys attend school longer than girls, and the earning power of males is usually higher. During the era of collective farming males earned more work points, and today rural factory wages are higher for boys and men than for girls and women.

The Chinese preference for male children, for both traditional and financial reasons, has been blamed for the alarming drop in the rate of live female births. Voluntary abortion and infanticide were not uncommon in past centuries in China, when they were a matter of survival for the rest of the family during desperate periods of famine or flood, but contemporary reports of infanticide persist. A young Mandarin-speaking British doctor who traveled throughout rural China in the 1980s told us he was appalled by the frank admissions to him of female infanticide by couples who absolved themselves, saying that if they were allowed to have only one child, that child must be a boy.

Although central planning authorities for the birth-control program had ignored or denied reports of female infanticide, concerned officials in Guangxi, a relatively prosperous but largely agrarian province, decided in the early 1990s to investigate the matter on their own with a rather unscientific study of marriageable males and females in the province (they never defined "marriageable"). Their findings that Guangxi males outnumbered the females 52 percent to 47 percent seems high compared to almost equal numbers of men and women (ages twenty-five to twenty-nine years old) counted during the American 1989 census. The provincial demographers concluded that the sex imbalance was due to "pernicious feudal influences" (female infanticide) and "alienation" caused by modern technology (ultrasound), and gloomily predicted at least 5 million males were doomed to bachelorhood.

A declining number of eligible young women may account for rising prostitution and kidnapping of young women. The *China Daily* reported 15,000 cases of gang kidnappings of women, sold as brides to peasants in 1993. During the same year, 240,000 prostitutes were arrested, according to the All-China Federation of Women, a government-controlled organization that enlists and mobilizes Chinese women in support of state policies.

The Chinese, enthusiastic consumers of the latest technology, computers, faxes, and cellular phones, now have ultrasound equipment to determine the gender of a fetus. Enterprising private businessmen have found it profitable to pay thousands of dollars for the imported machines. Whether the clients are affluent urban couples or rural couples who can afford the procedure, whether they feel compelled to observe the one-child policy or are inclined to agree with it, detection of a female fetus usually leads to voluntary abortion.

ONE CHILD OR MORE

The All-China Women's Federation, in a survey of Beijing and Shanghai women, reported that 25 percent of married Chinese women had had at least one abortion. Eight percent had two or more. During the same period, however, the Family Planning Commission noted a rise in the birth rate, which it attributed at least partly to adverse publicity in the Western media. Foreign press reports of infanticide and abandonment of baby girls, graphic stories of forced abortions and sterilization caused relaxation of the campaign in China and a corresponding population spurt, it believes.

The Family Planning Commission, analyzing its failure to limit population growth successfully in the past, places a portion of the blame on the local officials who are the educators and enforcers of the family planning policy. Some, according to reports in the Chinese press, have been too lax. Other officials and doctors have deliberately flouted directives about birth control.

Overzealous local officials also have jeopardized the population policy through the adverse publicity that their actions have caused. It is they, defenders of the current policy claim, who should be blamed for the cases reported in the Western press about women forcefully aborted late in their pregnancies, others unwillingly sterilized, or couples who had their homes destroyed and heavy fines imposed after the birth of a second or third child. Responsibility for birth control programs is handed down from Beijing to provincial authorities to local leaders who, planning officials say, sometimes administer the program with a vengeance.

During the past forty years, the Chinese Communist Party

poured considerable money and human resources into health education and medical care, cutting high rates of infant mortality and deaths from preventable parasitic and communicable diseases. Peasants in villages and towns are exposed to public health education, usually in the form of bright cartoon-style posters, designed to instruct illiterates as well as literates, plastered on village and town walls, and trained first aid personnel or paramedics (the Chinese frown on the term "barefoot doctor") are responsible for minor health problems and family planning education.

When birth control education, enforcement, and free contraception fail, the couple will be referred to the nearest clinic, which is sometimes miles away, where doctors and surgeons perform abortions, serving as the last gatekeepers for population control.

The chief surgeon in a South China county clinic explained how he and his staff coordinated their work in the field and in the clinic. They were responsible for not only population control but also preventive health programs, general medical care, and surgery, relying on Western-style and traditional medicine.

He acknowledged the importance of population control, particularly among his poor, backward patients. He explained that after first babies, he encourages new mothers to have tubal ligations, the preferred method of sterilization in China, or new fathers to have vasectomies. "I perform only four vasectomies for ever 300 tubal ligations," he admitted ruefully. Chinese research suggests that there is some evidence that vasectomies improve male longevity, but local men aren't convinced, he said.

Since the new campaign to enforce population control, however, hospital personnel and officials have been reported overlooking extra births once again, sometimes out of sympathy for couples who want forbidden babies or because they have been bribed. Initially, banquets and small gifts from parents sufficed to persuade the people in charge of enforcement to overlook the birth of a second or even third child. In a single village in Gansu Province, women admitted that at least half of them had paid bribes as high as $400 to have a second child. Apparently, the frenzy to get rich that has gripped most Chinese has also affected the birth control enforcers.

Beijing takes laxity or corruption by officials of the birth control program extremely seriously because it is another indicator of the loosening of central party control. Punishment has been severe and widely publicized. Prison sentences from two years to life and a death penalty were meted out in a town in Henan, a densely populated province, for falsifying sterilization papers and taking bribes. In other regions, both parents and officials have been jailed for such violations and had property confiscated.

Couples who have been unable to persuade or bribe local officials have sought other ways to have second or third babies. Sometimes the pregnant woman simply slips away to another village or town, hiding out until after the birth. Others head toward large urban areas, husbands seeking work, would-be mothers seeking invisibility.

A further drawback to the birth policy is the unraveling of the forty-five-year-old system of household registration and urban resident permits that was designed to control unauthorized movements. The lure of wages as laborers, cooks, street sellers that are double or triple what they could earn as farmers have enticed married couples and whole families, as well as single men and women, to abandon their villages for metropolitan areas without permission from village officials.

Once they arrive in the cities, they still can manage food and housing without complying with current regulations to register with the police. Official food ration cards are no longer an obstacle with the availability of rice, grain, and oil as well as other foodstuffs in the free markets. Every Chinese city has its squalid crowded quarter of temporary shacks and mazes of shabby little houses that provide cheap living arrangements. Living in one of these teeming quarters has the advantages of avoiding police resident checks and the appointed monitors who report unauthorized pregnancies in less crowded and better regulated neighborhoods. As a result, migrant couples are held responsible for nearly one in eight "illegal" multiple births.

The flourishing business of smuggling cigarettes, cars, and televisions now includes even a small but apparently lucrative business of spiriting pregnant women across the border to Hong Kong, despite strong protests by officials there. Some persistent women have paid large sums to be smuggled into Hong Kong to give birth, believing, erroneously, that their babies will receive Hong Kong citizenship. The smugglers transport pregnant women by taxi to waiting speedboats along China's coast that quickly take them to Hong Kong. There they receive free medical care to deliver their babies, but, without citizenship papers, are soon repatriated to the mainland.

The Chinese have an extraordinary passion for statistics and a fondness for promoting national campaigns with numbers: the Four Modernizations or the Five Good Families. In spite of One Couple, One Child, the birth control slogan that has been promoted since 1979, Peng, the minister of the State Family Planning Commission, admitted that by 1990, the average Chinese family had 2.3 children.

Since the imposition of the new incentives, statistics published in the official *Population News* show that the birth rate dropped to 18.2 births per thousand by 1993, a decline that portends the average family will shrink to 1.9 children before 2000. The new "more flexible" approach and financial and material incentives, planners say, is already lowering the birth rate. But the population continues to increase. Even though families are becoming smaller, there are growing numbers of women of childbearing age.

Every year since the early 1980s, a cohort of approximately 13 million women, born in the baby boom years of the 1950s and 1960s when Mao encouraged large families, have entered their marriage and childbearing years. The number of fertile women will total approximately 350 million by 2000. If the birth control policy is not strictly adhered to, there could be as many 23 million newborns annually.

According to modern calculations, overpopulation has cursed China periodically. The population grew from about 150 million people in 1700 to 430 million in 1850. Despite famine, inflation, epidemics, floods, droughts, and wars, it continued to climb in the present century. By 1949 it stood at 540 million.

During the first Five-Year Plan (1953–1957) under the young Communist government, Mao insisted on one of his many extreme miscalculations. He positively encouraged large families, even to the extent of paying food subsidies and providing wet nurses. Thousands of Chinese men and women, particularly those who were raised in peasant families, now in their late thirties, had as many as seven, eight, and even ten siblings.

It was obvious to central planners, if not to Mao, that providing enough food, transportation, housing, or anything else would be impossible if the population continued to multiply at such alarming rates.

China's first birth control campaign, mounted in 1957, was called off the following year when Mao launched the Great Leap Forward to transform China from an agricultural to an industrial nation. He boasted of the strength of China's huge population, which had grown to 600 million people. Some experts agreed that it was a figure that China could cope with, considering its resources and arable land.

The disastrous policies of the Great Leap Forward, emphasizing manufacturing over food production, caused famine and chaos; birth rates dropped precipitously. But by 1965 the population began to renew itself again, peaking alarmingly at 37 births per 1,000. Somehow statisticians and demographers managed to prevail over Mao, and there was some enforcement of birth control in succeeding years. The campaigns were never uniformly strict. Each of China's fifty-five minorities has always been allowed to have at least three children per family. Since the minorities total only 6.7 percent of the population, that has not opened too great a gap in the program. During the 1970s officials in some provinces permitted the birth of a second baby, especially if the first child was a girl or handicapped.

National campaigns and reforms always have produced some unexpected results. The one-child policy is no exception. It caused a curious social phenomenon, the "Little Emperors." The government had no intention of eliminating traditional values of docility, obedience, and group cooperation through its one-child policy, but nursery school instructors and schoolteachers complain that these only children are willful, disobedient, and unruly, spoiled by parents and grandparents. The accusations mount: Little Emperors, literally spoon-fed, can't handle their chopsticks by the age of five; they are uncooperative and selfish with their peers; rude and demanding to their elders, anathema in China.

OLD AND NEW CHINA

The old habits of Chinese society are clashing increasingly with the rules of the Communists in many other issues besides birth control. Individuals and communities are becoming increasingly assertive, and the party is quietly retreating from many conflicts in which its word once was unquestioned.

Little Emperors are but a single minor phenomenon in the burst of changes that have affected China in the past decade and a half. Stock exchanges now contrast with Buddhist temples; jazz is as familiar as Chinese opera, Coca-Cola and Pierre Cardin advertisements as common as posters of the Kitchen God. Mercedeses, Fiats, and Volvos compete for road space with Phoenix bicycles, and tractors are gradually replacing water buffalo and donkeys in the countryside.

Many characteristics of Old China endure. The strong Chinese inclination to have sons and several children is only one of the traditions, customs, and examples of "backward thinking" that persist in modern China. When the Chinese Communist Party came to power, it banned ancestor worship, arranged marriages, the binding of women's feet, and other "holdovers of feudalism." Strait-laced Communists continue to rail against the many traditions and customs of Old China that are reviving in today's villages, towns, and cities.

The party press constantly scolds the extravagance of citizens who spend too much on lavish weddings, banquets with a staggering number of dishes, or old-fashioned elaborate funerals, imploring them to practice simplicity and economy. A fireworks ban in 1994 on grounds of safety proved difficult to enforce in the face of centuries of tradition. Celebrations of all sorts, from the Lunar New Year to completion of a building project, have always been the occasion for noisy outbursts of fireworks, from strings of tiny crackers to brilliant and expensive pyrotechnics.

Prosperity has renewed the celebration of traditional weddings, funerals, and celebrations. In the countryside, wedding processions with musicians leading the way and the bride dressed in the customary red for happiness and good luck, riding on a cart piled with gifts of quilts, Thermoses, and the inevitable sewing machine, have become common. Scarlet paper posters embossed in gold with the double happiness symbol, a multicourse banquet, and much toasting with orange soda, beer, sweet Chinese wines, and fiery Mao Tai are all part of the festivities.

In towns and cities, twentieth-century touches have been added to the traditional Chinese ceremonies. Photography shop windows feature portraits of brides in rented Western-style wedding dresses alongside their bridegrooms in Western suits. The young office worker who boasted of spending almost a year's salary on his wedding, adding disco music to the usual banquet, is one example of young Chinese who combine what they believe is the best of both worlds.

To counter these practices, party propaganda sessions sternly remind would-be brides that they should be at least twenty years old, bridegrooms twenty-two years, and that citizens' savings are better spent on things other than banquets and extravagant entertaining. Even official three-day holidays for bridal couples who are at least the minimum marrying age, magnanimously extended to ten days for couples over twenty-five and twenty-seven, are not sufficient inducements to observe age limits or curtail expenses for China's young men and women or their parents, who are customarily involved in the arrangement of marriages and nuptial celebrations.

In a further move to control the birth rate, the government now intends to monitor marriages more carefully. About 20 percent of the 10 million marriages that take place each year are illegal, according to reports. Bigamy, arranged marriages, and couples who are living together without registering with the proper authorities face fines, separation, and reeducation.

Despite disapproval by the government, old funeral customs also persist. Cremation has generally replaced coffin burials, as much for lack of available land for graves and the traditionally desirable sites that face in a prescribed direction as acceptance of the party guideline for cremation. At considerable expense, many bereaved families still outfit the mourners with white coverings from head to toe. Then, bearing wreaths of gaudy paper flowers, some the size of cartwheels, packed in the backs of trucks or on foot, the mourners accompany the dead to burial or (government encouraged) cremation.

Although the Chinese constitution guarantees freedom of religion, incidents of arrests and imprisonment of Muslims, Tibetan nuns and monks, Catholic priests, and foreign evangelists indicate that the Communist Party still considers religion a threat. Freedom to practice religion, in fact, is tolerated only as long as the religion does not challenge the authority of the Communist Party. Chinese Catholics, for instance, have been permitted to elect their own hierarchy of archbishops and bishops but are forbidden to acknowledge or submit to the higher authority of the Catholic Pope in Rome. Many underground Roman Catholics, of course, do just that.

After the arrest and expulsion of seven fundamentalists, some of them Americans, who were proselytizing in Henan Province, a spokesman for the Religious Affairs Bureau called the missionaries an "international influence that could harm or damage China's integrity and safety in the country."

About 8 million Protestants and Catholics worship in state-approved churches, but there are unofficial estimates that the number of worshippers in underground or home churches is much higher. Untold numbers prefer to worship undetected and constrained by the authorities. Still, every Sunday and holy day brings large congregations of Chinese openly worshipping in the officially restored and reopened temples, monasteries, and Catholic churches.

Among crowds of the sightseers and the simply curious, men and women unself-consciously light tiny tapers in front of regilded statues of Buddhas or kneel on handmade cushions before a gorgeously repainted Goddess of Fertility. Buddhist priests, seated around long tables heaped with offerings of cakes and fruit, chant prayers for the dead and burn paper money for the departed, as the family and strangers solemnly watch. Thousands flock to Christmas mass in Beijing's Catholic cathedral. The Han presence in Tibet has not discouraged devout Tibetans who make arduous pilgrimages on their hands and knees to the Jokharta Temple in Lhasa or visit the monasteries, hauntingly empty, with saffron robes thrown over the prayer cushions of the hundreds of monks murdered during the Cultural Revolution.

An enormous attraction for tourists, some of the temples, monasteries, and churches destroyed by the Red Guards during the Cultural Revolution have been restored with government money. But once opened to the public, the religious buildings rely heavily for support on admission tickets, donations, and small shops that sell religious articles and books. Moon cakes, delicacies stuffed with nuts and lotus seeds and a traditional must for the autumn Moon Festival, are the lucrative specialty of Shanghai's biggest Buddhist vegetarian restaurant, outside the temple courtyard. The restaurant closes for weeks to bake tins and tins of the moon cakes for locals who would buy no others.

There is a building boom for new mosques in the western provinces and regions of Ningxia, Qinghai, Xinjiang, and Gansu, whose large Muslim populations coexist uneasily with the Han Chinese who have been resettled in many of their communities.

ABORTION, ACUPUNCTURE, AND ANTIBIOTICS

If the 52-million-member Communist Party is in conflict with the rest of society on many questions of the old ways against the new, there is consensus on the ancient problem of the nation's health. A World Bank team found in the mid-1980s that the pattern of Chinese health problems has changed from that of a low-income developing country. High rates of infant mortality and of deaths from preventable parasitic and infectious causes have been dealt with in a remarkably short time, a tribute to the financial and human resources party and government have allocated, despite other pressing priorities.

In a county clinic we visited sixty miles from Ningbo, the South China port city, the tubby chief surgeon, dressed in the same white cotton coat and bun-shaped cap that is also the uniform of Chinese sanitation workers, kitchen help, and factory technicians, warmed to the subject of preventive health measures.

Government preventive health campaigns in the past forty years have all but wiped out the epidemics and plagues that killed millions in Old China. Better sanitation, food supplies, and immunization programs have vastly improved the general health and longevity of the population. The leading causes of death in China today are no longer infectious diseases but, as in industrialized nations, cardiovascular diseases, stroke, and cancer.

Every community is exposed to public health education. The chief surgeon reported that his team working with the medical aides or paramedics in the eight villages of his district had made certain that all children under the age of three years had their shots, but safe running water that met World Health Organization standards was still a problem.

The latest health campaigns are aimed at curbing smoking, spitting, and drinking. China, according to official accounts, has relatively few cases of AIDS and drug addiction, which are carefully watched and controlled.

In the direct Chinese way, economics, not persuasion, is expected to discourage smoking, spitting, and drinking. Fines of a few cents have noticeably cut the number of citizens who hawk and spit on the sidewalks and smokers who light up in railway stations. China, the world's biggest cigarette producer and consumer, turns out 228 billion cigarettes annually for its 300 million smokers, mostly men who seem to smoke constantly, between courses at banquets, at work, in the trains, on the streets.

Health officials expect that cigarette consumption will fall as the cost of cigarettes rises with the removal of price ceilings. The favorite foreign brands, Marlboro and the British 555, which have the double purpose of tips or tokens of gratitude, may not be tucked so prominently in shirt pockets of successful officials or well-paid employees when prices rise from their current $3 a pack.

The government decision to raise the price of Mao Tai liquor from $5 a bottle to as much as $30 and the $1-a-liter Chinese beer, brewed according to old Czech and German formulas, to similar heights was based mainly on the need to conserve precious grain, rather than to discourage excessive drinking or alcoholism. A spokesman claimed that the price rises "will not have much social impact, because most buyers are government organizations and those individuals with high incomes." China boosters expressed hope that the same price curbs would be applied to another favorite beverage, expensive imported Coca-Cola, in favor of the domestically produced imitation, the Lucky brand.

As the chief surgeon spoke of these health campaigns, a narrow skiff drew up along the riverbank fronting the clinic. A village paramedic and the helmsman carefully lifted out a frail old woman and carried her into the hospital. Trailing behind was the daughter-in-law who, according to custom, will stay to feed and wait on the invalid, a strange arrangement in the land of surplus labor, but perhaps a psychological plus for the sick.

The paramedic, a thirty-two-year-old former laborer with six months' medical training, tends to the first aid needs of her fellow villagers in a small office furnished with a large cabinet of simple remedies and Chinese herbs, a scale, a large antique pier glass, and an examining table covered with straw matting. After taking care of colds and scrapes and bruises, her most difficult task is checking on proper waste disposal from the local industry, eels, boiled, stripped, and pickled for export to Japan, she quickly explained before pushing off in the skiff for the return to her village.

The clinic, like most medical facilities outside of major cities, was very simply, minimally equipped. The hospital chief was obviously proud of the spare, airy, four-bed wards, the emergency room, the Western-style operating room, and the pharmacy for traditional Chinese medicine, lined from top to bottom on all four walls with tiny drawers filled with herbs.

The operating room and the pharmacy represent one of the few deliberate policies of the Communist government to combine Old and New China by financing and promoting the practice of both modern (Western) medicine and traditional Chinese medical treatment with herbs and acupuncture. A quarter of all Chinese doctors, approximately 350,000, practice traditional medicine exclusively, but increasingly, city as well as rural doctors prevent and treat diseases with both therapies.

The surgeon described the case of one of his patients whose cancer is now in remission after state-of-the-art surgery and radiation treatments at a nearby metropolitan hospital. But doctor and patient both put great faith in the therapeutic effects of the patient's daily doses of Chinese herbal medicine.

Public pharmacies, stocked with very expensive Western pharmaceuticals, frequently advertise them with large signs lettered in English across their store fronts: ERYTHROMYCIN or PENICILLIN. They also sell very inexpensive imitations of Western drugs, as well as herbs, which are ladled out of their drawers, weighed, and bundled up in plain paper with instructions to boil, shred, swallow. Self-prescribing Chinese are devoted consumers of the herbal wines, powdered deer horn, ginseng, and "heart" medicine tastefully boxed in heart-shaped packages, available in gift shops and apothecaries.

As the chief surgeon led a tour through the spacious halls of the new clinic, he acted out some of his own ambiguous feelings about abortion, feelings shared by many of the Chinese medical profession. Darting into the nursery for newborns, he emerged beaming with a tiny baby in his arms, obviously as enchanted with it as his visitors were.

HOUSES, HUTONGS, AND HIGH-RISES

China has been working hard to catch up with the needs and demands of its population, sweeping more and more consumer goods, roads, housing, and services into the tidal wave of its millions. Its rapidly expanding population continues to create new shortages and exacerbate old ones. Electric power, transportation, land, raw materials, sometimes even food, are in short supply. Only the relatively privileged few in China are not affected in some way in their daily lives by the distortions and shortages caused by over-population.

The shortage of housing and inadequate housing affect both city and country people. The whitewashed houses of Lhasa with bright striped cotton pelmets over the windows, flying red, blue, and green Buddhist prayer flags from their flat roofs, or the thatched houses flanked with enormous cones of drying ears of corn on tiny islands in a Shandong lake village may be picturesque, and fine old courtyard houses with tiled roofs and heavy carved beams may have architectural value, but the odds are that none have indoor running water, toilets, or adequate heating. A third of the Chinese population lives in substandard housing, according to Chinese housing authorities, and in a poor country, much of what is rated as adequate housing would be below industrialized nations' standards.

The average peasant family may enjoy triple the living space of their urban counterparts, but the first visible signs of prosperity in the countryside are the new houses that boast indoor water and sanitary plumbing. Even if circumstances permit and the community has electricity, many peasant homeowners prefer to rely on the traditional oven that accommodates woks and sends heat to the underside of the *kangs* (platforms that serve as beds). The new money peasants are earning is invested in remodeling or new home construction, a good investment according to the laborers who can now buy and sell their houses, or pass them along to children, even if the land beneath still belongs to the state.

In overpopulated cities, adequate housing is one of the most acutely felt shortages. While the population manages to cope with the crowded stores, packed buses, and pedestrian traffic that spills over from sidewalks to the streets, people yearn for privacy and space in their living quarters. Single adults and students are housed, four to a room, in dormitories provided by their work units, the municipal governments, or their schools.

Only families merit assignment to apartments or to houses that have been subdivided to accommodate more than one family.

Young couples who wish to marry and live outside their parental homes say it is easier to find a good mate than any kind of apartment.

Every city has its old *hutongs*—lanes of century-old houses, built around walled-off courtyards. Over the past decades, the spirit walls intended to confound the egress of bad demons who enter the main gates have been torn down and the courtyards have grown additions like barnacles to provide room for several families who share communal outside toilets and water faucets.

"At the time of the liberation, one generation of the family lived in the four rooms in this courtyard. The older generation lived behind in the next courtyard," a Beijing blue-collar worker said. "Later there was one family in each room of the courtyard. Even then, some of them managed to take in a needy relative or two."

North and central China have bitter continental winters, followed by blazing summers. In the south, winters are mild but summers so extreme that Shanghai and Wuhan are called "furnace cities." Chinese cope with the cold with little coal stoves that appear in rusty heaps every autumn at the local hardware stores. The acrid smoke from perforated cakes of compacted coal commonly used for fuel pollutes gray winter skies and, according to newspaper accounts, occasionally asphyxiates families whose makeshift stovepipes fail to function properly.

Residents in the gray cement blocks of apartments built during the 1950s and '60s have amenities such as central heating and electricity, but some must fetch their hot water in kettles and Thermoses from central community boilers. The only adornment of most buildings are the balconies, which serve as storerooms for wicker trunks, bicycles, umbrellas, spittoons, piles of stored winter vegetables, drying laundry, or any paraphernalia that can't be squeezed into cramped indoor living quarters. The overflow is piled on staircases.

If urban houses and apartments are inadequate, at least they are inexpensive. Rents paid to the municipal governments or to work units average only 1 or 2 percent of wages. The rents, of course, have never covered the cost of construction, let along taken into account the value of the land on which they stand. Broken windows, scaling cement, and peeling paint are obvious signs of maintenance that is minimal, sometimes nonexistent.

The central government is now looking for new ways to get out from under the burden of nearly $7 billion a year for new construction and rent subsidies and still provide more housing and realistically finance existing housing.

A fairly successful experiment in the port city of Yantai raised the government rents to six times their original sums, while the basic wages of the renters were increased by 24 percent. Wage raises, however, were in the form of housing coupons, not cash. Brand-new housing is being sold to applicants on installment plans at discount prices of two-thirds their actual cost. Old houses, offered for sale in this experiment in Yantai and other cities, have attracted few buyers, since most have no running water, indoor toilets, or electricity.

As desperate as many Chinese citizens are for housing, the principle of government-subsidized basics dies hard, and some citizens are very disgruntled with the housing reforms. A Shanghai resident wrote to his local newspaper, a frequent outlet for citizens' complaints:

> Housing is an absolute necessity, like grain, for people's existence. Low rents suit the prevailing low incomes in our country. In a socialist country, housing is part of the universal social welfare. It is not meant to make a profit, at the expense of the people. Reform is aimed at changing what is irrational, not the fine tradition of safeguarding the interests of the people.

But Shanghai is pushing ahead with plans to make housing pay for itself. Five to 10 percent of the municipal housing stock will be sold each year, and, in the meantime, rents will be doubled from their current average monthly rate of $4 to $5.

Public response has been mixed. Large majorities of the public in several municipalities and provinces surveyed by the *People's Daily* welcomed the new plans because they believe that the reforms will encourage people to save their money for housing, rather than spend it on scarce consumer goods. They also felt that "backdoor allocations" that place some applicants unfairly at the head of housing lists would be eliminated.

CHINESE CONSUMERISM

More Chinese are better fed and better clothed and possess more modern conveniences than ever before in their history. So well fed, in fact, that the minister of health cautioned citizens not to eat so much meat, an exhortation that may have more to do with conserving precious grain from use as swine or cattle feed than anxiety about cholesterol. Still, 80 million urban and rural citizens have inadequate diets, due to inflation, poor harvests, inefficient or inadequate distribution of foodstuffs, or simply poverty.

Inflation that has reached 30 percent in some areas has taken a terrible toll among urban families and pensioners. Buffered by state-subsidized rents, utilities, and medical care, the average family spends more than half its monthly income on food, even when the prices of grains, cooking oil, and other food items have been controlled. Since the free markets appeared, the abundance and variety of food in China has improved. If they can afford to spend a few pennies more per kilo than state store prices, Chinese food shoppers will fill their shopping nets and baskets in the free market, passing up the state-run stores with their piles of fruit and vegetables, which are never quite so fresh or available in such great variety.

Peasants now have incentives to grow all sorts of produce, and Chinese agriculturists claim that there are more than 100 varieties of fruits and vegetables available in South China and an average of twenty varieties in northern cities. But for the 200 million urban Chinese whose meals are composed mainly of rice or noodles and vegetables, the choice of fresh produce, meat, or fish is still limited not only by price but also by the seasons and by the availability of transport.

The arrival of the first persimmons in the autumn or fresh young beans in the spring is cause for lines of shoppers. Trains and planes from lush tropical South China or livestock-rearing Northwest China are filled with travelers bearing huge bundles of pineapples, whole stalks of little green bananas, or cartons of meat, to the delight of city friends and relatives and, sometimes, the discomfiture of their fellow passengers. The pilot for the government airline who refused to take off from Kunming until one of the passengers jettisoned an enormous sack of too-aromatic garlic dealt with a common problem.

Most Chinese in cities, towns, and villages shop for food in neighborhood state stores, free markets, and the small specialty shops, such as the tea stores with shelves of beautifully decorated canisters, offering a variety of teas from the very cheap to the very expensive, purchased for special occasions.

Supermarkets are gradually being introduced, and like many other ideas adopted from the Western world, they have distinctive Chinese characteristics. An enormous metropolitan "supermarket" accommodates its masses of shoppers with aisles wide enough for trucks to drive in and simply dump huge loads of cabbages or scrawny frozen chickens into large tiled bins in the middle of the store. Counters for pickled vegetables in barrel-size stoneware crocks, racks of spicy sausages and flattened preserved pigs' heads are ranged around the edges. Impassive clerks in the standard white coat and bun-shaped caps stand by; there is no hard sell in state stores.

Consumer surveys claim that more than half of Chinese households have television sets and one in eight families has a washing machine. Floor electric fans are a coveted item in sultry southern China, and electric rice cookers are popular additions to tiny city kitchens equipped with the typical two-burner stoves.

Due to China's shortage of electricity, household consumers are accustomed to using their proudly acquired electric appliances sparingly. Householders must pay a stiff surcharge for any electricity used over a basic level. Houses and apartments wired for electricity are lit with low-wattage bulbs. On hot summer evenings in cities, families move outside to dimly lit sidewalks to read, gossip, and play cards. In some cities such as Chongqing, neighborhoods of very old houses have never been wired for electricity. Resourceful housewives simply hook up their washing machines to the street's electric poles and hang their laundry on horizontal bamboo poles that stretch above the sidewalks like colorful banners.

There appears to be no shortage of consumer goods or buyers for them. The big-city department stores have special features to allow for the enormous crowds they attract. Extra-broad staircases permit streams of customers, eight and ten abreast, to move up and down from floor to floor. Pensioners with official red armbands and bullhorns control the constant pressure of shoppers going in and out extra-wide doorways.

Chinese shoppers pay for expensive purchases with enormous piles of banknotes. Checks and credit cards are virtually unknown, except in hotels, restaurants, and shops that cater to foreigners. Sales clerks reckon the sums with lightning speed and a furious clacking of beads on an abacus, which is still China's cash register and calculator. Even bank clerks, slightly mistrustful of their Japanese-made calculators, will double-check their figures on an abacus.

Favorite consumer purchases are the traditional Chinese decorative products that people were unable to find or afford during the austere Mao years: pink silk lampshades, lacquerware from Fuzhou, gorgeous brocades from Suzhou, scrolls of classic Chinese paintings and the Eight Immortals, and chopsticks of jade or ivory. Gaudy mass-produced posters of Kitchen Gods, paper lanterns, and garlands are purchased to celebrate holidays properly.

New department stores, with elegant mannequins and piped-in classical music, stocked with latest upscale merchandise, are modeled after Western stores. Older shops have updated their appearance with large plate-glass windows and shiny aluminum doorways. Local and provincial stores display a profusion of modern and traditional wares: tools; stacks of rice bowls, packed for shipping with intricate nets of hemp and straw; bamboo graters; cast-iron woks alongside electric rice cookers; hot plates; brassieres; and nail polish. Work gloves stacked next to giant pots of bright pink face cream and bottles of black hair dye, blankets made of real dog fur (smelly for a year or two, the saleswoman advises, but unsurpassed for warmth), next to shock absorbers, vacuum cleaners, and straw brooms are the eclectic jumble of available merchandise. Leather shoes have replaced the heaps of cheap, serviceable cotton shoes for men, women, and children.

For Chinese who have the money and special preference, there are now merchandise choices unavailable just a few short years ago. Across the street from the tinsmith who used to have a steady business of mending blackened, battered pots, pans, and woks, there is a new store with handsome, gleaming stainless steel cutlery, pots, pans, and even large pieces of restaurant equipment. Stereos, cellular phones, computers with Chinese-character keyboards, and exercise machines are all available to buyers with enough yuan in their pockets. The Chinese walking out of a store with a little red rectangular object clutched to his breast is not carrying the *Thoughts of Mao,* but a new transistor radio.

Clothing stores are crammed with modern fashionable clothing—jogging shoes, fur coats, elegant lingerie with familiar American or European labels—manufactured in China for the domestic market and export. Economy, rather than preference, probably accounts for the numbers of peasants and workers who still wear blue cotton, baggy pants, loose jackets, and the ubiquitous Mao caps. They cost a fraction of the price of the jeans, colored T-shirts, and sweatshirts with improbable slogans in English printed across their fronts that are beginning to make their appearance in fields and at work sites.

Older officials continue to order trim hand-tailored Mao suits and tuck a ballpoint or two in their breast pockets, a sort of badge of importance, but Western-style suits, windbreakers, and wool trousers are the choice of young men, China's new breed of businessmen and even politicians, in spite of the fact that dry cleaning is expensive and can take as long as six weeks.

The first chilly days of autumn used to signal the gradual ballooning of the silhouettes of Chinese men, women, and children. As the temperatures steadily dropped, layer after layer of shirts, sweaters, jackets were added and startling cerise long underwear peeped out from under padded trousers. The final layer, a bulky army green greatcoat with artificial fur collar or a padded jacket, has been replaced, along with the many layers of clothing, with an export-quality down coat or jacket by Chinese who can afford them.

Minority women such as the Dai in the South or the Caucasian types, such as the Uighurs in the Northwest, never traded their colorful native dresses and delicate jewelry for the drab, monotonous shapeless pants and blouses that were de rigueur for Han women after the revolution. Each year since the reforms, cautiously at first, then more and more unconcerned with conservative criticism, Chinese women have abandoned the uniform slacks and blouses for smart gaily colored skirts and dresses. Gold jewelry is particularly fashionable, justified as a hedge against inflation and a perfect opportunity for women to indulge in luxury that was considered bourgeois and unseemly during sterner Communist days.

A booming market economy as well as a growing population has put tremendous pressures on China's transportation system. Trucks and buses, transporting produce, people, and goods, travel at almost the pace of the herds of bicycles that weave in and out of the traffic along two-lane roads that connect villages and towns with cities. At bus stops and railway stations, clusters of would-be passengers squat patiently on their heels, ready to storm them, managing to squeeze thirteen people into ten square feet of a bus or train by one quasi-official count.

Excess labor is substituted for shortages of power and equipment. Massive projects of laying sewer pipes or digging tunnels are accomplished by scores of men and women, doing the work of nonexistent ditch-digging machines. They work barefoot or in cotton shoes, with shovels and picks, transferring dirt and rubble from hand to hand in wicker baskets and trundling it in wheelbarrows along narrow planks. A half-mile-long goods conveyor belt stands silent in one of China's ports, while hired part-time laborers haul crates from warehouses and docks to waiting freighters. The advantages are twofold: jobs for the unemployed and saving scarce electric power.

POPULATION AND PLANNING

Many of China's projections of income, living space, and infrastructure for the turn of the century are based on the stated goal of 1.2 billion population. Uncontrolled population growth and unpredictable numbers of citizens threaten to undermine all these goals.

The city of Xian, undergoing restoration, is typical of the dilemma that faces demographers, social engineers, and economists all over China. Formerly called Chang'an, a capital through nine dynasties, Xian is a favorite tourist site since the 1974 discovery of the army of terra-cotta soldiers in the third-century B.C. tomb of the emperor Qin.

Historians and restorers have pored over ancient plans and sketches dating back to the Tang Dynasty to decide what must be done to restore the inner city, its imposing city gates, and the drum tower to their former imperial grandeur. Restoration has already begun on the ramparts of the intact surrounding city walls, tourist-worthy attractions in themselves. Most city walls were destroyed long ago by wars or used as quarries for houses and temples. Beijing kept most of its walls, including a section used as the imperial elephant stables, until the 1950s. But then they were torn down to make way for broad boulevards and rows of apartments, a decision that some older residents of the capital still regret.

In Xian, the urban planners and engineers agree that the walls will stay, but they are frustrated by their lack of information for other phases of their planning. The city that once was one of the largest in the world with 1 million inhabitants must now move some of its present 2.5 million citizens to new, multistoried buildings outside the city walls.

"It is very difficult. In fact, it is impossible for us to plan and to build for even the near future, unless we know how big our population will be," one of the architects complained. "Our industry and economy are improving, but we don't have unlimited resources. We must plan very carefully. If our population grows by leaps and bounds, how can we know how many apartments, schools, or shops we must build, or how much sewage and power lines we must provide?"

That is China's dilemma and its challenge.

FOUR

A BRIEF OVERVIEW OF 5,000 YEARS

OF CHINESE HISTORY

Chinese history is remote, monotonous, obscure and, worst of all, there is too much of it.

—ARTHUR H. SMITH, *North China Herald*, 1908

A history that begins in the fourth millennium B.C. may seem remote, the Neolithic period obscure, a succession of dynasties monotonous. But 5,000 years of history explain much about modern China. Many of the present-day Chinese concepts of the relationship between the ruler and the ruled; the reliance on patriarchal, familial, or personal connections; the traditional family and its role; attitudes toward anybody who is not Chinese; and religious eclecticism can be traced back at least to the third and second millennium B.C.

Since adopting a republican form of government early in this century and then declaring a socialist state in 1949, China has had a long struggle to come to terms with some of these distinctly Chinese social and political relationships as well as customs and attitudes deeply embedded in the national culture. Some, labeled feudalistic, have been banned or legislated out of existence. Others are simply tolerated and continue to endure in the Chinese psyche and way of life.

According to tradition, the "Father of China," Huangdi or August Sovereign, reigned 5,000 years ago. Although the 1921 discovery of Peking Man (now commemorated in a dusty museum thirty miles from Beijing) indicates traces of human existence in China a half million years ago, Chinese history books begin with Huangdi's reign during the Neolithic era, the fourth millennium B.C. He was the head of one of the many small tribes that settled along the rich alluvial plains of the Yellow River. Unearthed artifacts, red, black, and gray pottery, stone knives and spearheads used by these tribes support the proud Chinese claim that not only their history but also a fairly high degree of culture already existed 5,000 years ago.

Ancient lore and tradition substitute for historical facts from the reign of Huangdi through the first and perhaps legendary Xia dynasty founded by the mythical hero Yu the Great, sometime between 2200 B.C. and 2000 B.C.

A more distinct picture of life and customs in ancient China emerges during the successor to the Xia, the Shang dynasty. In recent times, archaeological excavations for canals, roads, and dams are serendipitously unearthing oracle bones and tortoise shells covered with pictograms, bronze ritual vessels, burial tombs, even remains of towns built during that dynasty. Historians don't agree on the span of Shang dynasty, which they date variously from 1800, 1600, or 1500 B.C. to 1000 B.C., but they have been able to reconstruct ancient social, political, and religious customs and relationships dating from that period. Much has endured or been adapted during successive dynasties and continues to exert a powerful influence on millions of Chinese in the twentieth century.

THE RULER AND THE RULED

From the legendary Xia dynasty up to 1912, when the last dynasty, the Qing, abdicated the Dragon Throne, China has been ruled by a succession of Chinese or foreign emperors. Aloof, awesome figures, the emperors always held a very special relationship to their subjects. As early as the Shang dynasty, the emperor was looked upon not only as the sovereign head of state, but also as a religious leader in a sense, the "Son of Heaven." He was considered a link between heaven and earth, or, more precisely, heaven and the people.

Dynasty after dynasty, the imperial government exerted its power through rigid customs and strict protocol, but above all it relied for its direction on the moral authority of the emperor, not a code of laws or institutions. The emperor was honored and respected not for his military prowess or administrative abilities but for his virtue, which served as the model for all citizens. Every Chinese citizen, from the highest official or nobleman to the lowest peasant, was expected to revere the emperor, obey his edicts, and follow his moral example.

Although Chinese emperors commanded extraordinary reverence and obedience from the masses, they suffered a certain lack of loyalty. Few emperors ruled unchallenged; most faced popular uprisings by the oppressed, heavily taxed peasantry or threats to their thrones from domestic rivals or alien invaders.

Since the emperor was responsible for the successful conduct of public affairs, he received little popular sympathy if he was overthrown by rebels, rivals, or foreign powers. In the Chinese view, a defeated emperor was an emperor somehow deficient, lacking in virtue, and deserving of his fate.

Historians have pointed out that the Chinese may have been the most rebellious of civilized races but the least revolutionary. Rebels assumed colorful names: The Red Eyebrows were desperate farmers dispossessed by floods; the Yellow Turbans were a group of disgruntled generals; the White Lotus Society was an underground band of religious or semireligious sects opposed to the ruling dynasty. Several domestic rebellions actually overthrew the ruling power, but they caused little or no change in the social order or methods of government.

After thousands of years of one emperor replacing another, however, rebels in the nineteenth century posed the first serious challenge to the traditional Chinese government. The prestige and the resources of the imperial government were seriously weakened after the British defeated China in the Opium War (1839–1842). Millions of Chinese workers were out of work, homeless, and hungry. Under the leadership of the Taiping rebels, they turned their anger against the emperor.

Some of the aspirations of the Taiping rebels were truly revolutionary: abolition of private ownership of land; abolition of concubinage; and equality of the sexes. In the end, the religious fanaticism of the Taiping leaders and the threat of completely overthrowing the established order frightened peasants, small landowners, and the rural poor. The rebellion, lacking the support of the masses, was suppressed by the emperor's army in 1864, but imperial power was secure for only another fifty years.

From the time of the Shang dynasty, the ruling class was dominated by a small group of noblemen whose titles were passed down to their sons. Wealthy landowners, scholar officials, and rich merchants eventually joined the privileged class, but this elite group probably numbered as few as 2 percent, never more than 10 percent, of the population at any time during imperial history.

The hereditary ruling class of the Shang dynasty hunted and waged war while the peasants toiled outside the town walls. The "great tradition," considered for centuries by the rest of the world as the Chinese way, consisted of a separate elite religion, celebrated by the Son of Heaven, and a nobility with the exclusive right to possess arms. Peasants practiced a completely separate culture of religious cults and customs—the "little tradition."

Ritual, privilege, and powerful mystique separated the masses from the emperor and the ruling class, according to an ancient dictums: "Ceremonial rites do not touch the common people; legal penalties do not touch high dignitaries"; "Those who earn their living by labor are destined to be ruled." The peasantry—more than 80 percent of the population—were regarded by emperors and nobility merely as taxpayers, forced labor, army conscripts, and potential rebels.

The teachings of Confucius (551–479 B.C.), not a religion but a code of social conduct, legitimized the enormous gap between the ruler and the ruled, solidified the social class system and influenced the moral order in China up to the twentieth century. The Confucian code laid down distinct obligations of obedience and respect from the younger to the elder, wives to husbands, sons to fathers, but, most important of all, subjects to their rulers.

Over the centuries, continued oppression by the hereditary nobility of the Zhou dynasty, successor to the Shang, led to open rebellions that splintered the kingdom into several city-states governed by leaders who won their power by force, not by noble claim. When the Han reunified the empire 500 years later, its first emperor, intent on preserving the power of a ruling aristocracy, reinstated the Confucian code.

As the Chinese population grew and the simple noble-peasant society became more diversified, four social classes emerged under the Han. The most important was the ruling class, the hereditary nobility. Next came the peasants. Craftsmen ranked third. Last, at the bottom of the social scale, were the merchants. The aristocracy, steeped in Confucianism, which loftily disdained the profit motive, feared that great landowning families or prosperous merchants would challenge their power.

Their fears were justified. In time, Confucianism made it possible for wealthy landowners and merchants to replace or supplement the nobility as the ruling class of China. In imperial China, men gained entry to the ruling class by becoming a member of the civil service. Originally, the mandatory rigorous civil service examination was based almost exclusively on Confucian teachings and was open only to the nobility.

The aspiring scholar-official was required to write "eight-legged essays" in a very formal manner on a theme from the Four Books, a group of canonical writings. To prepare for the difficult examination required leisure and education possible only for the wealthy. Rich merchants and landowners invested some of their fortunes in education for their sons to pass the civil service examinations and enter the ruling circle. Such entry not only enhanced their social status, but also protected their commercial interests.

The emphasis on a Confucian education had another and very damaging effect on Chinese society up to the twentieth century. The Chinese scholar-official was not concerned with political or scientific developments, nor was he required to know anything about economics, finance, or technology.

By the mid-nineteenth century, after the British had overwhelmed the Chinese with the superiority of Western technology and arms in the Opium War, many Chinese realized that their educational system had to be modernized. Over the objections of Confucian traditionalists, the examination system was abolished in 1905, and subjects such as mathematics and science were finally introduced in colleges and the nation's single university in Beijing.

THE CENTER OF THE WORLD

For centuries, the Chinese were convinced that they possessed a culture superior to all others, and they stubbornly remained aloof from and ignorant of the rest of the world. Since the founding of the first small kingdom, the Chinese believed that all mankind revolved around their emperor, just as the stars revolved around the Pole Star. Their country, the Middle Kingdom, or Zhongguo, was the center of the world, the source of all culture and civilization, in the Chinese estimate. An agricultural people living in the plains and along rivers, the Chinese looked upon the tribes living in the desert and mountain regions on the northern and western borders of the Middle Kingdom as foreigners and as barbarians.

In fact, these "barbarians" were backward, unsophisticated people who willingly acknowledged the Chinese claim to superior culture. They were impressed by the Chinese script, monetary system, palaces, roads, canals, and organized society. Many of these foreigners—Tobas, Kitans, Tangut Tibetans, Jurchen, or Mongols and Manchu, who eventually invaded and ruled the nation—so admired the Chinese culture and civilization that they assumed Chinese customs and characteristics. Alien conquerors found it expedient and efficient to adopt the Chinese bureaucracy, institutions, organization of government, and even the language in order to rule the enormous territories of imperial China.

According to the Chinese, the moral superiority and the beneficent favor of their emperor could be enjoyed by the barbarians as well as Chinese citizens, but there were very explicit conditions. When a new category of foreigners from beyond the mountains and deserts—merchants and traders from Persia and Arabia—began to arrive in China in the seventh century, they were required to recognize the suzerainty of the emperor and superiority of China by bringing tribute, usually elaborate gifts, and kowtowing before the emperor.

The traditional kowtow, a threefold genuflection that involves touching the ground nine times with the forehead, did not come as easily to Western visitors as it had with deferential Middle Easterners. When the British ambassador George Macartney in 1793 and British envoy William Amherst in 1816 refused to prostrate themselves before the emperor, it simply confirmed Chinese beliefs that all foreigners were barbarians.

However, from the seventh century on, the obligatory tribute system and the kowtow embodied the Chinese imperial attitude toward trade and foreigners. Any trading privileges granted by the imperial court in exchange for tribute were purely incidental, a minor issue, in Chinese eyes, up until the nineteenth century, when Western powers extracted extraordinary trading and territorial concessions from the imperial government with the use or threat of force.

Haughtily sure of their superiority, dynasty after dynasty chose to be isolated and uninformed about developments in the rest of the world. And, in fact, up until the fifteenth century, China *was* far more advanced than the barbarians surrounding the Middle Kingdom and than even the West. The magnetic compass, paper, printing, movable type, the wheelbarrow, the sailing carriage, the crossbow, the iron chain suspension bridge, kites, porcelain, gunpowder, were invented and used in the Middle Kingdom long before they were known in Europe. Early accounts of the splendor and luxury of Chinese civilization by Marco Polo and other Western travelers dumbfounded skeptical Christian Westerners who knew little or nothing about that vast advanced world in the Far East.

However, by the thirteenth century, Western scientific knowledge had begun to surpass that of the circle of astronomers, seers, prophets, and diviners that advised the Chinese emperors. According to the Chinese notion of the world, what happened in the heavens bore a tremendous influence on earthly events. Private affairs and imperial decrees were determined by auspicious dates and omens. Therefore, great importance was laid on the calculation of the calendar and the study of astronomy, astrology, and mathematics. More likely the imperial welcome offered the first Western travelers, emissaries of the pope, soon followed by a few adventuresome merchants, was due to their advanced scientific knowledge rather than any Chinese interest in Christianity or desire to expand trade.

If the earliest Western travelers returned home without any Chinese converts to Christianity or advances in international trade, neither did they incur the enmity or distrust of the Chinese. In fact, the most famous of these early travelers to the medieval imperial court, Marco Polo, became a trusted favorite, ambassador, and advisor of Kublai Khan, founder of the Mongol dynasty in China, grandson of Genghis Khan, in the late thirteenth century.

In 1245 Pope Innocent IV sent the Italian Franciscan monk, Giovanni Carpini, with an official letter to the court of Kublai Khan. The pope, aware of the communities of Nestorian Christians already living in China, probably hoped for more converts. While the emissary returned without any converts he did bring back wonderful tales of a country "very rich in cereals, wine, gold, silver, silk and everything that human nature needs for its sustenance."

A few years later, another Franciscan, the Fleming William of Rubrik, arrived in the Far East, this time in hopes of persuading the Mongols to join European Christians in liberating the Holy Land from the Muslims. His mission was also a failure, but he added to the lore about China: cities with walls of silver and gold, silks and the Chinese currency, "cotton cloth, as long and as wide as a hand, on which lines of writing are impressed."

Almost two centuries passed before Europe rediscovered the Far East. At the end of the fifteenth century, the Portuguese and Spanish set sail on their voyages of exploration, rounding the Cape of Good Hope in 1497. The Portuguese arrival in the Bay of Canton in

1517 created an incident that deepened Chinese antipathy and distrust toward Westerners for the next 400 years.

As the Portuguese ship, the first official representative of the Portuguese king, sailed into the bay and up the river to Canton, the captain fired the ship's cannon in a salute, as was Portuguese custom. Unfortunately, it was a serious breach of Chinese regulations, which banned any armaments in the harbor of Canton. The Chinese considered the cannon firing and the Portuguese barbaric.

The mistrust, suspicion, and contempt that the Chinese heaped on the Portuguese was soon turned on the Spanish, Dutch, and, much later, the British and American merchants and mariners who arrived in China in search of trade. The Westerners, who were competing fiercely for trade and business, frequently fought each other. Jealousy, intrigues, and conflicts that sometimes burst into violence were the normal state of affairs between the rivals. The Chinese considered them all uncouth, brutal, and uncivilized and played them off one against the other, a common Chinese diplomatic tactic in dealing with enemies.

One hundred years passed before the Christian missionary movement followed Western traders. The arrival of the Italian Jesuit Matteo Ricci in China at the end of the sixteenth century was an auspicious beginning. Ricci wisely began by first studying and conforming to Chinese customs and culture, precisely what the Chinese expected an uncultured foreigner to do. Only after he had earned respect from the Chinese did he attempt to convert them.

He and followers had limited successes as well as setbacks. Less diplomatic Jesuit priests than Ricci were imprisoned or deported. Then, a few decades later, fellow Jesuits were accepted into the inner circle of the imperial courts of the Ming and later the Manchu because of their much-admired technical abilities and scientific knowledge of mathematics, astronomy, and weapons technology. Large bronze astronomical instruments designed by the Jesuit Father Ferdinand Verbiest can still be seen on the platform of the Beijing Observatory.

If the acceptance of the Christian missionaries who lived and worked in China in the sixteenth, seventeenth, and eighteenth centuries was due largely to their tactful diplomacy or technical skills rather than to their theology, the Chinese opinion of foreign pastors and priests changed drastically in the nineteenth century. Missionaries all over the country were challenging age-old Chinese traditions and the social order when they called for Western-inspired rights for peasants, women, and children. Incidents such as that of a missionary distributing Christian tracts from one side of a British ship moored in Canton harbor while opium was being unloaded on the other side appalled and enraged the Chinese.

A series of treaties beginning with the Treaty of Nanking in 1843 forced China to grant concessions in its ports and along the coast to Great Britain and other Western powers. One of the treaty provisions readmitted Christian missions, which the emperor had previously banned. The foreign powers insisted on imperial toleration of the missionaries and their activities, including the right to buy land and to build churches and schools outside the treaty ports, a flagrant disregard for Chinese sovereignty. What's more, the Westerners were perfectly willing to enforce their demands with the threat of arms when they thought it necessary.

No wonder that the imperial court of nineteenth-century China looked on Christianity as a political tool of the West, introduced by trickery and force and associated with all manner of pernicious evils. To the Chinese emperor, foreign merchants and foreign missionaries inspired the same distrust, suspicion, and scorn as other alien visitors had before them.

THE FAMILY

In traditional China, the family was not only a domestic unit but also an economic and a political unit. Under the feudal system of ancient China, local lords commanded allegiance and tribute in the form of produce or grain from small groups of peasant families. When the Han dynasty eventually adopted Confucianism as the model for public and social conduct, the importance of the family as an economic and political unit was settled for centuries.

All through dynastic history, the family, not the individual, was considered the smallest social unit; Chinese were responsible for taxes, forced labor, and army conscripts as a family, not as individuals. Imperial decrees and the command for peace, harmony, and obedience reached down, step by step, from the emperor through various levels of administrators to the family, which answered for all its members.

Since the family, not the individual, was the main unit of responsibility, every Chinese was expected to be completely integrated into his or her group. Any originality or deviation from tradition was considered abhorrent and disruptive. Individual Chinese owned very little personal property, but if they did attain good fortune, wealth, power, or honor, it was expected that they would share that with the family. This loyalty spread to relatives once, twice, or even thrice removed, a practice that led to the considerable nepotism that has always characterized Chinese public life and government.

The dark side of the Chinese concept of collective family responsibility was that the Chinese authorities also held an entire family legally responsible for all its members' actions, bad as well as good. This meant that shame, dishonor, and even execution for the misdeeds of one member was also the lot of the rest of the family.

The family of imperial China was not necessarily large, but it was certainly extended, traditionally comprising five generations with five degrees of kinship that reached as far as third cousins. Even the dead who remained in "spirit" were counted in the family. The rituals of ancestor worship, offerings, and annual sweeping of the graves, symbols of family unity, are still observed in modern China.

The nobility of the Zhou dynasty created ancestor worship to perpetuate hereditary lines and to guarantee their power. Only nobles bore surnames *(xing),* and the family name could be handed down only through males. Since male heirs, never female, performed the rituals of ancestor worship, a succession of sons was considered of utmost importance. Couples would adopt sons if they were unfortunate enough to have none of their own.

Eventually, all classes of Chinese society acquired surnames, and millions adopted ancestor worship, placing names of their ancestors on wooden tablets on a family altar, where offerings of food, money, and clothes were made to the dead. The present-day dearth of Chinese surnames and the persisting Chinese desire for male heirs can be traced back through centuries of tradition.

The Confucian social hierarchy and rules for respect and obedience were strictly observed within families, particularly aristocratic or prosperous ones, as well as in the government structure. Peasants toiling in fields or paddies to support elderly parents were less likely than nobles to be ruled by their fathers, but were expected to show great respect nonetheless.

On the traditional Chinese social scale where the young deferred to elders, sons to fathers, women ranked at the bottom, even among the wealthy and educated gentry. No matter what their class, females led tightly circumscribed lives, deferring to fathers, brothers, and husbands. Perhaps the mothers-in-law who were permitted to dominate their sons' wives were the only women who had any real power in the Confucian pecking order.

Through marriages—always arranged, either by parents or by matchmakers—daughters could enhance their parents' holdings or status. According to custom, the young bride lived with the groom's family, and if she was a peasant, she worked for them. After feeding and raising girl children, peasants considered the loss of their daughters' working power a serious matter.

RELIGION

Buddhism, Taoism, and Confucianism were the three dominant theologies or philosophies of traditional China. An old Chinese saying, "Three ways to one goal," refers to the traditional Chinese belief that all three could coexist and mingle, as they did for centuries. It was not considered unusual in imperial China for a Chinese who practiced Confucian ideals in his official duties to go home and worship in a Buddhist temple and believe in Taoism.

Official toleration usually accompanied this personal eclectic attitude toward religion. Chinese emperors never launched holy wars or engaged in the bitter clashes between temporal and spiritual powers that flared up between kings and popes in Western history.

In fact, the imperial view was one of detached tolerance to all religions, including Judaism and Nestorian Christianity, which reached China by the seventh century. Many of the traders and merchants from the Middle East who settled in small communities in China's trading ports were either Jews or Christians who believed that the Virgin was the mother of man.

According to one simplified definition of the three doctrines, Confucianism defines the position of man in an orderly social hierarchy; the mysticism of Taoism explains man's relationship to the entire universe; and Buddhism shows man a path of individual redemption, even of release, from the miseries or unhappiness of earthly life. Despite occasional clashes, one set of beliefs did not contradict or deny another's. In fact, they were compatible enough that they borrowed from each other. The Taoists, for instance, were inspired to create a pantheon of deities like the Buddhists.

Although all three doctrines have been part of the Chinese culture since the early dynasties, it is Confucianism that has made the deepest impression on Chinese thought and values, right up to the twentieth century. Confucius intended to construct a philosophy for a social order and government, based on morality, not a religion. Only long after he died and his philosophy had been adopted by Chinese rulers as the official code of conduct for Chinese citizens as well as the government did Chinese emperors raise Confucius (and his descendants) to the nobility and did his doctrine take on the aura of religion.

Although China avoided holy wars, Chinese emperors did suppress or regulate religion when it interfered with imperial policies or revenues. Up until the ninth century, Buddhist monasteries were exempt from taxation. Shrewd peasants who wished to escape taxation, forced labor, and military service gave their land to the monasteries and then worked for them as tenants. Monasteries became so rich and powerful that, in 845, they were closed and monks were ordered to return to civilian life, by imperial decree.

During the same period, the Tang imperial administration also strengthened their control over Taoist monasteries to limit their social power and wealth. Eventually monasteries were reopened and training for the monkhood resumed. Although both religions contributed magnificent sculpture, art, and literature to the Chinese culture, they never regained the same political or economic power in Chinese society.

The Catholic and Protestant missionaries who arrived in China in the mid-nineteenth century in the wake of European traders never made many converts. At any time, Chinese Christians probably numbered 2 or 3 million at most. It has been suggested that Chinese Christians were as interested in the educational opportunities offered by good mission schools as they were in spiritual salvation. Others undoubtedly viewed Christianity as an answer to their increasing dissatisfaction with the centuries-old Chinese values and political system. Christian missionaries' sermons that called for equality of the sexes, the abolition of the binding of women's feet, and freedom for the oppressed peasantry appealed to progressive Chinese. These challenges to tradition and the Chinese way of life were more than the imperial government could tolerate. Many missionaries were persecuted, imprisoned, or forcibly ejected from China during the last dynasty in the late nineteenth and early twentieth centuries.

A SHORT CHRONICLE OF THE DYNASTIES

Little is known about the legendary **Xia dynasty (2205–1766 B.C.)**, but the **Shang dynasty (1766–1122 B.C.)** left the written records of a small feudal society cast in bronze and inscribed on shells and bones. Shang nobles spent their time hunting the plentiful game, and peasants scratched out a living along the Yellow River, in a kingdom not much larger than Connecticut.

Neighboring tribes overthrew the Shang and established the **Zhou dynasty (1122–770 B.C.)**. The Western Zhou, with a capital in Chang'An, the present Xian, was known as the Eastern Zhou when the capital was moved east to Luoyang. The kingdom of the Zhou, the size of Pennsylvania, was the heart of China until the reign of the **ninth-century Tang dynasty.** Despite the transformation from the hunting society of the Shang to a prosperous feudal agricultural society with increasingly sophisticated rituals and regulations, the Zhou dynasty was overcome and destroyed by powerful city-states on its borders.

For the next 500 years, the empire that had been built up by the Zhou remained divided among these rival city-states. A Chinese chronicle that recorded the events between **770 and 476 B.C.,** known as the **Spring and Autumn Period,** describes the worsening life of the peasants and the military and economic difficulties of their rulers. Constant wars encouraged internal state organization such as tax reforms and penal laws and gave rise to a form of diplomacy between the states.

The philosopher Confucius lived during this period, when the traditional aristocracy was fast losing its influence to a class of men who seized power by military strength and political cunning. To combat this unsettling state of affairs, Confucius, an aristocrat himself, maintained that the nobles could retain their power if it was based on a framework of moral principles, instead of hereditary claims. His philosophy was only one of many schools of thought that were trying to devise a system of legitimate and successful government.

The concepts of government and social order developed by Confucius were never accepted by any of the city-state princes during his lifetime or during the continued warfare and political crises of the next 200 years. In fact, Confucianism was banned by the Qin, the short-lived dynasty that emerged as victor after the next era, the **Warring States (476–221 B.C.).**

As the name suggests, the rivalry between the states continued during this period in Chinese history. In spite, or perhaps because, of constant war, remarkable advances and changes mark this turbulent period. Princes and leaders of the several kingdoms, vying for superiority, competed for the most able diplomats and advisors they could find and supported a flourishing intellectual circle of painters, poets, and musicians.

Reform measures eroded the power of the nobility and strengthened central power. Families of peasants were grouped into regiments, the first example of collective responsibility that successive dynasties found extremely useful for governing a large and growing population.

Discovery of the technique of casting iron (almost 1,600 years before it was known in Europe) improved agricultural tools, and the introduction of irrigation systems made the expansion of farming possible. As a defense against the ever-present threat of barbarian invaders, the separate kingdoms built walls along their borders.

The powerful emperor Shi conquered the states and ascended the throne as emperor of a united empire, the **Qin dynasty (220–206 B.C.)**. By 206 B.C. the Qin dynasty was replaced by another dynasty, the Han. During his short fifteen-year reign, the Qin emperor had established absolute power as sovereign of all China, and had given the nation the name foreigners know it by—Qin or Chin-a.

Banning all teachings of Confucius, the Qin emperor organized a highly centralized state, administered by appointed officials rather than the hereditary nobility. From his capital in Chang'An, he ordered the development of communications, a unified written language, currency, and weights and measures, which were adopted by succeeding dynasties. But the best-known known legacy from the Qin dynasty is the beginning of the Great Wall. During the reign of Emperor Shi, a force of 300,000 laborers linked up the walls built by the separate kingdoms during the Warring States period.

The **Han dynasty (206 B.C. to A.D. 220)** rose out of the popular rebellion against the harsh laws and physical and financial strains of the huge works projects ordered by the Qin emperor. The next 400 years of Han rule were interrupted only once, by the "usurper," Wang Mang, who wanted to ban slavery and redistribute land from the wealthy to the poor. The Han restoration of Confucianism as the official code of private and public conduct firmly entrenched the power of the great landowning families. The introduction of a state examination system, based on Confucian teachings, created the scholar-official class, a social hierarchy that ruled China until 1905 when reform and revolutionary influences insisted on European-style education.

The Han then embarked on a period of expansion westward.

During the second and first centuries B.C., the Han opened up the Silk Road, the route over which Buddhism arrived from India. The arts flourished, agriculture was expanded and improved, and trade grew. Despite Confucian distrust of the merchant class, the Chinese merchants also pressed westward, making contacts in central and western Asia and Europe, as far away as Rome. A combination of internal rebellion from peasants and from wealthy landowners, threats from covetous barbarians on its borders, even plotting of court eunuchs (a pattern that led to the demise of other dynasties) finally weakened and broke up the Han empire.

The short period of succession to the Han Dynasty was an omen of the disunity that was to follow. The **Three Kingdoms (220–280 A.D.)** were three rival states, ruled by the Wei, the Shu Han, and the Wu.

For the next four centuries, China was divided, partially reunited, and then split again among overlapping claims to sovereignty by Chinese and alien conquerors. The domestic rebellions and barbarian invasions that caused the disintegration and collapse of the Han dynasty continued in the rival states and competing dynasties, eventually leading each to the same fate.

The **Jin dynasty** is known as the Western Jin as long as its capital remained in Luoyang (265–316) and then the Eastern Jin when the capital was moved to Nanjing after the unification of the empire (317–420).

The **Southern and Northern dynasties (386–589)** divided the empire yet again.

The **Wei dynasty (386–543)** was the first to be ruled by aliens, the Toba, Mongolian warriors from the north. Although they ruled by the traditional Chinese administrative system with Chinese officials, the imperial army was made up entirely of Toba. From separation between a Chinese civil arm and an alien army there arose a Chinese distaste for the military as an institution to look down on, suitable only for barbarians.

Despite the fragmentation of the former Chinese empire until reunification under the Sui dynasty in 581, agriculture expanded, trade and handicrafts continued to develop, and Buddhism took root and flourished. Successive conquerors, rather than imposing their alien cultures, became completely assimilated, adopting Chinese dress, customs, and language.

The **Sui dynasty (581–618)** reunited China for the third time. Although measures were taken to stabilize and strengthen the country internally, massive projects such as the building of the 1,200-mile Grand Canal, which eventually linked Hangzhou with Beijing, required millions of laborers and enormous sums of money. The common people and the upper classes, overburdened and overtaxed, rebelled and the Sui gave way to a new dynasty.

The **Tang dynasty (618–907)** saw a united China reach new heights as one of the most powerful nations in Asia. A great blossoming of the arts, the introduction of block printing, and advances in cartography and astronomy accompanied a determined expansion of the empire. Tibet was brought into the Chinese sphere of influence, and China's borders were pushed to Yunnan in the southwest, northeast toward Korea, and northwest toward the territories of the Turks.

The expansionist ambitions of Tang emperors eventually led to the downfall of the dynasty. According to traditional imperial policy, the Chinese controlled a vastly expanded empire by installing native figureheads over a conquered tribe or minority, with only a small but powerful group of Chinese officials to hand down the imperial decrees. After 300 years of war and expansion, the Tang emperors had overextended the imperial resources and found it impossible to garrison alien territory; more and more of it fell back into the hands of foreign tribes. The growing power of ambitious Chinese generals and the inevitable peasant unrest and rebellion undermined the empire from within, while aliens threatened her from the outside.

The **Five dynasties (907–960)** marked the last breakup of the empire. Dynasties headed by alien rulers and reigns that overlapped each other in different parts of the fragmented nation followed.

The **Liao dynasty (937–1125)** was ruled by the alien Kitan, who established their capital on the site of Beijing. Meanwhile the

Tangut-Tibetans established the **Western Xia dynasty (990–1227),** and another alien people, the Jurchen, proclaimed the **Jin dynasty (1115–1234)** in northern China.

The **Song dynasty (960–1279)** flourished in spite of invasion from the Mongols in the north that forced the imperial court to move from its capital in Kaifeng in 1175. Reestablished in the southern capital, Hangzhou, one of the most magnificent cities of its day, the imperial court encouraged the flowering of the arts, philosophy, and literature. With the loss of the northern empire, the Song government looked to the southeast for revenue.

The inventions of movable type, the magnetic compass, and gunpowder aided the dynasty's expansion of trade. Enormous ships with crews of 1,000 built in Guangzhou (Canton), sailed out from four important ports, Ningbo, Guangzhou, Hangzhou, and Quanzhou to the South China Sea and the Indian Ocean. During this period of consolidation and peace, a prosperous urban society of merchants and traders sprang up and the scholar-official class grew. A highly developed system of maritime regulation degenerated into graft and bribery, but even more powerful forces finally brought down the Song dynasty.

When Kublai Khan established the **Yuan dynasty (1280–1368),** he finally accomplished what his grandfather Ghenghis Khan had started out to do when he swept down from the North in the thirteenth century and conquered almost all of the region of central and northern Asia bordering the Chinese heartland. Kublai Khan managed to bring China itself under control after first forcing the Song dynasty move to the South. Although the southern Chinese were treated particularly harshly, the Mongol conqueror adopted the Chinese system of government and followed the Song policy of open foreign trade, reaping enormous benefits.

Unlike his Chinese predecessors, Kublai Khan welcomed foreign merchants and missionaries, most notably Marco Polo, who became his ambassador and advisor. But he tightened maritime control to keep out "criminals or spies," particularly the Chinese who had fled the Mongol invasion. Land was confiscated and turned over to

Mongols, leading to the inevitable domestic rebellion, this time led by the Red Turbans, which spelled the end of Mongol rule after less than a century.

Under the **Ming dynasty (1368–1644)** Beijing became the permanent capital. Ming emperors, determined to expand and to push the Mongols back north, began the rebuilding of the Great Wall. But Japanese pirates were already ranging along the Chinese coast, and the arrival of the Westerners—the Portuguese in 1517, the Spaniards in 1557, the Dutch in 1606, and the British in 1637— began to threaten imperial power from a different direction.

Harassed on all sides, the emperor banned all private trade, thereby acquiring a state monopoly of all imported goods. Foreign countries wishing to trade with China had to go through an elaborate procedure of establishing relations with the imperial government before receiving permission. This government monopoly of trade had a long-lasting, stifling effect on the growth of private commercial activities and capitalism. When the restrictions were partially lifted, gentry merchants acquired great wealth and, through bribery, political power.

The reorganization of the economy and agriculture caused disturbances among all classes of Chinese—wealthy landowners, peasants, and workers—that further weakened the imperial government and provided the opportunity for the Manchus in the North to march into Beijing and establish a new dynasty. The last of the Ming emperors committed suicide on the Coal Hill behind the Forbidden City, the 250-acre walled and moated park surrounding the Imperial Palace in the heart of Beijing.

The Manchu **Qing Dynasty (1644–1912)** brought a new period of stability and expansion of power until the middle of the nineteenth century. During this dynasty, the empire included not only China's traditional interior territory but also Manchuria, Mongolia, Taiwan, and the Central Asian region of Turkestan. Tibet, conquered by the Mongols when they ruled China, also came under Manchu control but those ties weakened during the last years of the Qing dynasty. The Manchus, like other alien rulers before them, tried to be more Chinese than the Chinese dynasty they replaced. Not only did they not tamper with the traditional Chinese concepts of order in society and the universe or with the administration of the government, they dogmatically reinforced them.

CHINA AND THE WEST

Up until the arrival of the Western powers in the mid-nineteenth century, the Manchu emperors and courts thought that all was going well in traditional China. There was respect and deference for the emperor, the arts and scholarship flourished, the economy prospered, and foreign relations were successful, according to their complacent assessment. However, China's self-imposed isolation from the rest of the world actually left it ill-informed and unable to comprehend the military strength or trading expectations of Western governments. China expected to receive their representatives as it had always received foreign emissaries, with tribute in exchange for controlled trade.

The British for one had an entirely different view of trade between the two countries. They wished to expand their exports to China, particularly opium. Anxious to balance a trade deficit with India, they decided to unload Indian opium on the Chinese market. The Chinese, incensed by the illegal import, finally destroyed a large shipment. The British seized the opportunity to launch a military campaign in 1839. The resultant Opium War ended in 1842 when China signed the Unequal Treaties that opened five ports to British trade and ceded Hong Kong to England.

Other nations, looking for new lucrative markets, took advantage of the weakened imperial government, demanding similar trading privileges, including immunity from Chinese courts. By the turn of the century, China had been divided into spheres of influence among the Russians in Xinjiang, Mongolia and Manchuria, the Germans in Shandong, the British in the Yangtze valley, the Japanese in Fujian, and the French in the southwest, near present-day Vietnam.

The United States also entered the competition for Chinese markets and privileges in the mid-nineteenth century. U.S. Minister

Anson Burlingame promoted business and encouraged American missionaries during his tenure in the Chinese capitol. He secured the same concessions that Britain had extracted from China after its Opium War victory, including extraterritorial rights and most-favored-nation treatment in five ports, for the American traders who made the long voyage to the Orient in the Yankee clipper ships.

Within a few years, the Chinese were exporting labor as well as tea, silk, and porcelain to the United States when American railroads began recruiting Chinese laborers for the construction of the transcontinental railway. With 100,000 mostly poor and illiterate Chinese in the country, men victimized by race riots and lynchings, Congress acted—not to right these injustices but to shut the gates to further Chinese immigration. In 1882, the Chinese Exclusion Act did just that; later restrictions limited immigration to only a few hundred Chinese per year until the 1960s when the law was liberalized.

Meanwhile, the dynasty was threatened from within by domestic uprisings by Mongols in Yunnan province and Turkestan. The most serious revolt was the Taiping rebellion that spread throughout southern China, actually establishing a capital in Nanking in 1853. Its aim to overthrow the dynasty and establish an entirely new, more modern and liberal society, was finally put down in 1864 by the Manchu military with the aid of the British and French who first demanded new concessions and privileges from the weakened and frightened imperial government in return. The fortunes of the Qing Dynasty continued to deteriorate. War broke out between the Chinese and the French, with the defeated Chinese ceding more trading rights to France. In 1895, after a brief war with Japan, China was forced to give up Formosa (Taiwan) and the Pescadores Islands to the victor. Beleaguered from without, the Imperial Court soon felt the continuous ferment of tensions and unrest within the country. Pressed for mild educational and administrative reforms by enlightened scholars, the aging Dowager Empress Ci Xi reasserted strict imperial authority and imprisoned the more liberal young emperor in a palace within the Forbidden City (where he remained until he died in 1908).

Most disastrously of all, the empress, in a desperate attempt to expel the foreign powers, directly supported the Boxers, one of many xenophobic societies that had sprung up in opposition to the power and presence of foreigners.

During the 1890s, the Boxers (literally, in Chinese, the Patriotic Fists) had harassed and attacked foreign traders, businessmen, missionaries, and diplomats throughout the country. The Boxer Rebellion began in June 1900, with an attack on the Beijing diplomatic quarter with an army of 140,000 men, including an imperial war party. The eight-week siege was finally lifted by an expeditionary force made up of all the foreign powers in China.

At the insistence of the United States, the treaty that ended the rebellion did not further carve up China with territorial rights to the foreign powers, but it required the Qing Dynasty to agree to increased trade privileges and to permit the stationing of foreign troops. The United States made a wise investment with its share of the $333 million indemnity demanded by the foreign victors, by returning the money to China as scholarships for Chinese to study in American universities. By example, they forced the Europeans to join in and by World War I, more than a thousand Chinese students had been subsidized by Boxer indemnity funds.

The Qing Dynasty's defeat and humiliation was followed by a decade of attempted reform of the imperial government, intrigue, and betrayal that finally ended in the abdication of China's last Emperor in 1912, shortly after the proclamation of the Republic in December 1911. A loose alliance of military men and the liberal intellectuals surrounding Dr. Sun Yat-sen, who had been working for reform or revolution since the turn of the century, succeeded in replacing China's imperial ruling circle with a parliamentary government.

The United States was the first nation to recognize the Republic of China in 1912, and, from the start, U.S. specialists began advising Sun's new government. The Americans quickly realized that Chinese society was far from ready for the sweeping democratic reforms they proposed. Legislators bought their seats and sold their votes openly while warlords grappled for power. General Yuan Shi-kai, who elbowed Sun and other liberals aside, talked a good deal about the power of the people, but eventually dissolved parliament on a pretext and tried to get himself proclaimed the new emperor.

As the power of the center withered with Yuan's death, warlords carved up the nation and ruled their territories like petty kings. Their mercenary armies were filled with peasants who could eat better and make more money than by working the land. They were allowed to pillage, pay for goods in the constantly inflating paper money, and traffic in drugs and prostitution.

In the cities, small groups of Communists began to organize, first as uneasy allies of Sun's Nationalists and then as bitter enemies, after the sudden Shanghai massacre of Communists directed by Chiang Kai-shek, Sun's former military aide. Chiang had become leader of the Nationalists after Sun's death, and after early battle-field successes he seemed to be in a position to end warlord rule and unify the country. The United States recognized Chiang's Nanking government in 1928.

When Japanese aggression began in Manchuria three years later, an isolationist America did little more than protest. Economic aid followed in 1937, and full alliance after the Japanese attack at Pearl Harbor in 1941. Chiang spent the war alternately negotiating with the Communists and fighting their forces, which he labeled "bandits" but which were becoming formidable guerrilla armies. The Communists had fled Nationalist onslaughts in the Long March of 1934–1935, regrouping in a remote headquarters at Yanan, where the first Western journalists reached them and began to write about their growing strength.

At war's end, in 1945, U.S. policymakers had to come to grips with a victorious but corrupt and authoritarian Nationalist government ready to resume full-scale warfare with the Communists. General George Marshall failed in long negotiations aimed at turning a tenuous cease-fire into an agreement to form a coalition government, and the civil war intensified.

The United States continued to pour money into the Nationalist cause: more than $2.5 billion in the four years between the Japanese defeat and the end of the civil war. As the Communists swept to victory, the Nationalists fled to Taiwan. A State Department White Paper blamed their defeat on corruption and incompetence.

Although Britain and other allied governments recognized Mao Zedong's People's Republic when it was proclaimed in Tiananmen Square October 1, 1949, the United States withheld recognition. But at the same time, it also drew back from its unequivocal support of Chiang. The outbreak of the Korean War half a year later and Mao's decision to commit "volunteers" to the fighting against the Americans restored Chiang to favor.

Two Asian wars, Korea and Vietnam, cast shadows on U.S.-Chinese relations for the next two decades. They affected domestic policy as well as foreign, Chinese internal concerns as well as American. Above all, they caused political conflicts based on faulty perceptions: The Chinese leaders were convinced that the Americans were about to attack them. Washington thought that China, which had attacked U.S. troops in Korea, was an expansionist threat, in Vietnam as well as Korea.

Chinese society suffered when Mao's harsh internal security measures, taken in large part because of this perceived threat, choked off any democracy or pluralism that might have followed victory in the civil war.

The United States found that McCarthyism was fueled in large part by the contention, never proven, that Communists and other traitors or weaklings in the State Department had not only "lost China" but helped create a new and awesome enemy in Asia.

Both nations found themselves in a circle of fear, hysteria, and mistrust. A great part of China's justification for the Great Leap Forward at the end of the 1950s was the buildup of military strength and the industrial capacity to make war against the Americans. According to Edgar Snow, the Maoists justified the repression of the Cultural Revolution in the form of "expunging all remaining bourgeois influences" as a defense against the U.S. and Soviet threats.

Only after these campaigns collapsed and the Chinese split with the Soviet Union did the United States emerge as the lesser foreign evil. The Chinese were able finally to begin the negotiations that led to President Nixon's historic 1972 visit.

In all this history of mutual misperceptions, the real loss has been to China. The United States got over the damage done by the foreign fears that led to McCarthyism. China's development was set back seriously by its overreaction to the perceived threat from abroad.

Now, more than eighty years after the fall of the empire, the imperial palaces are austere museums in the heart of Beijing and the last dynasty's successors, the Communists, are still trying to come to grips with the same kinds of problems the emperors faced over the centuries: how to rule a country now 3,705,390 square miles, populated with more than 1 billion people, including fifty-five minorities.

Many of their problems can be traced to the centuries of indifferent or simply bad rule the population was subjected to. But many of the answers to those problems also may be found in an understanding of the history.

PART TWO

THE ECONOMY

An agricultural country for all of its five millennia, China has begun the transformation that all other developed countries underwent much earlier in their histories. County by county, province by province, region by region, it is industrializing. The process is complicated enormously by another change going on at the same time: abandoning the stringent market regulations decreed by communism and adopting many of the features of capitalism. The people are responding in many ways familiar from Chinese history. In both city and countryside, some are prospering honestly; some are getting rich through position and corruption. And on the bottom rungs of society, in factories and farm villages, people are beginning to demand a bigger share for themselves and to protest against those abusing the economic reforms.

FIVE

AGRICULTURE

Poverty is not socialism.

— DENG XIAOPING, IN A 1992 STATEMENT
DEFENDING HIS REFORMS AGAINST HARDLINERS

CRISIS IN THE COUNTRYSIDE

Peasant protests and disturbances that have erupted in the 1990s in many areas of rural China are causing as much concern among officials as did the student demonstrations of 1989 that led to the Tiananmen Square tragedy.

Throughout Chinese history, bloody peasant rebellions had never deposed an emperor, but the furor inevitably signaled the end of a dynasty. Peasant resentment over decades of neglect and mistreatment under Maoist policies led reformers to act quickly on agricultural policy when they began their changes at the end of 1978. They knew that a disaffected and rebellious peasant population was a risk that could not be endured. Their first efforts paid off handsomely, but, after a time, the living conditions and wages of the rural residents again began to fall behind those of people in the cities. Now the party is taking another look at rural reform, after a decade of devoting most of its resources and attention to the successful industrial and business economy. Struggling to keep control in the face of the rural protests, central and provincial governments have begun to address the complex of issues that set off the rural protests.

What had begun as a promising start to prosperity for rural China was beginning to sink into crisis for millions of peasants. Harvests dropped precipitously in 1985 and were disappointing the following two years. By the early 1990s the central government could no longer ignore agriculture's problems: inflation, unemployment, growing peasant discontent, corruption, the mass migration of peasants to cities, and shrinking arable land.

Inflation that has spiraled dangerously upward in urban areas also has affected peasants, who are paying higher prices for seed, fertilizer, and farm tools, sometimes 50 percent more in a single season. And the central government has been discouragingly slow to raise the prices it pays for contracted quotas of agricultural products. The average annual income of peasants, even those who initially had enjoyed growing prosperity, is slipping far behind those of urban workers.

Although during the first half of the 1980s, peasant incomes were increasing each year by at least 10 percent, and once by a remarkable 30 percent, the rate slowed abruptly in succeeding years to about 2 percent. In the meantime, urban incomes were growing at 5 percent a year from a higher base. Bonuses and subsidies from employers and the state blunted to some extent the impact of rising inflation for urban workers, but self-employed peasants had no such relief.

Surveys showed that the average urban worker was making four times as much as the rural worker and in fact huge numbers of peasants were still struggling in deep poverty. In 1993, officials launched a program to reduce poverty among 80 million citizens, the majority of them living in the inland provinces, who suffer shortages of both food and clothing.

On a tour of relatively poor Shanxi Province, President Jiang Zemin urged village leaders to "take good care of the poor . . . keep the poverty-stricken areas in mind and share the comforts and hardships of the masses." His concern may be as much economic as compassionate or political. Raising income levels and buying power of all the peasant population is essential not only to the economy but to social stability. The continued growth and success of the industrial market will depend on rural consumers as well as customers abroad.

MIGRANT MILLIONS

The industrialization of the countryside is considered the panacea for surplus rural labor. To a certain extent it has already been successful. More than 116 million former farmers have become workers in one of 20 million rural enterprises. By the early 1990s, in the province of Hunan alone, 760,000 peasants are self-employed and more than 1 million farmers are employed in 6,300 private enterprises. They produced so much that traditionally agricultural Hunan in 1992 earned more than half its income from industry. But there is much to do before the rest of the rural unemployed can be absorbed into rural industry. Although surplus farm labor has been freed from the commune system for fifteen years, at least 100 million peasants have not been able to find industrial or service work, and demographics suggest that at least 13 million more will be entering the job market annually for the forseeable future.

Staggering numbers of these unemployed peasants in search of work and the promise of high wages have descended in tidal waves on cities. It has been estimated that at least 1 million migrant peasants are now living in Beijing. City governments frequently close down railway stations at peak migration seasons, unable to handle the crowds.

Major cities and enterprise zones along China's prosperous eastern seaboard are magnets for peasants. Since the relaxation of residency permits and elimination of ration coupons, it has become remarkably easy for job seekers to leave the countryside for the metropolis and almost impossible for city authorities to calculate their numbers. Cities large and small have their hordes of shabby itinerants, single men and women, sometimes whole families, with bedding rolls of quilts and straw mats on their backs, huddled at railway stations or sleeping in squalid dormitories.

In Guangdong, China's most prosperous province and the gateway to Hong Kong, more than a million peasants have flocked to the booming clusters of factories and building sites seeking work. Many of the families and relatives left behind live in areas so poor that they depend almost totally on the wages sent home to them by the transplanted relative.

In the industrial area of Dongguan not far from the capital city, Guangzhou, the weekly lines of these inland workers mailing home wages from the local post offices were so long that the local government had to step in and provide extra post offices. Sending off money to families was so time-consuming that one sympathetic Taiwanese employer gave his workers special days off to mail their remittances.

The solution to the uncontrolled migrations, Chinese planners hope, is to build entire new urban areas to resettle the unemployed rural population. Already on the drawing board are plans to build medium-size towns for 1 million inhabitants and smaller communities for 500,000 people with all the necessary infrastructure of roads, sewage, water, and electricity, but above all nonfarming job opportunities.

An early example of the "instant" town was built along the two-lane crowded highway between Fuzhou and its port. The smokestacks spewing black flumes of polluting smoke from the factories, the sameness of all the housing, the shops bordering directly on the noisy, busy road, are not particularly appealing. In one field, even the oxen used for plowing wore kerchiefs over their snouts as protection from the polluted air. But the town has the advantage of ready access to transportation for its products, and the factories have provided work and wages for hundreds of peasants from the surrounding countryside.

Chinese farmers do remarkably well in feeding such a huge population in a country where the arable land has dropped from 12 percent of the nation's area to only 7 percent. Improved seed, increased use of chemical fertilizers, even some mechanization have boosted crop yields. However in 1993 alone, building, erosion, and desertification erased another 9 percent of the existing farmland. For centuries, peasants have struggled to protect their fields and paddies from floods, droughts, and pestilence, but the growing population, the new economic policies, and the burgeoning factory and business zones they have brought are new threats to crop-producing land.

Although rural factories and enterprises provide jobs and income for unemployed peasants, they have encroached on land that once raised crops. Peasants with new wealth have rushed to build fine houses, two storied, with beautifully carved roof beams and colorful tiles. Prosperous villages have built schools, clinics, and recreation halls on fertile land.

Truck farms that once surrounded cities such as Beijing and Tianjin and other metropolitan areas like green belts have disappeared under rings of highways or have been plowed up to make way for the growing demand for offices, factories, apartment buildings, and villas for rich entrepreneurs. The early-morning stream of bicycles or donkey carts piled high with fresh fruits and vegetables for the city's free markets have been replaced with truckloads that come from farther and farther distances.

Billboards on the outskirts of the growing cities now advertise building sites and housing developments rather than Communist Party campaigns. To the consternation of the Agriculture Department, even golf courses, laid out by Western experts near cities that welcome foreign businessmen, have become such a popular status symbol for modern, probusiness China that directives have now limited their construction to no more than two per metropolitan area.

Falling harvests of grain (which includes rice, wheat, corn, sorghum, millet, soybeans, and tubers such as cassava and taro) is a matter of serious concern. Main crops such as wheat, corn, and rice have dropped by big margins, particularly in South China, where peasants have found it more profitable to switch from farming to other occupations. Zhangzhou, about fifteen miles west of Xiamen, across the strait from Taiwan, has decided to shed its reputation as a flower and fruit village in exchange for more lucrative real estate development for incoming businessmen.

Inefficient storage and distribution facilities have aggravated shortages caused by smaller harvests. Rising industrial demand for the transport of raw materials from cement to coal as well as foodstuffs has put extra burdens on China's inadequate rail and highway network. The lack of sufficient grain storage may waste enough grain to feed a million people a year, according to some agricultural experts.

All too frequently China's solution to one problem is one step forward, one, even two backward. The highly controversial proposed damming up of the Three Gorges on the Yangtze River for muchneeded hydroelectric power has the double disadvantage of displacing at least 1 million inhabitants and inundating large stretches of precious rich farmland.

But recent food shortages and soaring food prices have caused such a public uproar that the state has had to abandon, at least temporarily, free-market agricultural policies and reinstate government purchase quotas. Premier Li Peng, defending the return to macrosupervision of agricultural products, said that by providing relatively stable prices for grain, oil, meat, vegetables, and eggs, the government was giving "special concern to those who are still poor or have grave difficulty making ends meet."

PEASANT PROTESTS

To Beijing's central authorities, agriculture's most dangerous and disturbing problem has been the growing unrest and rebellion among the peasants toward corrupt party officials, which burst out in defiant demonstrations in many of the provinces. During 1993, in Hubei, Shanxi, Anhui, Guizhou, Guangxi, even the more prosperous provinces of Shandong and Jiangsu, over 200 incidents of surly and angry peasants storming Communist Party offices and confronting officials required police intervention.

The peasants accuse party officials from village to provincial levels of imposing unreasonable and numerous taxes and levies, which they claim they cannot afford. In Shanxi Province alone, the party has cracked down on over 1,000 cases of gross and unreasonable charges. Censured in public meetings, some of the accused officials were expelled from the party. Others have had to pay fines (which reverted to the peasants) of up to $500.

Many of the fees, levies, or taxes were for schools, roads, or irrigation projects, but many were frivolous and bizarre: fees for a job recommendation, an appointment, a transfer, even for watching donkey carts at the village fair. The most serious clashes came when local officials paid peasants for their quotas of state grain or cotton with IOUs instead of cash, a practice officials later banned. Party officials also had appropriated community financial resources for business ventures, some of them impractical and worthless, for their own benefit.

Peasant unrest, growing disparity between rich and poor, the uncontrolled migrations, and declining harvests all threaten social stability. In recent years, maintaining this stability has been the rationale for every new measure adopted by Chinese leaders to deal with runaway inflation, to curb the overly ambitious plans of provincial leaders who disregarded central directives, to punish the corruption that extended from the local to highest levels, and to suppress political dissidence.

In 1994 the minister of agriculture, Liu Jiang, announced that boosting the farmers' incomes should be "the core of agriculture and rural work at the present and for the rest of the decade—the foundation for stabilizing the whole of society."

To accomplish this, Finance Minister Liu Zhongli proposed raising agricultural expenditures by a sizable 17 percent. The government conceded that the 10 percent of the national budget formerly allocated to the training of agricultural technicians, upgrading of farm equipment, water maintenance, and flood control had been decreased drastically to approximately 3 percent during the 1980s as funds were devoted to other priorities such as the military and urban infrastructure.

Under the new budget, every year until the year 2000, $1.75 billion will be invested in Central and West China for increased rural aid. The added funds will support measures to raise the farmers' incomes by at least 5 percent a year. A large proportion will go to 500 grain-producing counties and 150 cotton-producing counties for subsidies that will guarantee farmers profits if market prices of grain or cotton should fall below the state protection levels.

New measures will be designed to ensure that no more arable land is swallowed up by unauthorized building. Approximately 3,000 development zones, 90 percent of them unauthorized and overburdened with debt, have usurped large quantities of farmland or leased urban land. Ambitious provincial and county governments, eager to attract investment, have looked on the creation of these zones, which typically offer tantalizing tax benefits and other incentives to developers, as the quickest way to become prosperous. Many of them have no suitable infrastructure or skilled workforce to offer other than the land. In ways unexplained, the government intends to reduce the numbers to 300 to 400 zones, reserving at least 100 as state-level zones.

THE END OF COMMUNES

In contrast to almost every other change in Chinese society, the rural reforms were a grassroots phenomenon, not the result of directives from central planners. The first changes in the countryside were introduced by local party officials. The disbanding of the 53,000 communes after the death of Mao was accomplished without any direction from Beijing or even any consistent provincial plans.

Many peasants have prospered from the first stage of reform and weathered the downturn that followed. Communist China's first "millionaires" were the Ten Thousand Yuan Farmers, whose annual incomes of about $1,250 made them millionaire equivalents by Chinese standards. The return to family farming after four decades of communes and the introduction of light industry in rural areas held out the prospect of achieving prosperity to 950 million peasants, 80 percent of China's population, a prospect they viewed skeptically at first and then pursued enthusiastically.

This prosperity seemed particularly fitting. The peasantry had made up the masses that first rallied to Mao Zedong and the Communist Party. Millions of them had fought the long bitter battles against the Japanese invaders and then Chiang Kai-shek's Nationalists, the party that represented the industrialists and landlords.

All through the 1980s, the Chinese media featured amazing get-rich stories of hard-working peasants who were making more money in a year than most peasants would have expected to see in their lifetimes: the farmer who started a profitable airline with one surplus Chinese air force plane; another who raised deer for their prized medicinal horns instead of raising cabbages; still another who cultivated exotic houseplants.

Soon even more successful ventures that raised the incomes of entire villages were being reported. The household contract responsibility system, which allowed families to farm their own plots, released multitudes of peasants from farmwork. By pooling resources; scrounging for loans; getting the cooperation of the local officials, approval of the central government, and sometimes the expertise of "Sunday engineers," peasants set up, managed, and worked in small factories, construction firms, and marketing enterprises.

Harvests improved year after year. The peasants who continued to farm worked with new energy and enthusiasm. Although fields of potatoes and cabbages, rice paddies, and tiered hills of tea look the same, peasants have eagerly invested in fertilizers, pesticides, and small tractors. Much of the countryside began to change, with bright new houses, small factories, schools, and clinics. Village fairs and city free markets sprang up, supplied with added abundance, quality, and variety.

One of the closest observers of the changes on the countryside has been China's eminent sociologist, the octogenarian Fei Xiaotong, whose reputation dates to the studies he did in the 1930s on his own poverty-stricken village in East China. "No single person or group of persons sat down and came up with the responsibility system, the core of the rural reforms," Fei said in a conversation in his Beijing home. "It began spontaneously and without authorization from above, when local cadres, in despair over the situation at the depths of the Cultural Revolution, decided to tolerate the beginning of reform as a way out of slumping production."

Agricultural output had surged with the Communist victory in 1949. The disruption of two decades of fighting civil wars and the Japanese occupation were over, and the landlords and rich farmers, the 12 percent of the population that had owned nearly half the farmland, were forced to redistribute their holdings.

But after this initial spurt, collectivization campaigns brought a new kind of disruption to the countryside. For twenty years the Communist Party used coercion and persuasion to get the new peasant landowners back under control, moving from "voluntary" work teams to cooperative farms, and finally to giant communes.

Peasants were forbidden to make their own decisions on what crops to raise. "Grow grain as the main link" and other directives determined their planting schedules, and often the results were disastrous. Fake model farming communes such as the much-propagandized Da Qai made the outside world believe for a time that miracles, not hunger, were the common condition of rural China.

Officials in the trading port of Xiamen on the South China Sea confess today that they were overjoyed when one of their harbors silted up. That gave them an additional opportunity to "grow grain as the main link." Free markets were banned in the cities as "capitalism's tail," forcing city people to deal only with the shortage-plagued state stores. Even rural fairs came under official disfavor, since the party had decreed that trade was ideologically backward, and the self-sufficient communes made it unnecessary.

"In the past, the peasants were not permitted to take part in management," an agricultural economist in Beijing said. Governments at all levels issued directives on crop planning. Percentages were fixed for cotton, grain, and other crops. Once an order was issued, the commune had to carry it out, whether it made sense or not. "In this way, many things were ordered that were unreasonable," the economist continued. "Some places were unsuitable for certain crops, but the commune had to follow the directives. Peasants found it difficult to do their work. Everything was arranged by the commune headquarters. Peasants didn't bother about improving the soil, or developing better seeds. Although they participated in farming every day, they didn't have the right even to think about it."

Peasants' contributions were kept track of not by their actual efforts, whether of ideas for improvement or a hard day's work, but by labor points, the old system copied from the Soviet collectives and not notable for its success. Points were awarded on the basis of hours worked; men received more than women, and young city people sent to the countryside often found it impossible to earn enough points to feed themselves. "Such accounting of the results of farming did not necessarily illustrate how much one actually contributed," the economist said. "This wasn't reasonable; it dampened the enthusiasm of the peasants."

When production dropped, no one was allowed to discuss it, he added: "People were only allowed to talk about revolution, not productivity, under left-leaning policies."

Marketing was similarly hemmed in by regulations. Conditions varied from province to province, but generally, no peasant had the right to sell to individuals. Hundreds of products had to be handled by the state, including grain, sugar, fruits, vegetables, and herbal medicines.

But to the party propagandists, their agricultural system put China in the forefront of ideological innovation. China, they said, had found a way to break forever the ancient capitalist instincts of the peasants. Admiring Western visitors agreed, praising China for "reducing the appeal of the money motive" as a successful path to development. "When everyone has enough to eat today and hope of improvement tomorrow," one wrote, "then it is possible to appeal to the people to combat egoism and eschew privilege."

Chinese propagandists were claiming a 35 percent increase in grain production in a single year, thanks to the sun of Mao Zedong thought that rivals the real sun. The communes were "a natural outcome of developments in China, superior in every way to the small co-ops, and the best form for the transition from socialism to Communism," they wrote. But as the figures grew less and less believable, they finally stopped publishing statistics.

What happened instead, Chinese and foreign agricultural analysts now agree, was that agricultural production all but stagnated in the twenty years between the Great Leap and the reforms of 1978.

Some official statistical accounts simply skip this period, using 1952, before large-scale collectivization, and 1979, after the reforms, as reference points. Some, including the graphs posted in offices and schools, are quite open about it. The graph line goes steadily upward after the end of the civil war, then dips like a ski run in 1957 to account for the Great Leap. There is a climb with the good harvests that followed those famine years, and then another sharp slide during the Cultural Revolution. Officials do not seem to be aware of the irony when they make statements such as "Of course, production slumped during the Great Leap Forward."

THE PATH TO REFORM

Fei, the sociologist, says this food production crisis caused many little bursts of local reforms in the late 1970s in many places in China, when the radicals in the party had begun to lose power. The province of Sichuan was in the forefront under Zhao Ziyang, a close disciple of Deng's who was then head of the provincial party and later became premier and party general secretary.

Elsewhere, many other party officials opposed the changes as capitalism, Fei said: "Often peasants would run afoul of local leadership and be drawn back, but then experimenting with the responsibility system would pop up in other places. Thus reform already had a very good track record when the new leaders in Beijing were ready to consider it as a national policy at the end of 1978."

What are the reforms? Their essence is contained in their name: the household responsibility system. Responsibility for the decisions on what to plant, how to plant it, who should cultivate it, who should market it, and where and at what price, was removed from the government, local, provincial, or national, and returned to the peasant household, where it had been for centuries. Communes became townships, brigades reverted to villages or, in large villages, to neighborhoods. Individual peasants or families received long land leases, in exchange for payment of a modest tax and the agreement to sell part of their production to the government marketing system. The market, sooner or later, told the family what was profitable to plant, how much to spend on fertilizer, and how much labor to devote to crops rather than sideline occupations.

"Simply put, the peasants have the right to determine when and where they should start doing something," a specialist at the State Agricultural Institute in Beijing said. "They have the final say."

The reformers told the peasants that they own whatever they produce. The old collective structure was retained, but its functions were radically changed. Instead of receiving orders, peasants now sign contracts, with the townships or villages. Not only crops but also services are contracted for. Peasants can conclude contracts to work in forestry, water conservancy, or erosion protection, and decide themselves how to divide their time between these chores and farming.

Land remains the property of the state, but the reforms divided it up in such a way as to be the personal property of the peasants who till it. While now it can be inherited but not sold, even that final barrier may not remain forever.

The physical transformation of the farms has been remarkable, say agricultural specialists who remember mismanaged land and wasteful storage facilities. Fields were neglected while labor was mobilized for giant projects—some of them useful, such as irrigation canals, but others grandiose arches or administrative buildings. Where the change is most noticeable, however, is in the revived markets in country and city.

There are no United Parcel trucks in China, and so everyone can see what their neighbors are buying at the markets. One stream of foot, cart, and bicycle traffic brings food and homemade goods to sell; another leaves with purchases. Coming into the markets are the products of Old China: the grain sacks and vegetables, red and yellow painted stools, bloody hunks of meat or sides of pork, and basketry. In the other direction go the television sets, balanced on the backs of bicycles with no regard for the English-language THIS SIDE UP on the cartons; a new washing machine or refrigerator, carried on the back of a freight tricycle, often with its proud owner riding beside it.

The peasant household wealthy enough to afford a small tractor can proceed to market at about 20 mph, a good speed on the narrow roads hemmed in with rows of poplars (the national reforestation project) and deep ditches (the national irrigation plans).

In some cases, Chinese customers, poor or better off, make purchases they would not seem to need very much, such as inflated plastic Bambi toys. For a society long denied such trifles by a state-run trading system, even frivolous purchases are important. But most of the new merchants are filling basic needs left by the great gaps in the centrally managed economic structure. And most of them come from the huge pool of surplus labor that the reforms freed from farmwork.

SUCCESS IN SHANDONG

A tour of model villages in Shandong showed how the return to family farming and the launching of rural enterprise can change the lives of ordinary peasants, examples that the government expects to be copied in some form all over the country.

The teacups were filled from brightly painted dragon-design Thermos bottles in the little reception hall of one farm, a prosperous hundred acres near Yantai on the Shandong peninsula. From the bent-iron-pipe archway to the farm grounds, we could already see the little shops and factories that showed that sideline occupations were important here. Most of the people were at work in these shops rather than in the fields. One group was kneading dough and frying it in fat twists to sell to passing truckers and bicyclists. Another was filling vials with a pharmaceutical, on contract to a local industry.

The brigade or village chairman (the terms are used interchangeably), a tanned and energetic man in his early fifties, had learned farming in a boyhood spent on a nearby collective and mechanical skills in a twenty-year career in the Chinese navy. During the Cultural Revolution, he said, the village raised only grain—although its site, not far from the Yellow Sea, makes it ideal for fruit, a more profitable crop. Grain yields were low, and annual income per person was only about $30 at current exchange rates. The 1,100 villagers managed to feed only themselves.

Then came the reforms.

"After the party began to encourage us to take up occupations

other than just farming, we started twelve industrial sideline projects," he said. Besides the fried bread and drug enterprises, they
include a lumberyard, a tile plant, and two garment workshops
where women stitch children's clothing on treadle-operated sewing
machines, while their own young children play in a day care center
close at hand. The farm rents trucks to the nearby Shengli oil fields.
It runs a small rural bank, lending money to Yellow Sea fishermen
to buy or equip boats and getting some of the payments in fish for
the village.

The same story, with local variations, could be told in almost all
of China's 700,000 villages, an optimistic official of the state agricultural institute in Beijing claimed. The institute is able to measure
the national as well as the local results, and it has found remarkable
changes.

"First, there has been a great increase in agricultural production.
Second, the livelihood of the peasants has been raised. Third, the
system of supply and marketing has been changed. All these
changes resulted in a fourth: the change of relationships between the
cadres and the masses, between the countryside and the city."

The Shandong village is unusual in its degree of industrialization. Only 2 percent of its income now comes from farming; the
other 98 percent is from its various manufacturing and commercial
projects.

At the agricultural institute, this trend is encouraged. "We want
the peasants to leave the land," the specialist explained. "Once a
peasant has left, the land is taken away by the commune and redis-
tributed for use by the other households. Those raising crops have a
bigger piece of land; the scale of farming will become larger. Those
who leave start other businesses."

But these shifts have left those at home at a disadvantage in many
cases. Village and township officials say they try to work out a system to keep peasants who have taken up other trades from getting
incomes too much higher than those on the land. If the gap is too
great, peasants aren't willing to stay home and grow grain. Some
truck-driving or merchant peasants are making three times the
income of those who stay with farming. Village leaders can decide

to divert profits from the sideline occupations and subsidize those who stay on the land.

The Shandong village sends out more than forty men and women to buy and sell, and they also serve as recruiters for skilled personnel who may be looking for off-the-books employment. Some of these specialists keep their state jobs, drawing no salary, so that they retain fringe benefits and pensions. Others are confident enough in the village's earning power that they break their iron rice bowls, in the words of the chairman: quit their jobs. The highest salary paid these specialists is about $130 a month, nearly half a year's pay for a villager. The paid experts take care of the village enterprises' accounting, management, quality control, and marketing.

Others are brought in to train peasants and workers in a technical school set up by the village. It is open to the whole county, but outsiders have to pay tuition. The school grants a certificate but does not provide an automatic job assignment, a factor the students say is an advantage in an expanding small city economy like the one around Yantai.

Freedom of choice is important to the village leaders as well. "The commune used to be able to order us to plant wheat, and you had to obey, no matter what the conditions were," the chairman said. "Now we make the decisions." Even with so very few villagers working in the field, the farm easily grows enough grain to feed itself and sells 50 metric tons to the state in an average year. After an initial grace period, it also has begun paying taxes at the rate of 10 percent of its earnings.

For the peasants, income has increased tenfold, to about $400 a year per capita. Although the enterprise profits would permit a higher payout, the village leaders divert some of that income to pensions and amenities. About $30,000 was spent on a youth center, and pensioners are paid 30 to 60 percent of their working wages. (There is no state pension for rural Chinese.) With retirement at fifty-five for women and sixty for men, and people living longer because of improved health care, the pensions, while quite a burden, are easily within the village's resources.

There is so much work in the sideline factories and shops that 500 extra people have had to be hired. They get the same pay as the villagers, but they don't have a claim to the common fund that builds up each year. Personal income stays relatively low because the village wants to concentrate on production, and this means money is needed for investment. Decisions are reached at annual meetings on the wage rate, the chairman says, and everyone has a chance to participate. The villagers have the right to change leaders if they don't like the way things are going, he insists.

The neat homes in the village, most of them newly constructed, have the usual number of television sets under embroidered maroon velvet dust covers, as well as bicycles, new furniture, refrigerators, and fans.

Villagers can buy the simple square houses built around the shops, fields, and fishponds for $800 to $6,000. The latter figure purchases a handsome two-story model. Even the cheapest home has 600 square feet of concrete-floored living space, many times the average space that city dwellers live in. The owners have three to five years to pay for their houses. They cannot sell them but can pass them on to children or other relatives.

As a working example of the success of the rural reforms, the experience of the village raises two points about the way the reforms have proceeded, a local leader explains. One is that although individual efforts are responsible for the success of the village's enterprises, there is still a large element of direction from the top—if not the top of the party anymore, at least the top of the village. It would be hard to imagine French or American farmers volunteering to keep their wages down for the sake of a bigger pot of money to pay for accountants and teachers. These farmers apparently do so; at this level, Chinese citizens have more than a theoretical right to change leaders if they are dissatisfied with their policies.

The second point is that the successes are built on a very low level of previous performance.

Only thirty to forty people now work in the fields, accomplishing more than the entire village workforce of several hundred did during the commune years. There are more machines, but, as national figures also show, the main reason for the gains is individual effort.

Since the responsibility system and signed contracts, people simply work harder.

A third consideration for the specific success of this village is its location. The nearby towns and cities provide both experts and markets. In per capita income, Shandong is in the middle rank of provinces—poorer than the Yangtze delta area, richer than the less fertile interior—and the village is in the top fifth of Shandong's farms.

It should also be noted that "rich" and "poor" are terms that apply only in comparisons within China. Rich peasants here would not be considered rich by the standards of the industrialized world. Shandong is not wealthy compared to Iowa, but to the sparsely populated and arid west of China.

EAST MEETS WEST

China has a national East-West problem, as an economist at Fudan University in Shanghai pointed out. Unlike the United States, the middle of the country is a dead end. There is no "Midwest" to serve as a bridge between its eastern and western borders. A long crescent of level, fertile land along China's eastern seaboard extends inland for about 600 miles. Then the country slopes westward in a series of plateaus and mountains that rise higher and higher to the "roof of the world," Tibet. To the North, the mountains descend to the wide stretches of desert, China's Far West, Qinghai and Xinjiang. Along the northern border, the provinces of Inner Mongolia, home to nomadic people, and Gansu lie within the Gobi Desert, which stretches in undulating waves, like a great golden sea, up to the edges of cultivated land.

Although there are pockets of good land in the interior, for the most part farming is a difficult occupation. Rainfall can be four times the average in one season and a quarter of the average the next. The 3,000-mile-long Yellow River, which bends through several provinces in giant hundred-mile loops, can dry up to the point at which irrigation is impossible, or suddenly gush to ten times its normal flow.

Despite its mineral deposits, mines, and processing plants, the interior remains far behind the coast by every economic measure. In the 1950s, the government tried to even up the disadvantage of the West by moving entire industries and technical schools westward and by diverting investment from the old coastal centers such as Shanghai and Guangzhou. Part of the reasoning was strategic: Mao wanted to have sources of aircraft, arms, and industrial products in China's heartland, secure from invaders. But the leaders of the mid-1980s decided that the coastal infrastructure and foreign trade links were too vital for the nation's economic reforms and opening to the world, and have been concentrating resources in the East once more.

The traditions of the West are also a factor limiting development, according to the Shanghai economist. Peasants from the mountains and desert are not used to trading or taking up other occupations. Although there appear to be many individual exceptions, western-ers are regarded as having no "business sense." "Tradition over-powers commerce, except on the coast, where foreign influence is an old tradition," the economist said.

SUNDAY ENGINEERS

The East-West difference shows up clearly in both farming and industry. In the coastal provinces, rural industries have grown up so fast that official statistics are always a year behind trying to keep track of them. In western China, such a rapid growth of industry is rare. The reasons include the traditional reluctance to change from farming, no matter how unremunerative; the distance from big-city domestic markets and opportunities for export; and the lack of a light industrial base that could supply professional advice.

These experts include the "Sunday engineers" who advise and teach, sometimes for a fee, sometimes for a share of the profits, and peasants who have had some experience with vehicles and machin-ery. The Sunday engineers get their name from the fact that they keep their secure state enterprise jobs for the benefits they offer and supposedly venture into the private sector only on their day off.

The drawbacks of location have not been insurmountable for imaginative and ingenious peasants. Traveling on a hot, crowded train through relatively poor agricultural Henan Province, a village party official and two peasants, in fresh white shirts and trousers nattily rolled to their knees, exposing their gray silk socks shoved into muddy sandals, explained how their village became the exclusive manufacturer of specially insulated uniforms.

Quite by chance, the villagers had read a newspaper report about the invention of a fabric that resisted extremely high temperatures by a professor in one of Luoyang's many technical institutes. After considerable correspondence and discussions with the inventor, consultations with a bank for a loan, and more experimentation on the part of their Sunday engineer, they were in business. The market for their wonder fabric was very good, the villagers reported, although sometimes orders were held up for lack of raw materials.

Other villages hit on manufacturing jeans or plastic toys, raised ducks for their feathers and down (much in demand for coats, jackets, and vests), cultivated eels (a delicacy for the Japanese market), or made Popsicles. There have been a thousand schemes, fulfilling pent-up demands for unusual or luxury items considered superfluous or frivolous during earlier austere years.

The southwestern province of Sichuan is a good example of the state of Chinese agriculture and those who live and work in the rural areas. A largely agricultural province the size of France, with more than twice as many inhabitants, Sichuan had the nation's fifth lowest income per person, in spite of ten years of agricultural reform and the growth of some rural enterprises.

Sichuan's economy grows but cannot catch up with the more prosperous provinces. In recent years its growth rates, along with other inland provinces such as Shanxi, Henan, and Yunnan, have been 9 to 12 percent, while coastal provinces such as Shandong, Jiangsu, Fujian, and Guangdong grew between 20 and 27 percent. The income gaps between western farmers and factory workers with easterners is also striking.

In Guangdong, the urban worker has an average wage of more than $500 a year, more than twice the farmer's average income of about $200. But that Guangdong farmer, in turn, is twice as well off as his or her counterpart in Shanxi. The peasant in Shanxi who is lucky enough to work in a rural factory, however, can count on about the same amount of money as the Guangdong farmer.

GOODS AND SERVICES

As one farm in the West's Yellow River region demonstrates, there is a fourth way to prosperity other than depending on crops, leaving the villages, or risking a manufacturing venture that the peasants might not be prepared to run successfully.

That is to fill some of the many gaps in services, either by creating new ones or by supplementing inadequate government efforts in transport, lodging, and repairs. A village outside Xian finds it profitable to provide a range of services to the local population.

The 350 people in the village had been pleased to see their farming income grow after the reforms took force, but under the leadership of a former army truck driver who had seen something of the world, they began to branch out. The truck driver started out by using the village farm trucks to haul for local concerns, and soon a boxy passenger cab was loaded onto the back, so there would be a country bus. A kind of jitney service was launched first, followed by regular routes.

So many peasants and traders were coming through the area on their bus line that the people decided to open a hotel. Peasant-operated hotels on the outskirts of major cities and market towns have since become a fixture, but theirs was the first in the area.

The villagers pooled their savings and negotiated a loan from county authorities to finance the hotel. They say they could have done the construction work themselves, since they all build their own houses, but they decided that paying an outside construction firm to build the hotel was less risky. Outsiders also are hired to work in the hotel, although many hotel employees are retired farmworkers from the village who are able to retain their $15 monthly pensions as well as collect a salary of about the same amount.

At the end of each year each investor gets a dividend and interest from the investments, which in the case of the army veteran was several thousand dollars he had saved during his career. The two-story hotel looks like an enlarged peasant house, with shiny varnished furniture, burgundy carpets, and orange and yellow velour couches. Its four-bed dormitory rooms rent for about $9 a night, and there is television in a common viewing room.

The villagers are proud that their hotel occasionally gets a foreign tourist from the overcrowded facilities in Xian, but their steady trade consists of the men and women traveling to visit provincial offices or buy or sell at the markets.

They are proud of their leader, the army veteran, who is at once their idea man, the political head of the village, manager of the hotel, and largest single investor.

In 1987, for the first time, the rural sector's production of industrial goods and provision of services such as the hotel and bus line surpassed agricultural production, and the trend points to an increasing emphasis on small industry and services.

"No one could have predicted this other rural revolution," Fei, the sociologist, said. "This was the growth of crafts and small industry and all the other societal effects that the release of farm labor brought about. In the richest part of Jiangsu, for example, only 10 percent of the original labor force is needed to farm the land—and to produce more than the 100 percent had been doing.

"As with everything else in Chinese history, the reforms began in the countryside and then came inexorably to encircle the cities and sweep them along with them. There had to be urban reforms once there had been rural reforms. A huge part of the economy had begun to function independently, guided almost solely by the pragmatic considerations of the market, and it wouldn't work in the long run to have it stop at city borders, or at the gates of the state enterprises.

"Just as the liberated areas finally engulfed the cities during the civil war, the free market did so in the middle eighties."

SIX

THE CITIES

_____

China is a nation in motion, and the Shanghai railway station is one of its collection points. Peasants sit or squat beside their stitched-together cloth bundles or cardboard boxes of purchases. Lines of hundreds wait to buy tickets, and others prowl the crowds to make deals. Passengers surge ten abreast along the platforms from the trains, and then push themselves and their bundles into city buses. At the peak of the annual migrations after the Lunar New Year holiday, half a million people a day crowd into Shanghai in search of work. The traffic is a little less dense but the scenes are much the same at the coastal steamer and riverboat terminals on the Huangpu River, which link Shanghai to the neighboring provinces of Jiangsu and Zhejiang. Across the nation, as many as 100 million Chinese have left their homes to find work in the cities, and countless other millions travel back and forth every day to buy and sell in urban markets.

GOING TO SHANGHAI

A floating workforce of 100 million is one of the unintended consequences of the economic reforms the Communist Party began a decade and a half ago. Most things went according to plan. Living standards have pushed upward, cities have renewed their skylines or created new ones, and billions of dollars of foreign investment have poured in to match the huge sums Chinese themselves are putting down as tokens of their faith in the new system.

More is yet to come. China has promised to reorganize its state enterprises into more efficient stockholding corporations and allow the worst money losers among them to go bankrupt; overhaul its antiquated tax and inadequate legal systems; and adopt independent central banking, employee-financed social security, market rents, and other features of capitalism.

Many problems remain, including a surge in crime, white collar and otherwise; pervasive corruption; the use of party position to help families and friends; the lack of regulation in companies and on stock exchanges; and spurts of inflation that touch off land and other buying frenzies. All these negative factors have affected foreign partners as well as Chinese investors.

What is surprising is not that these obstacles to reorganizing China's nonfarm economy have slowed progress, but that the process has advanced so swiftly despite them. China has a long way to go in catching up with the industrial nations, but the record of the first decade and a half of reform shows that that goal, in time, is realistic.

The success of the reforms is the result of a combination of careful planning, effective political infighting against the Old Guard, and a large measure of luck and unintended consequences. The roving population is an example of the latter. The way the planners had it figured, the economically liberated peasants would either stay on the land or close to it, and the 20 percent of the population that lived in the cities would be dealt with in a separate round of reforms.

Instead, huge numbers of peasants decided to join the city folk. For decades the communes in the countryside and the work units in the city had served as control and discipline organs. Suddenly, with the reforms, their function of keeping people in place disappeared. Country people were allowed to leave the farms; city people, the state enterprises. Although the migrant peasants have become an added burden on social services and already overcrowded housing, they are also a good source of cheap labor and a pool of ready and willing consumers.

Now anyone can go anywhere, or try to—first to bigger villages, then, if they're lucky, to the provincial capital, Shanghai or Beijing, and even to the United States.

The Zou family, from a village named Xikou in Jiangsu Province, is on the way. Zou Quifen first got a job as a housemaid in Shanghai and a room with the professional couple who hired her. They permitted her to work a second job during the day, when they were gone, as long as she was back in the evening to cook and clean. Room and two jobs added up to $125 a month, more than many civil servants earn. Mrs. Zou then summoned her husband, who found a fifteen-by-fifteen-foot room to share with eight others and a job as a cook. In describing his accommodations, they talk not of beds or rooms but of sleeping space.

One hot summer night, sixteen-year-old Xiumei, their daughter, arrived at the Shanghai station from Xikou village, unannounced. But she had something that most other members of the peasant stream in the station didn't: a telephone number. She called her mother's employers. They told her to go back home. She told them there were no more trains. Aware of the stories of gangs that rape young peasant women or sell them into prostitution, the couple told her to stay put, hired a pedicab, and returned from the station an hour later with a grinning and triumphant Xiumei.

Shanghai's permanent transient population of more than a million thus grew by one. Mr. Zou said he would look for a scullery job for his daughter. Xiumei is barely literate, with a grade-school education, but that puts her ahead of her parents and many other peasant competitors. The family is likely to end up in a neighborhood where people from their province have congregated. The Jiangsu and Zhejiang neighborhoods, where people from the two closest provinces live in Shanghai, are as big as major cities in some countries.

The Zou family's achievements in transforming themselves from farm laborers to city laborers may not seem like much, but their ability to do so is the heart of the success of the reforms.

Not only have they improved their economic status—to a level not very high by Western standards, but unimaginable to them a few years ago—but they have broken out of the cycle of regimentation that still characterizes so much of Chinese society. Individual liberty is being expressed all over China, whether as a chance for a few square feet of one's own in a worker barracks or for a partnership with an American or European entrepreneur. These individual efforts at all levels are the real force behind the growth of the Chinese economy.

THE URBAN REFORMS

In the first three decades of Communist rule, initiative was not much in evidence. Both the communal farms and the state industry kept people fed and supplied, but performed sluggishly. China's consumption of goods and services for that thirty-year period had a zero rate of growth when adjusted for population increases. Maoist slogans proclaimed that China was blazing a path for the world to follow, but when the pragmatic Deng Xiaoping defeated Mao's heirs and returned to power, he told the nation that socialism did not have to be equated with poverty or backwardness.

Even isolated China was aware that its neighbors in Asia, not to mention the West, were pushing toward much higher living standards. After Mao's death, party leaders realized that unless they tried to catch up, they would lose their legitimacy.

The economy had lagged behind that of industrial states because of the massive problems of poverty and underdevelopment that the Communists inherited. In its first decades, the party had worked to correct those inequities, providing low and stable prices, full employment, and growth through construction of new plants and infrastructure. Each of these achievements had its negative side.

Price controls meant scarcity. Guaranteed jobs and social services were a drain on enterprise funds and a barrier to efficiency. The constant expansion of the facilities meant that there was little concern for growth through improving the productivity of the existing plants.

This Chinese welfare state economy was adequate for the needs of the People's Republic in its early bootstrap years, but it could not keep up with expanding population and demand.

Conservative economists argued that all that was needed was to make the traditional system more efficient—to increase productivity in old plants, paying workers bonuses to produce more but not threatening their job security. Equipment and processes could be brought in from abroad by the "airlock" method, they argued: The highest technology could be purchased from foreign firms and set up by foreign experts who would then leave China. There would be no contamination from Western ideas and no Western investment in or ownership of Chinese enterprises.

The reformers disagreed. They said that to catch up, China must move out of the welfare stage of its economy and adopt a whole range of measures no Communist nation had ever tried before. Management would be modernized and the party's grip relaxed. The open door would replace the airlock and foreign partners the temporary technicians. These foreigners would be trusted to invest and participate. Otherwise, China would continue to be left behind in technology, research and development, level of investment, and competitive chances on international markets. The reformers won this crucial argument.

As a result, after dissolving the rural communes, they were able to move ahead to the second step of reform: opening trade doors to the outside world, creating special economic zones, and permitting foreign companies to operate on Chinese territory for the first time since the old ones were driven out in the 1950s.

Next they began the difficult task of dismantling the old system of price controls and subsidies, letting market forces set many prices, both for retail sales and transactions between state enterprises. They gave those enterprises more independence from party control and began to curtail the benefits of a system of lifelong labor tenure that made it hard to promote the industrious and impossible to fire the incompetent.

The fourth reform was to create, or permit the growth of, free enterprise. Millions of little businesses sprang up, offering goods and services customers could not find in the state sector and providing their owner-workers with additional income. As they grew, they were joined by the international giants not seen in China since Communist rule began: Du Pont, General Motors, and IBM.

The fifth reform happened by itself, when the peasants no longer needed as farm labor, with the help of some specialists from the state enterprises, cobbled together a vast and undisciplined system of rural industry or moved to the cities as the Zou family did.

Two other unintended offshoots of reform proved more difficult to deal with. Inflation began to go out of control in the mid-1980s and became one of the bundle of grievances that set off nationwide waves of student protests that culminated in the Tiananmen Square turmoil. Those protests, in turn, nearly sank the reforms, when party hard-liners charged that opening the economy had opened the country to dangerous and hostile influences that could overthrow Communist rule.

At the age of eighty-seven, Deng Xiaoping took up the second challenge himself, putting his reputation behind reform. Tired of party squabbles, he announced that "ideology cannot buy rice" and left in January 1992 on a trip to Shanghai, South China's booming Guangdong Province, and the special economic zones near Hong Kong.

The factional fighting among the "eight immortals"—Deng's ancient party colleagues—was threatening the further course of reform. Some Old Guard leaders, headed by octogenarian Chen Yun, the formidable exponent of old-style government control, argued that the abandonment of a planned economy for Western-style markets, private trade, foreign investment, and education abroad might have made people more prosperous but also created an entering wedge for capitalism.

With the fall of the Soviet Union, these were times of greatest danger for Communists, the hard-liners warned. Chinese officials found it hard to understand how the Soviets had permitted their own destruction by their capitalist enemies. They thought they saw the same elements encroaching on their own territory, in the banks and stock exchange of the Shenzhen special economic zone, for example. Some even demanded that Shenzhen and the other special economic zones be swept away and the economy directed back to the safety of the state plan and state industry. Economic success, they said, was all very well, but not at the risk of slackening controls over society.

But Deng went to Shenzhen and Zuhai and praised their achievements. They and the rest of Guangdong Province had become "the leading force for economic development" in China, he said; the region could catch up with Asia's little tigers: Singapore, Hong Kong, Taiwan, and South Korea.

"If we do not uphold socialism, do not carry out reform and opening, do not develop the economy, and do not try to improve the people's livelihood, then there will only be the road to ruin," he said. "This basic line should be valid for 100 years."

Deng's views were set down in a widely read and quoted "Central Document No. 2." Although the conservatives continued to grumble about the threat, Deng carried the day, and subsequent party shuffles pushed aside many of the most recalcitrant and strengthened the reformers.

Both winners and losers worked out ideological formulas to justify their new "socialist market economic system." President Jiang, summing up, said that "foreign capital, technology, and personnel, and the foreign funded economy and the private economy, can and should be used by Socialism. The political power is in the hands of the people and there is a powerful public ownership system."

Foreign business executives and bankers were less concerned about the rationalization than the clear signal that market-oriented reform had won a crucial test in China. They responded with the biggest surge in investment in China's history. Contracted foreign direct investment went from $12 billion in 1991 to $58 billion in 1992, then nearly doubled to $110 billion in 1993.

IN THE ZONES

The party's renewed invitation for capital, technology, and personnel was extended for all of China, not just the special zones created for foreign investment. After an initial rush to the zones, the American, European, and Asian companies eager to form joint ventures or establish wholly owned enterprises had been branching out, in any case, to older industrial centers such as Shanghai and Manchuria. The special economic zones, however, had served as a valuable laboratory for fifteen years. At first, the experiments they conducted seemed quite radical.

"Self-reliance does not mean a closed door on imports," the *People's Daily* wrote a month after Mao's death in 1976. "We learn from the good experience and advanced science and technology of other countries and absorb them for our own use." The editorial was a gentle repudiation of the Maoist doctrine of self-sufficiency (which *had* meant a closed door to most imports) as well as a notice to the world that from then on, China would resume its position as an important international trader.

China needed technology and processes from the West, Japan, and its newly industrialized neighbors in Asia to bring up the productivity of its backward factories, energy, and transport enterprises. The Four Modernizations—in agriculture, industry, science-technology, and the military—could not succeed without such infusions.

These economic gains, however, had a political price. China had denounced the capitalists for so many years that explaining why their exploitation was being invited once again was difficult. Older Chinese had clear memories of the privileges foreigners enjoyed in Shanghai, Qingdao, and other enclaves from the early nineteenth century until the rise of Communism.

Importing equipment, machinery, or complete plants from foreign suppliers and then running them with Chinese engineers and specialists was a way around the ideological problems. Even Lenin had approved of these kinds of dealings with the capitalists, the party explained.

Trade trebled in the first five post-Mao years, with Japan, Hong Kong, and the United States taking the three leading positions. The United States' trade embargo kept it out of the China market for twenty-one years, until 1971, but it moved quickly to catch up, selling both grain and high-technology items such as airliners. Japan and Germany delivered steel plants, refineries, and mining equipment, with some of the payment to be made in coal and oil.

But China's reformers decided that these one-shot purchases, despite the boost they gave the economy, would have to be supplemented by a closer form of cooperation with the outside world. They provided no real opportunity for China to continue to modernize its industry through sharing in research and development with foreign partners.

The means of trying out this closer cooperation was the creation of four special economic zones in 1980, and of a fifth, Hainan Island, added in 1987. Two of the first SEZs are on the borders of Hong Kong and Macau; the others are farther up the coast in Guangdong and Fujian provinces. In addition, a coastal economic open zone, comprising 140 cities and counties in the Shanghai area, and individual open ports on the coast and up the major rivers have been established, with many of the investment incentives the SEZs offer foreign businesses.

Chinese officials say the zones have nothing in common with the concessions granted foreigners in prewar times, since the agreements were not forced on the Chinese as they were in the past; the investors and technicians are there by invitation. A second point they stress is that the benefits are mutual: If the foreign companies profit from cheap labor, China profits from absorbing the technology and marketing skills they provide.

National priorities are clear from the kinds of plants the authorities are trying to attract. First on the list is electronics, including computers, peripherals, and integrated circuits. Petrochemical and plastics come next, followed by building materials, textiles, and consumer goods.

Politically, culturally, or ideologically, officials say, the SEZ on one side of the fence is no different from the mainland province on the other side. Numerous scandals and shakeups of SEZ politicians, however, show that fencing off the influence of foreign wealth on a poor country isn't easy.

The zones are special because they have the state's permission to practice special economic policies, "led by the socialist economy." Preferential treatment is given outsiders on taxes, land use, fees, and visas. Foreign companies normally pay 30 percent income tax; in the zones, that amount is halved. Managers are granted special powers of decision, a euphemism for the right to hire and fire.

Visits to Shenzhen, Zuhai, Xiamen, and Shantou, the four original zones on the coast, brought out the following reasons why China first concentrated investment in the SEZs rather than spreading it more generally through the economy.

- The geographical position of the zones, close to Hong Kong and Macau, makes it easier to attract Hong Kong–based foreigners to arrange for investments and check on their progress. They can do business in the two border zones all day and be home for supper.

- The zones provide flexibility for new enterprises and are closely geared to export markets. Foreign businesspeople must deal with zone bureaucracies, but the red tape is minor compared to the problems elsewhere on the mainland.

- The managers of the state economy profit from using the zones to observe the international market, study the business and financial methods of the capitalists, and even experiment with some of them. The experiments can be contained in the zones before being tried in the country at large, thus reducing the risks of failure. "The SEZ system is a filter for the socialist system to absorb capitalist experience," an economist in Shenzhen said. "It's a window for technology, a window for knowledge, a window for management, a window for foreign economic policy."

- Finally, officials concede, a good part of South China's population was trying to flee to Hong Kong before the zones were set up. Now no one wants to leave, they say, and hundreds have already returned, with a few more arriving every day on visits from Hong Kong, to check out conditions.

Shenzhen, across a creek from Hong Kong's rural New Territories, is a frontier town, with the tracks of the Kowloon–Canton railway paralleling its main street and piles of construction dirt trampled into the permanence and hardness of concrete.

The piledrivers work through the lunch hours and late into the evening; carpenters and masons scramble over precarious-looking bamboo scaffolding as the apartment and office towers rise. The new buildings are pushing back the colonies of dormitory shacks, where workers play cards, shave, and wash in the packed-mud courtyards.

Shenzhen's neon isn't so bright as Hong Kong's, but it outshines that of most mainland cities. Restaurants stay open and sidewalks stay crowded with shoppers far later than they do in Beijing. Shenzhen is a trading place, for Hong Kong investors shopping for cheap labor and mainland officials gaining new industries, but also for ordinary Chinese on both sides of the border.

Hong Kong residents arrive by interurban train and use their Hong Kong dollars to take advantage of Shenzhen's low prices, set in Chinese *renminbi,* or people's money, to eat at restaurants or buy porcelain and furniture. The Shenzhen residents negotiate with the Hong Kong visitors to buy goods not yet available or cheaper than those in China. Although the once flagrant black marketing at the railway station under the eyes of the police has abated, many deals are still being made. Chinese from the interior come to Shenzhen to trade with American dollars sent by relatives abroad or siphoned from their state enterprises.

Other Chinese use contacts in the zone or visits to try to play the Shenzhen stock market, the only one in the country besides Shanghai. The market is so popular that potential shareholders rioted when denied the chance to participate in a lottery that would have allocated a new share issue. Although 5 million stock application forms were being issued, they became so scarce that black marketers sold them for ten times their $20 face value. The turmoil seemed worth it; previous Shenzhen stock issues had rocketed to values six to eight times their purchase price.

Outside of buying and exchanging, people don't seem to go to Shenzhen to have a good time. Unlike other frontier towns, including Hong Kong and Macau, Shenzhen has banned prostitution and gambling.

The Shenzhen economist and other officials stress that the existence of this and other zones is thoroughly consistent with communism. Marx and Engels said mutual economic contacts would gradually replace closed and self-sufficient economies, according to the officials. Their arguments sound more like a party ideological lecture than a sales pitch, but after the preliminaries, they turn to the realities of the market.

China says it is ahead of its stated goal to quadruple production between 1980 and 2000. If it is to continue the pace, Shenzhen officials say, it must overcome technological backwardness and a capital shortage to attain this goal. The zones were established to attract technology and capital. China also must learn from the West, but not in directly copying its capitalism, the officials stress. The same techniques can be applied to a socialist system with special Chinese characteristics.

"We must absorb the new technologies from other countries and narrow the gap that separates us from them," the economist said. "We are twenty to thirty years behind the advanced countries. If we go on closing the door, as we've done in the past, we'll be even more backward."

But he and other Chinese analysts concede that all is not well in the zones, that they have been slow to reach the level of investment that had been planned, that the benefit of the foreign technology has not spread inland as quickly as the planners had hoped.

"We lack talent; we lack people. Our legal system isn't completed," a researcher in a Beijing think tank said. "We doubt that the average businessman abroad understands our policies. We have promised to maintain our agreements and make our guarantees work, but that may not be generally accepted by our foreign partners. We need better laws for protection of investment."

The researcher was responding to questions about foreign traders' complaints about bureaucratic delays, slow returns on their capital, and, above all, the impression that the zones are more a haven for wheeling-and-dealing mainlanders than serious places to do business. A Dutch oilman who buys from both Zuhai and Shenzhen said he had trouble getting his equipment on time from joint ventures there because the employees seemed to be busy with other, not always legal, tasks.

Chinese provincial enterprises set up offices in the zones to sell their products, often at cut rates. But instead of buying machines and equipment to modernize their plants, they spend their foreign exchange on consumer goods to distribute to friends or customers back home. The Chinese Academy of Social Sciences found that "smuggling, fraudulent shipments, bribery, and embezzlement" had hurt the effectiveness of the zones.

Chinese investigations have criticized "briefcase" offices in Shenzhen, where mainland entrepreneurs arrange paper exports and reimports of the same Chinese manufactures, collecting subsidies on both transactions and kicking back some of the profits to their Hong Kong partners. Economic planners found that the early goals of creating a strong export base and sharing technology with foreign companies were being neglected. Instead, Shenzhen was generating most of its income through trade and real estate.

Nevertheless, the zones, with Shenzhen in the forefront, continue to thrive. They may suffer from lack of direction or inefficiency, but, to the Chinese, as the stock market rioting showed, they are the best chance available on the mainland to make a quick fortune.

THE DRAGON'S HEAD

In Shanghai, not far from the restaurant where the Zous work, a glass-and-chrome tower that would fit in handsomely with the skyline of New York or Hong Kong is rising from a backdrop of small alleys and Chinese-style courtyard houses. Floodlights illuminate the construction site all night as the procession of trucks, heavy equipment, and handcarts carry in material for the building. Not only the peasants are flocking to Shanghai. Even when the national leadership poured resources and investment into the special economic zones, Shanghai never lost its status as the nation's commercial, industrial, and shipping center. But now it is set for another takeoff. From year to year the figures for foreign investment, new hotels, apartment buildings, and road construction double, treble, and quadruple.

With a population of 13 million and an economy long stalled by state enterprise domination and overregulation, Shanghai epitomizes the pent-up demand for goods and services that has brought nearly 4,000 foreign firms there. It also possesses the other element of China's attraction to foreign investors: the best-educated and highest-skilled workforce in the nation. Companies such as McDonnell-Douglas and Volkswagen have been taking advantage of these twin incentives of markets and production forces for more than a decade. Many other business leaders think Shanghai's future growth will overshadow these previous achievements.

The glass-and-chrome building will house, among other tenants, local representatives of Motorola and AT&T, and the potential business that these companies stand to gain is a good way of explaining the attraction of China to foreign investors as well as Shanghai's central role in fulfilling their plans. Nearly 400,000 customers are on waiting lists for telephones in Shanghai alone. Nationwide, the figure is about 10 million. But Shanghai also possesses the electronic companies, laboratories, and university research facilities to help end the shortage, whether it is through installing lines and digital switching equipment or manufacturing cellular phones. China is the world's fastest growing market for what the Chinese call the "thread between heaven and earth"—the cellular phone. There were only 20,000 such threads in 1990; in three years the figure grew to half a million. The eventual number that China will need can only be dreamed about by the bright young cellular phone–equipped sales and technical men and women Shanghai is attracting.

Shanghai has two skylines, one brick and stone dating from the 1920s and '30s, when foreign businesses ran the city like a colony, one mirrored and bright, home to the new generation of businesses. Some of the new arrivals have bought or rented old villas in the city's international quarters. New executive neighborhoods are going up on the edges of the city, with lawns, canal frontage, and Italian names to match. This day-and-night, workday-and-weekend building boom is creating entire new business districts and transforming Shanghai, much as the British, French, Germans, and Japanese did with their riverfront Bund earlier in the century.

That city stopped at the river. Across the Huangpu was Pudong, which means "east of the river," flat farmland with a few dockyards and industries. On a 1987 trip to the area, we traveled at the pace of the horsecart in front of us, with trucks, cars, and other horsecarts in a long, slow line behind us on the two-lane road. Since then Shanghai has built two bridges across the river to unclog traffic through the only other crossing, a tunnel. The stunning harp-shaped single-suspension bridges carry traffic high over the river and its strings of little barges, chugging sampans, and foreign-flag container vessels. More and more of that commerce will be shipped in and out of Pudong, as the farmland is chewed up for construction sites.

Shanghai must become a "dragon's head" of development in China, regaining its place as financial capital of Asia, Mayor Huang Ju says. President and party general secretary Jiang Zemin, a former Shanghai mayor, also calls his city a "dragon's head," but stresses its position as a trading center for a region of 300 million people in the Yangtze valley and delta.

Both descriptions of the city's potential are right. Shanghai has not only banks but factories, not only one of China's two stock exchanges but its largest port, not only its biggest population but its biggest workforce, which accounts for 10 percent of the national industrial production and 30 percent of the nation's exports.

Shanghai's towers are monuments to international trade and business, tourism, and shopping. They overshadow the few Soviet-style spires still remaining, not to mention the Mao statues, although one still greets the students at the main gate of Fudan University.

Even communism's greatest critics among the Chinese—and there are many—concede that the new towers are based on the old economy, built up in the years of hard work for egalitarian pay under Mao's direction and often despite it. But their next argument, buttressed by the growth figures in every morning's newspaper, is that the economy then took off only under the current leadership.

Five years after it had launched the rural reforms, the party unveiled its program for restructuring the state-run economy, a giant of a million different manufacturing, construction, transport, and service enterprises. The momentum of the changes in agriculture would be lost, the party statement on the urban reforms said, if reform had to stop at factory gates and city limits: "there is an urgent need to unclog the channels of circulation between town and country." The reformers wanted to adjust prices and wages so that the urban dwellers would have benefits equal to those the rural population was beginning to enjoy.

The reformers introduced a detailed program to reduce the role of central planning, give individual enterprises more power, and begin to dismantle price controls, both for retail customers and the huge enterprise transactions in raw materials and components. All these measures were related, they stressed: Trying to regulate every transaction by a plan disregarded the market forces and was "seriously out of step with reality." The plan's grip on the state industry led to lack of vitality, which could be restored by enlarging the decision-making power of those on the spot. And if market forces were to supplement planning in guiding the economy, then there must be realistic prices, not, as the document said, the kind set by the state that reflected neither the value of the goods nor the relation of supply to demand.

A decade later, the state economy and the cities are still struggling with all of these problems. The urban reforms have not had the instant success of decollectivization. Price freedom brought inflation; the party resisted the surrender of control in the state industry, and workers objected to threats to their job security. People were better off, but the problem of dismantling state management proved far greater than the reformers had thought. Instead of ten years, official predictions were that the urban reforms might take until the middle of the next century.

Even though the reformers had been careful to move a few steps at a time, keeping price controls on basic needs and going very slowly in permitting enterprises to shake off state controls, the explosion of market forces that the introduction of the reforms set off was startling in its impact. China went on a spending and buying spree. Enterprises passed out generous bonuses and ordered expensive machines and equipment. Customers crowded the stores with bonus money, eager to spend it before the rules changed or inflation ate it up. So many new refrigerators, washing machines, fans, and television sets were plugged in that power failures occurred throughout the country.

Since that early burst of a truly free market, the government has had to move several times with emergency steps to contain the overheating of the economy. It has raised interest rates, tightened credit, and ordered enterprises to submit to bank monitoring of their bonus payments. But inflation has remained a problem for both local and central governments. Price reforms have been postponed, implemented piecemeal, and then, in some cases, rescinded. Every time the state apparatus intervened to impose price limits, it was a setback for the eventual goal of free markets.

State enterprise managers took advantage of their new independence to grant raises and bonus, often bowing to the threat of labor unrest. Inflation was a leading issue in the student demonstrations in 1986 and 1989. Since then there have been many wildcat strikes in industry, construction, and services, some of them minor, as when city bus drivers stage slowdowns to force wage parity with the free-enterprise taxi drivers, some of them major. In 1993 officials admitted that 10,000 industrial actions took place across the nation. Almost all of them were illegal, since labor law permits strikes only against private businesses, which account for less than 5 percent of the nation's enterprises. Some strike leaders have been arrested, but officials have had to give in in certain situations, as when the strike is too large to confront. Such was the case in the walkout of thousands of construction workers on the Ertan Dam in Sichuan. After halting construction for two weeks, the workers won 30 percent wage increases.

The rural reforms had worked from the start because everyone was given a stake in prosperity. There were no major state-owned institutions to get in the way of this individual quest for wealth. But in the cities, workers in the giant enterprises owned by the state were harder to reach. Their jobs were guaranteed for life; on retirement they could even pass them on to their children. While wages were low, they were augmented by a complex system of bonuses and subsidies that increased their buying power. And government-set prices were supposed to protect them against inflation. The enterprises, too, were protected: If they fulfilled their state production plan, no one cared if they made a profit.

Inflation took away some of the security of the state workforce. Many workers dealt with their reduced purchasing power by taking second jobs after hours—and sometimes during hours—at their state enterprises. The enterprises themselves seemed as sheltered from inflation as from the other realities of the marketplace.

WORKING FOR THE STATE

In Beijing, the Fang family feels the pinch of inflation but still manages a comfortable existence with two incomes from guaranteed jobs in state enterprises. Mr. Fang, a middle-age engineer employed by a state construction enterprise, his wife, Meidi, a government employee, two school-age children, and retired mother-in-law, have moved into a brand-new, centrally heated apartment. Construction workers in wicker hard hats had erected the compound of six-story buildings rapidly, earning a bonus for its early completion.

The new tenants are thrilled with the private toilet and overhead shower pipe, the cement floors, the tiny kitchen large enough for a two-burner gas stove, shelves for pickled foods, and a sink. There are three more rooms large enough to hold their beds piled with brilliant quilts, a bookcase, a television, a new leatherette sofa, and space-saving round table and stools that fold up between meals. Their Snow Flake refrigerator just fits in the entranceway. The small balcony will store the family bicycles and winter supplies of cabbages, pomegranates, and onions.

A private telephone and piped-in gas for the kitchen stove to replace the 2-burner propane stove will not be available in the fore-seeable future. Telephones are allotted only to those with connections or high positions, as well as to government offices, listed in a perfunctory way in Beijing's quarter-inch-thick phone book. China has 1.2 telephones per thousand population, compared to Hong Kong's 560 and the United States' 600. Telephoning is done from the corner kiosk, which also sells cigarettes, candy, and newspapers. Incoming calls and the arrival of visitors are announced by neighbors on the floors below, who shout the messages from balcony to balcony. The ancient telephone lines make local conversations hard to understand without shouting, too, but overseas calls, relayed by satellite, sound as if they're coming from the next block.

Despite the municipal government's citywide project to pipe natural gas to all households eventually, it has been rumored that the management of Fang's work unit failed to arrange the almost obligatory banquet for the proper officials to ensure that the gas lines would reach the unit's new compound soon. The Fangs and their neighbors will continue to wheel carts of propane gas tanks for their stoves from a local depot, or buy pressed coal-dust cylinders from the coal man who wheels his platform bike from neighborhood to neighborhood, calling out his wares in a singsong.

The engineer has an easy commute to his work unit, which built the apartment buildings adjacent to its offices on the edge of the city. But Meidi now has a forty-five-minute bike ride from their new apartment to her government office in the center of Beijing. Buses, although very cheap, are unbearably crowded and slow.

It is a tortuous journey for her, riding three and four abreast with other bicyclists, some of them looking mute and anonymous with surgical masks across their faces, defense against fumes from the stream of buses, trucks, and taxis alongside, or dusty winds blowing down from the Gobi Desert.

Meidi could ask for a transfer to another work unit, closer to her new home. Even if her superiors were willing for her to leave—and often managers are not—she would be reluctant to change. It is a good work unit that provides many of the perks and benefits that work units are supposed to provide. Some state-owned enterprises are so poorly managed or generate such meager profits that they cannot afford the workers' clinic, the day care nursery, or the housing that is theoretically the responsibility of each unit for its workers.

Meidi felt fortunate when she was assigned to her work unit fourteen years ago after graduation from middle school. In those days, when the authorities made the assignments for graduates of schools and universities, it was without regard for family ties or personal preferences or, sometimes, even talents or education.

Until the reforms began, citizens were assigned where the government decided their labor or expertise were needed. During the Cultural Revolution, millions of experts and intellectuals, teachers, engineers, doctors, and students were sent to the countryside for "reeducation" in the ways of socialism. Often their expertise was wasted; doctors became field hands and teachers cleaned pigsties. There are no such abuses now, but China's rural development needs are great, and large numbers of specialists remain at jobs in backward regions, along with laborers (some of them sent there as punishment), and soldiers.

Many recall using *guanxi* (connections), a small banquet, a generous gift to persuade the right official to make assignments more to the taste and liking of a young student or worker, and others found more ingenious ways to outmaneuver the authorities.

A medical intern whose parents were sent to work in a remote part of Gansu Province, one of China's most backward, when he was a baby considered himself wildly fortunate to be back in Shanghai. He found it easier to get accepted at the university because quotas are more generous for the poorer provinces. Once there, he discovered a foolproof way to avoid going back. "I studied very hard and chose microsurgery as my specialty," he said. Since only big-city hospitals have such a specialty, he knew he was in the city to stay.

Well-run state enterprises like Meidi's offer many compensations to their employees to make up for low pay and long hours. The work day for Meidi and her colleagues has a predictable, almost leisurely, rhythm from the time she enters the compound of her work unit and fills several Thermoses at the communal hot water boiler for the innumerable cups of tea she and officemates will drink throughout the day. An assortment of teacups sit on a table just inside the door of her office, furnished with an odd collection of desks and calculators and typewriters of various vintage and makes. She and her six officemates take turns napping in the two over-stuffed armchairs during the lunch hour.

During the midmorning fifteen-minute break, she can join col-leagues in the courtyard for a little badminton or a routine of exer-cises, pick up her canteen meal tickets, check out a book from the unit's library, or visit the clinic nurse for an herbal medicine. She can even use the communal shower room, patronized chiefly by the single workers who live four to a room in the dormitories behind the office building.

Well before the official noon lunch hour, her fellow employees pull out enamel bowls and chopsticks from desk drawers and pour out of their offices and down the broad staircases to the bright, airy central canteen. Older employees, with the privilege of seniority, fetch their eating utensils from tiny lockers lining the canteen's pantry where everyone washes bowls and chopsticks under cold-water taps ranged down the long, troughlike sink after lunch.

In an astonishingly short time, the long lines of lunchers have moved from counter to counter, exchanging meal tickets for bowls of rice, vegetables, or meat from the kitchen workers who ladle out generous portions from steaming, barrel-size woks. Seated on sturdy little stools around one of the many round tables, they quickly dispense with lunch to allow seating for the next wave of employees and to take advantage of the long noontime break for napping or doing errands.

Numerous diversions break up the rest of the work days. Occa-sionally employees are recruited to perform volunteer work, such as planting tree seedlings on the outskirts of Beijing, part of China's nationwide reforestation project. From time to time a special ship-ment of live chickens, the first persimmons, or a rare delicacy such as pineapples from the South arrives at the unit gates, and office workers rush to buy, chattering gaily, pleased with the unexpected treat. Their purchases of squawking poultry and net bags of produce line the cement-floored corridors until quitting time.

CUTTING LOSSES

The reforms have tried to restore the state enterprises to profitability in two main stages. The current one, not fully implemented, borrows more from capitalism by using bankruptcy, corporate forms of organization, and legal reforms to push the enterprises into the marketplace. The earlier stage tried to accomplish the same effect by instituting labor contracts, manager responsibility, and contracts between enterprises and state bureaus.

Most of the nation's industrial plants have these contracts specifying output, earnings, and taxes. They are a way the state can monitor the efficiency of an enterprise and also control overgenerous bonus payments. Managers get to keep a share of their profits for investment and also may have to make up losses.

At the Wuhan Iron and Steel works on the Yangtze, these economic reforms are greeted with pleasure. The devolution of many decision-making powers, a state manager says, gives him much more flexibility and benefits not only the plant but its workers. As thick slabs of red-hot steel clatter along the lines of the rolling mill, disappearing into baths of steam and emerging thinner, a handful of attendants monitor the Mitsubishi equipment.

The manager said that under the old system, if he wanted to order another set of Japanese equipment, he would have to compete with the other mills for Beijing's approval. Under the contract system, he can finance the new equipment with investment funds retained by the Wuhan mill after paying taxes.

The workers benefit from bonuses geared to productivity, which have been running as high as 30 percent of their base pay. As more machines move in, the plant will shorten the present five-and-one-half-day week rather than laying off anyone. But the reforms make firing at least theoretically possible. "Some of our workers have enjoyed the 'everyone eating out of the same big pot' conditions," the manager said. "Some don't want to work very much." The first step is education, to convince these poorly motivated workers of the benefits of the reforms. If that fails, their pay is reduced. The manager admitted that no one had yet got to the third stage, which is dismissal.

Some reformers criticize the contract system as a backdoor way of keeping bureaucratic controls on enterprise managers. After years of struggle between advocates of manager independence from party rule, the system of factory responsibility was introduced as something both sides could accept. The factory director is now in charge of production, operations, and administration. The task of the formerly all-powerful party secretary is merely to ensure that the enterprise adheres to policy, and he or she is supposed to do this only through advice or persuasion, not orders.

The manager has the right to draw up plans, hire and fire administrators, change plant rules, issue raises and bonuses, and decide on new equipment. His or her obligations are set by the contract with the government. Managers also are supposed to listen to the advice of the party committee, a staff management committee, and a staff workers' congress, but none of these bodies has a direct role in decision making.

Another reform idea, the contract labor system, was greeted with less than enthusiasm from many workers. Giving workers contracts of two to twenty years, instead of lifetime tenure, was seen as a way of reducing the huge welfare and services burden on enterprises and promoting efficiency. Pilot programs showed productivity increases by contract workers, whose social service needs are picked up by the state.

Experience to date has showed that in boom areas, where opportunities for new jobs are plentiful, the contracts are popular with young workers, who can move around and improve their chances.

Workers with tenure have been assured that their status would not change; only newly hired workers would go on contract. But so many oppose the system that it has not expanded much beyond the pilot program stage, covering only about 3 million workers.

Reform in the cities and the state enterprises has not yet lived up to the expectations of the leadership. Shifting from the unrealistic but safe and slow system of government-dictated prices to the unpredictability of the market had never been attempted before on such a vast scale. It turned out to be a much bigger task than the planners had expected. No matter what incentives or contracts are held out to the elephantine state enterprises, it seems, they are largely resistant to change and continue to pile up losses.

There were hopes for improvement in 1994, when the government began plans to transform state enterprises into shareholding companies. This had the smell of privatization to some investors, foreign and domestic, but the party Old Guard prevailed. The state will retain at least 50 percent of the shares of the reorganized companies, officials stressed, and Chen Yun added that "the principle of state ownership as the mainstay of the economy cannot change."

Foreign investors responded by simply bypassing the old state enterprises and setting up entirely new plants. Foreign managers of joint venture agreements with Chinese partners don't want to wrestle with the inefficiency of the old plants or be bound to hire their padded workforces. By starting anew, they avoid much of the responsibility for the welfare of workers and their families. They say that the taxes they pay (after a two- or three-year initial no-tax period) should take care of that.

If reorganization doesn't work, more drastic methods for facing up to state enterprise losses are now legally possible, although still politically unwise. Party directives permit local authorities to close consistently unprofitable state enterprises, which means laying off workers. Mayor Huang of Shanghai has warned that some of his city's laggard performers may be first: "We will experiment with bankruptcy for a minority of enterprises, who, after hard efforts, have no hope of stemming losses," he told Chinese journalists.

FREE ENTERPRISE

Many Chinese have left the security of state jobs to "swim in the sea" of the private sector, the more than 20 million individual enterprises that form a third economic entity, alongside the state and the mostly rural collective industries. Individually owned businesses have flourished, sometimes on the edge of legality, since the reforms began, but only after they were seen to fill such a great need with such efficiency did they get the leadership's full blessing. In 1988 the Chinese constitution was changed to legalize these family or individually run operations and to permit them to hire labor without worrying about the old Marxist penalties for exploitation. A few factories are privately owned by Chinese, many of them in the Zhejiang province port city of Wenzhou, and many thousands are foreign-owned private businesses, but the most visible effect of private entrepreneurship is in services. Tiny Japanese taxi vans, already crowded with only the driver, help reduce the waiting lines at railway stations. In the Central Asian city of Kashgar, woodworkers, metalworkers, furriers, and rug weavers have restored the bazaars to their traditional central function in the economy. Free-enterprise cooks who own little beach restaurants on Shantou's Puyu island display their freshly caught crabs and fish and wok them on the spot.

Shanghai resident Shishun is a slim, bright twenty-three-year-old free-market businessman who wears a green silk shirt with his Western-label blue jeans, a current fad among young men in a city that claims to be the Paris of China. Unlike his thirty-five-year-old brother whose state-owned factory job provides the relative security of housing, medical care, and a steady salary of about $80 a month, Shishun is self-employed. He has a small stake borrowed from family and friends and the blessing of the government, which once considered peddlers and street merchants counterrevolutionary.

Shishun sells blue jeans similar to the ones he wears, a curious brand named Bronco Bust, made in Taiwan. His merchandise and some of the other free-market goods are smuggled in from an off-shore island where Taiwanese arrive to exchange jeans, pop tune tapes, and other manufactured items with coastal Chinese traders who deal in the medicinal herbs that are highly prized by all Chinese, bamboo furniture, jade, and other mainland specialties.

The young businessman sets up his stand, a simple folding table with a canvas umbrella, alongside dozens of other stands on a city side street at least six days a week. Every day is a good shopping day in China. Business is great, he claims, although he has to pay a daily tax to the official inspectors with red armbands who regularly patrol the free markets. The tax can be as high as 20 to 30 percent of his daily profits, but the final sum is subject to considerable negotiation and minimizing of sales on his part.

On a good day, he makes as much as $150, he claims. He can easily afford the $80 he may spend in an evening, a month's pay for his factory worker brother. That would include the admission charge to one of the discos that have sprung up all over the city and treating his friends to a five- and six-course restaurant meal, with plenty of beer and clear white liquor, with much of the food left on the plates uneaten as a sign of wealth.

He still lives with his parents, his brother, and two unmarried sisters in a three-room apartment, because even a handsome sum of money doesn't buy privacy in this city. He can easily afford a wristwatch, a camera, or a stereo set. For years he could afford a motorcycle, too, but could not buy one because a local policy limited licenses to cut down on traffic. Now his new Chinese/Japanese motorcycle stands with rows of others near the market. Some are covered from the rain with old Communist Party banners that used to stretch across the market street.

Medical care? He's not entitled to the free or very low-cost services his brother and other state employees get. He can always use a registered worker's name to get free care, he says.

Individual enterprises such as Shishun's are as traditional as card-playing and chopsticks in China, and they flourish so naturally in the cities and along the roads that it is hard to imagine their being banned as "the long tail of capitalism." Their comeback is universally welcomed.

Shanghai still has fewer restaurants than it had before 1949, and although new ones open daily, supply and demand is a problem. Until a few years ago, the solution was to crowd more people into the barrackslike dining halls and let them eat standing up in the spaces between the tables. (Chopsticks are admirably suited to such maneuvers.) Private entrepreneurs are contributing much of the

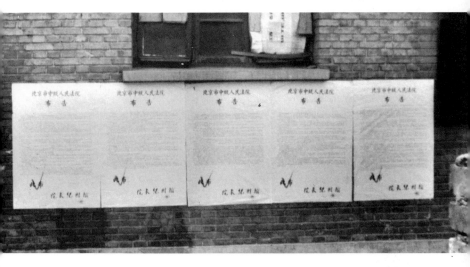

Execution posters are grim reminders of the harshness of Chinese justice. Corruption, rape, murder, even "hooliganism," are punishable by death. A red check below the text about the criminal and crime means the death sentence has been carried out.

The large white wreath, handmade of paper and bamboo, is one of the indispensable items for traditional Chinese funeral rites. Like old-style wedding ceremonies, they are increasingly popular despite official disapproval of extravagance and "feudalism."

Chinese, young and old, are insatiable readers. Bookstores, particularly the science and technology sections, are always crowded. The sidewalk rental library offers a good read of adventure or love stories for its youthful patrons, perched on tiny stools. The cheaply produced books could be banned quickly if judged to be too lurid.

A Tibetan farmer cheerfully hauls water and night soil to his fields, like millions of other peasants throughout China. Campaigns to ensure safe drinking water and to encourage modern fertilization have improved rural health conditions.

In overcrowded cities, balconies of apartments and houses spill over with drying laundry, piles of vegetables, and bicycles. Drab new apartments and old houses subdivided to accommodate several families provide an average of only twenty-one square feet of living space per person.

Well padded against the cold, these nursery school youngsters are already accustomed to group living and discipline. In a nation where both parents work, government work units—offices, factories, and collective farms—are expected to provide day, and sometimes night, care for their employees' children. But the reforms have lured many parents to private companies, where they do not automatically enjoy such perks.

Ping-Pong, a sport at which the Chinese excel, ranks in popularity with cards and billiards. Concrete Ping-Pong tables take up less precious space in parks than soccer fields.

Delivery men, fighting the heat, relax on a Beijing sidewalk. Urban workers take full advantage of their two-hour lunch breaks during their long work weeks.

Saffron-robed boys in Yunnan Province take a break from their Buddhist studies. Despite government-funded restoration of some temples, monasteries, mosques, and churches, Buddhists, Muslims, and Christians suffer an uneasy and precarious relationship with the Chinese Communist Party.

Surplus manpower equipped only with shovels and baskets make up for the lack of earth-moving equipment, a situation worsened by China's current building boom, to complete mammoth undertakings such as this sewer project in Sichuan.

Supermarkets, still rare in China, attract enormous crowds seven days a week. Trucks drive down the wide aisles to replenish produce, canned goods, frozen poultry, and sweets.

Peasants who find that they have become surplus labor in the countryside, and urban workers who leave the relative security of low-paying government jobs, cheerfully put up with squalid living conditions for the sake of high wages in booming special economic zones such as Shenzhen.

A successful worker, nattily fitted out from wicker hat to wheeled luggage, will join millions of others traveling back to their home provinces for the Spring Festival. Members of the million-plus transient population of Shanghai, these wicker-hard-hatted workers are seeking work in construction projects in the booming Chinese coastal provinces.

Propaganda banners used as dust protectors for the gleaming new motorcycles, symbols of affluence of well-paid construction workers, are a sign of increasing public disregard for Communist Party slogans and exhortations.

A bicyclist pauses before the construction site of Shanghai's television tower, one of the tallest buildings in Asia.

The pedicab is still a popular means of transportation. Here an elderly passenger rides down a street in an old section of Beijing.

Despite streets and avenues clogged with noisy taxis and trucks, the quiet bicycle is still the main means of transportation in Beijing.

This bicycle parking lot in Beijing shows how the capital copes with 3 million daily bike commuters. Parking fees, collected by pensioners, are a few pennies.

growth in eating capacity, opening little restaurants such as the Green Bamboo, not far from the downtown banks and office buildings on the Bund, the riverfront avenue built by foreign capitalists in the 1920s. It is owned by a former state employee who was so underutilized in his clerical job that he could hardly wait to quit, and his wife, who was famous in their neighborhood for her sauces and seafood recipes. They charge a little more than their subsidized competitors, but by every other measure—cleanliness, charm, freshness and attractiveness of food, and courtesy, they are far ahead.

In Shenyang, the Manchurian steel city that used to be called Mukden, restaurants play an important part in the revival of the private economy. In the 1950s Shenyang counted around 9,000 private restaurants. The Cultural Revolution and other campaigns forced them all out of business. Now the private sector is flourishing again. There are 9,000 restaurants once again and thousands of small shops, repair stalls, laundries, pedicabs, pushcarts, lending libraries, bamboo and wicker shops, and enterprises for the fluffing up of the quilting in bedding and jackets.

We watched the birth of a new fast food restaurant in a residential neighborhood of Beijing, a combination of American ideas, Taiwanese investment, and a slightly puzzled Chinese workforce who seemed ill at ease in their red-and-white-striped jackets modeled on those of Kentucky Fried Chicken. The entrepreneur was a Taiwanese who had studied business in California and carried thick rolls of U.S. dollars. The help were young men and women from the neighborhood who found their training in counter-style service so challenging that some slept during the entrepreneur's lectures. The food was no match for the fare of the outdoor wok stands down the street, but people from the neighborhood filled the chrome-and-glass restaurant on opening night, enjoying the glitter.

In Beijing, Shengyang, and elsewhere, free enterprise has brought great improvement in restaurants, services, and the production of goods such as scouring brushes and other necessities that do not fit into national plans. The private ventures have provided employment for peasants made redundant and urban youth "waiting for job assignments," the Chinese euphemism for unemployed.

They have come into being without the need for a new ministry or department to plan their work and supervise its execution. And finally, they have had some effect on the performance of the state enterprises, in marketing and in services.

The private traders have activated supply systems and influenced the decisions of factories, both state and private, on what goods to produce. They are close to the market and thus able to move faster than the slow state purchasing system. No state store manager is going to travel to South China to stock up on the latest Hong Kong–influenced nylon jackets, but the overnight trains are filled with individual entrepreneurs doing just that. A private-market intelligence service works with remarkable speed in the Yangtze delta area, using production data to alert suppliers. A private button factory put on extra shifts when its managers learned from the service that Western suit production in the Shanghai region was being increased by 2,000 a day.

The growing private competition is one reason that state department stores now give sales-related bonuses and reward employees for being courteous and helpful. A Shanghai resident says she has noticed the clerks in her state stores have become more polite and that the managers have been stocking a wider variety to keep from losing customers to the private businesses, which are opening in the city at the rate of twenty a day.

But bureaucratic obstacles abound. Officials' demands for multiple licenses, often accompanied by under-the-table payments, are common.

"I have to get fifteen chops just to sell bean curd," a Beijing peddler complained, referring to the orange or red official stamps on his permits. "Even then I can't go into the really good areas in the middle of town." Although there are periodic drives to streamline procedures, practicing free enterprise in a largely collective society is complicated. Not everyone can qualify; as an official of the Beijing municipality explained, peddlers must pass examinations on professional knowledge and managerial ability. The examinations appear to be more a way of controlling the number of traders than advancing professional standards; when the local or national policy is to cut down the numbers of unemployed youth, the tests are less stringent. Those who pass the examinations are granted licenses, which give them the right to buy goods from the state wholesale distribution system, if they do not produce them themselves or buy from other private traders. Some traders complain that even with the licenses, back-door connections help in getting more attractive or scarce goods.

Traders and artisans pay income as well as commercial or industrial tax, although they are exempt from income tax in their first year of business. Trading and manufacturing standards are enforced both by full-time local officials and the red-banded volunteers who make sure prices and weights are right. Sometimes the enforcement seems overzealous, and traders say this is a sign that the officials or volunteers want a banquet or a gift.

The private entrepreneurs account for less than 10 percent of China's industrial production, but their role in the services, although not measured by state statistics, seems much higher. Large cities devote entire markets to tailor shops that fit, cut, and sew on the spot. Hobbyists are served by shopkeepers who sell songbirds, their cages, their food, the heavy brass hardware to hang up the delicate bamboo cages, and the miniature porcelain dishes to hold their food and water. Fish fanciers can buy aquariums with tiny china underwater villages. Houseplant owners are supplied with handmade sprinkling cans.

Tangshan, site of a devastating 1976 earthquake, has a section of private dealers in used doors and windows. Shengfang, near Beijing, has 2,000 families working at home tailoring. Their weekly markets attract buyers from hundreds of miles away.

In every city market, there are two kinds of private traders: the regulars, with permanent stalls and licenses for food, clothing, and housewares; and the freelancers, who unload their small retail stock on a piece of cloth on the ground and keep an eye open for the authorities. Usually the regulars outnumber the freelancers, who are more likely to stock items such as comic books, Hong Kong movie star pictures, plastic pistols, and Buddha decals. There are periodic sweeps to check licenses and measure. Although customers sometimes question their absolute accuracy, Chinese scales are works of art: polished wooden rods with inlaid markings in brass, a weight attached to a sliding loop of string, and a pan or hook on the other end. Some of the traders have done so well that they have replaced their traditional balances with expensive digital scales from Hong Kong.

These small businessmen and -women work closely with rural industry, which, like free enterprise, is a sector of the Chinese economy that was spawned and developed without much participation from the planners.

RURAL INDUSTRY

Rural industry was born early in the reform period, when the changed economic circumstances in rural China began to create solutions for some of the theoreticians' problems. Farmworkers no longer needed on the land began pooling tools and savings and families expanded farm workshops into small factories. Local governments, deprived of most of their supervisory functions in agriculture, found a way to continue to exercise authority, earn money, create jobs, and fill consumer needs all at once.

These small factories and shops have sprung up on the edges of towns and cities, on the geographical and administrative dividing line that separates China's city and rural populations. The single-story buildings, often only partly constructed, and their cluttered yards sprawl along highways, rail lines, and canals. The seventy-five miles between Guangzhou and the Shenzhen special economic zone is taking on the look of a Western industrial strip; the same is true in the rich provinces of the delta in the semicircle around Shanghai.

These provinces, Jiangsu and Zhejiang, and the rural outskirts of the Shanghai municipality on both sides of the Huangpu River have all the advantages of location that made Shanghai one of the world's industrial and trade centers and, to date, few of the disadvantages. They have good connections by road, rail, and canal to sources of supply and marketing, a large and relatively skilled labor pool, access to consultants and foreign buyers, and opportunities to obtain credit and investment. But the new rural managers are not saddled with the ancient machinery, entrenched labor force, and bureaucracy of the state enterprises they compete with.

As a result, they are outpacing the state industrial enterprises in every way: growth rate (often double), productivity, and profits. In Jiangsu and Zhejiang, collective industries account for more than half the industrial output.

Parts of Jiangsu, north of Shanghai, have become China's most productive light industrial belt, with industrial and agricultural output nearly eight times that of a decade ago and earnings more than double the national average for peasants.

The region has been rich over the centuries because of silkworm culture and textile factories, but its new prosperity is also based on diversifying: instrument factories, metalworking plants, and service industries for textiles. Officials recall that shops and factories had to be started secretly in the early 1970s, even though surplus farm labor had been a problem for years. In Wuxi County, 80 percent of the population works in the county's rural industries, producing 94 percent of the county's income. The other 20 percent works on the farms.

Singapore's Economic Development Board chose the nearby garden city of Suzhou for its Singapore II industrial township, a project on the city's outskirts that will house 600,000 people and provide jobs for 360,000. A consortium of nineteen Singapore companies is investing $200 million in the area. The money is for infrastructure, training of workers, and export promotion—all of which will give Singapore II advantages that the local rural industries cannot possibly hope to match.

Shaoxing is at the other end of the crescent of booming small industries around Shanghai. This old canal city is known across China as the home of the great writer Lu Xun and of the amber rice wine served warm in tiny cups. But to the locals, textiles are Shaoxing's claim to fame—since the Tang dynasty in the seventh to tenth centuries, as one proud factory manager said.

The county's collective enterprises include transport and construction companies, but most are industrial, tied in with the production of silk and other fabrics. Its rural factories compete with Shanghai's state sector in supplying the textile industry with everything from knitting machinery and looms to dyeing and printing equipment.

At one textile machinery factory, profits have been increasing at nearly 30 percent a year, its manager said, despite a rate of taxation that would cause Western entrepreneurs to gag: 46 percent of earnings.

The factory, on the edge of the city, has plain but not unpleasant two-story dormitories for the 125 single men and women who come from distant parts of the county to work there on contract. Conversations with some of them showed that their reasons for leaving the farm were the same as those offered in other societies: Life is dull there, and the money in town is better.

No one goes back, one twenty-year-old-technician said. They like to work in the factory, because they earn twice as much, and the income, in addition, is stable. The average wage is around $90 a month.

These peasants who have become workers live a good life, particularly when their living standards are contrasted to those before the reforms, the manager said. They have color television in common rooms in the dormitories. There is a washing machine. All own bicycles, and some also have motorcycles.

Back in their villages, the land is being farmed by professional farmers, who are paid by the peasants-turned-workers, and who in turn pay them land rent in the form of food.

Those peasants who were alloted land in the distributions of the 1980s can charge rent for it, even though the state is the land's ultimate owner and they cannot sell it. The factory chips in with a subsidy to keep the professional farmers' pay up to that of the factory workers.

The factory gets some of its tax payments back in the form of credits from the district government. Other funding for new equipment comes from banks and the investment of the individual peasants, who are paid back over a long term with interest.

The factory allots a good part of its earnings to retirement accounts, since its workers are not covered by the state welfare and pension system. Workers with thirty years' service can retire at 85 percent of their pay. Hospitalization and life insurance also are provided by the factory. Women who have babies get lighter work and a two-month paid leave; the factory also pays for day care.

Not all cooperative enterprises are so generous, the manager concedes. He places his in the top 10 percent in the county for benefits. But since there is no lifetime tenure in cooperative ventures, workers in other plants can easily switch to his if they are dissatisfied.

With all these advantages, there must be some drawbacks to rural industry, and there are indeed. Local officials concede that the technical level of some of the rural plants lags behind that of the longer-established state enterprises, but consultant and training programs are in place to improve it.

Despite the local successes and production claims, there is evidence that the easy years of growth for rural industry may be over, now that the pent-up demand for almost any manufactured product is slackening.

Experts in the national and provincial government also are concerned about the amount of arable land disappearing for rural factories and housing for workers. Pollution is a special concern: The small factories are generally less careful than the state industries, although the record of the latter certainly has not been exemplary.

A further concern is the uncertainty that rural industries nationwide cause for the central planning process. They do not operate under the strictures of the plan, and yet they compete in domestic and to an extent foreign markets for sales and raw materials, and investment funds. Their energy consumption has sapped the overworked electric power grids of the nation; frequently we found factories closed for a morning or a day because of the power shortage. The booming manufacturing and trading activity also has strained the overcrowded rail lines and roads.

World Bank specialists are concerned about the inefficiency of some of the rural industry and the Chinese practice of duplicating similar factories in several counties or provinces, instead of pooling resources for fewer but larger and more efficient ones. Chinese analysts, too, praise the growth of rural industry as a means of absorbing excess farm labor and providing more goods but are concerned that it may not be able to compete in the long run with those small entrepreneurs of neighboring Asian countries who have had a twenty- or thirty-year head start.

PART THREE

CHINA AND THE WORLD

China's relations with the outside world are troubled, after more than twenty years of foreign policy successes. China has opened the door to the West but has not been able to contain the Western influences, from television broadcasts to demands for human rights, that it worries will weaken Communist rule. Its giant neighbor, Russia, and the former Central Asian republics are still shaken by the political and economic crisis that followed the Soviet breakup, and some of the instability has already spilled over to Chinese territory. Negotiations on the future of Hong Kong, once praised as a success for Chinese diplomacy, have instead cast new doubts on Beijing's commitment to democracy in the British colony. Further damage to China's image comes from the cycles of repression that follow political outbursts in the territories it already controls, Tibet and Xinjiang. All these actions make it even less likely that the people or leaders of Taiwan will agree to unite with the mainland any time in the near future.

China is proud of its modernization and economic gains, but it is responding to new ideas from abroad and other nationalities with an inflexibility more suited to imperial times than the modern world.

SEVEN

WRITERS, TEACHERS, AND CENSORS

It's book-banning time on a downtown street in Xian, not far from the gray, forty-foot walls built 500 years ago to protect China's former capital from invaders. Hostile influences from outside are again the target. Martial music from loudspeakers and banners denouncing bourgeois tendencies draw in the crowds, mostly peasants who have someone hold their place in line at the nearby railway station. They stare at the covers of the books and some of the piles of raunchy tabloids. Politics doesn't seem to be a big issue in Xian. The local censors are concerned about some rather mild accounts of sex and violence, considered lurid by Chinese standards, and blamed on Western influences. Bored-looking policemen stand next to the stacks of banned paperbacks and newspapers, letting the party's posters do the explaining: These writings support superstition, violence, and illicit sex. Authors and journalists should turn their energies to educating the people to adhere to the Four Cardinal Principles: upholding the socialist road, the people's democratic dictatorship, the Communist Party's leadership, and Marxism-Leninism and Mao Zedong thought. The real message of the event is that the party knows what readers should read and writers should write, and has the censors and political prisons to make sure it is obeyed.

THE HEAVENLY THREAD

In the classroom, on movie and television screens, and in newspapers, magazines, and books, China's intellectuals learn their lesson early. Control of what is taught, written, screened, and broadcast is considered as important to the Communist Party as its other main controls, the police, the army, and the security apparatus.

But China's audiences, readers, and students are fortunate that the book banning and censorship employed by the regime are becoming as outmoded a defense as Xian's walls. Across the nation, satellite dishes have been appearing on house and apartment roofs in numbers greater than the party flags and banners below, bringing viewers in touch with the rest of the world and bypassing the huge bureaucracies trying to blockade or filter information.

For years, and despite jamming, the ubiquitous transistor radio has linked Chinese listeners with the Voice of America, the British Broadcasting Corporation, and many independent Chinese voices from Taiwan, Hong Kong, and farther afield. The United States will soon add a Radio Free Asia to the information sources available.

Now the transistor has been joined by the much more powerful medium of television from abroad, beamed down to the mainland from satellites on what the Chinese call the heavenly thread. Hong Kong–based StarTV, which carries news as well as MTV, sports, and Chinese opera, reaches 30 million homes in China. Hong Kong's Chinese-language television stations send overland signals to 65 million more in the mainland areas it borders. China has 230 million television sets, ten times the number a decade ago, and StarTV and its competitors from around the world, including CNN, Time-Warner, and Home Box Office, are trying to fill these screens.

China's nervous leadership, in the meantime, is trying to keep them empty, at least of programs that don't originate in the People's

Republic. Laws banning satellite dishes, long on the books but unenforced, have been revived, with threats of confiscation of the dishes and fines for those who watch the broadcasts from abroad. Exceptions have been made for hotels, businesses, and those in mountainous or other inaccessible regions. Wang Feng, vice minister in charge of radio, cinema, and television, said the aim is "protecting the excellent cultural heritage of the Chinese nation, . . . promoting socialist spiritual civilization, and maintaining social stability."

But the Chinese censors face two obstacles in controlling what goes into viewers' homes. Enforcing a ban on satellite dishes might cause more social unrest than would permitting free choice of programs, particularly when viewers have invested $500 or $600 in their equipment. Even the most repressive regimes in Eastern Europe looked the other way when their citizens pointed antennae to the West because of the political cost of admitting their propaganda had failed. China may have to do the same. The second obstacle is technical: StarTV uses the same satellite as the government's China Central Television (CCTV). In areas where the CCTV signal is strong, no one would need a dish, but in much of China, there is no way for the authorities to know whether rooftop dishes were put up to pull in news broadcasts from Hong Kong, Kung Fu dramas, or their own propaganda.

With constantly improving technology, detection will be harder. Satellites are getting more powerful, permitting dishes to shrink from ten-foot to eighteen-inch diameters. The new systems developed in the United States are sure to be copied by the thousands of small electronic workshops on the mainland.

In addition, the international business and investment links brought on by the economic reforms created a censorship-free information network that has spun off into Chinese homes. Dissidents as well as bankers send fax messages across the Pacific; electronic bulletin boards and electronic mail are as common in some parts of China as they are in the West.

For this reason, some in the government question the attempts the leadership is making to block the free flow of information. Not surprising because of its importance as an international trade and financial center, Shanghai is taking the lead. Cutting citizens off from satellite television transmissions and other information sources would slow economic modernization, Shanghai authorities said in a confidential briefing paper obtained by Patrick Tyler of *The New York Times:* "We should have confidence in the viewers. We shouldn't seal the window just because a fly might slip in."

EMANCIPATING THE MIND

These differences among the leaders on the wisdom of providing or withholding information from the people of China has long been reflected in the ranks of the nation's reporters and editors. From the first days of Communist rule, they have had to survive through alternating periods of censorship and permissiveness, official lies and openness.

As in any society, the vast majority went along with those in power. But even at times of the worst repression, many journalists risked imprisonment to tell the truth.

Chinese journalists always have been a puzzle to the Communist leaders, who see them as a strange group of state employees who often do not behave as the other docile bureaucrats do. Yet the leaders need the press to get information and policies before the people, as well as to get information *from* the people. Good reporters can tell officials what is wrong in the nation and can call attention to corruption, mismanagement, waste, and injustice.

The officials also want their media to be lively and attractive, so that the people will read, listen, and watch without coercion or without switching over to MTV. To achieve this, they pay well and attract some of the nation's brightest minds. But they also insist on control, which is where the trouble begins.

The ambivalence of the leadership means that there are repeated crackdowns on free expression, but also periods when journalists sense that they can be a little bolder. Many of them then pay for this boldness with loss of their job or prison. China leads the world in imprisoned journalists, according to the New York–based Committee to Protect Journalists, with twenty-two, ahead of Kuwait and Ethiopia.

Mao Zedong's 1942 orders to the intellectuals are still used to define media policy in the satellite age. Writers and other creative people "must necessarily obey the political demands of class and party," Mao said.

How those demands are executed, however, has been open to wide interpretation. Whether journalists must work as direct propaganda conduits or be more independent depends on how far party officials dare to go in loosening restrictions and how far authors and reporters are willing to risk pushing the limits.

Such daring often is based on desperation. When an economy deteriorates to the point that vigorous, independent criticism from the press is needed, or where there is so much social disquiet that drastic policy changes are needed, both officials and journalists are emboldened. In these periods, and only then, all the paper guarantees of press freedom in authoritarian constitutions come to life.

At other times, these guarantees are canceled out by multiple controls on what reaches the public. All Chinese media, from the *People's Daily* to the village loudspeaker systems that broadcast provincial or national news and announcements, are supervised by the party. Its propaganda department—the Communists do not shy away from this term—sets the strategy for press campaigns as well as passing on content in the national media. Propaganda departments at the provincial and municipal levels take care of regional and local media. As an additional safeguard, party members fill all important editorial positions.

Nevertheless, there are conflicts of opinion, and editors are allowed some freedom in resisting these controls, depending on the political climate. The chief editor of one of China's leading newspapers described this process in conversations with the authors. He said he employed a strategy of placating the officials by agreeing without question to give front-page play to their campaigns and, indeed, to go beyond what is required. He assigned his top reporters to cover party themes, creating real reader interest in them.

In exchange, he said, he often got his way when he insisted that a sensitive story—more often than not a corruption scandal involving party officials—must be run.

"Don't lump all propaganda department people with conservatives and bureaucrats," a young party official in Shanghai said. "Some of us are reformers, committed to helping the press serve the people. That means permitting the widest possible freedom for journalists."

What is wide and what is possible has varied with the times. The low point for Chinese journalism was surely the Cultural Revolution, when the radicals seized the media and used them to fight their political battles. But the end of that period of turmoil was also the beginning of a resurgence of independence. The Red Guards had forced out many veteran journalists, persecuting some until they committed suicide, forcing hundreds of others to work as laborers. "I was quite fortunate," a *People's Daily* editor said in a conversation. "I had only to work as a chef, cooking for 190 people, laborers, as I had become."

All these journalists were rehabilitated in the realignment of power that followed Mao's death. Deng Xiaoping's reformers dismissed the propaganda teams from the papers and broadcast stations and eliminated the obligatory Mao pictures and quotations. Most important, Deng called for the "emancipation of the mind" to revitalize society.

"The call had the almost magical effect of opening the floodgates for a sudden surge of pent-up intellectual activity," a Beijing intellectual recalled. "Having been told to emancipate their minds, some of the old professionals and their younger colleagues began to question the rules that had governed what they wrote and reported."

The press created by that first burst of reform was neither truly independent nor wholly controlled. It was instead a press directed by the party to be more independent. In common with the zealots of the Cultural Revolution, Deng clung to the dictum that those in power determine what the people read.

Openness in the media served Deng's reformers in their campaign to modernize. According to Liu Binyan, China's best investigative journalist, Deng used the press against his party opposition:

"He had to permit the media to publicize, to a limited extent, the true, devasting economic situation. He had to rehabilitate the victims . . . and allow the media to make public the party's past mistakes. Thus, the party's taboos began to be violated. Chinese journalists used this opportunity to expand press freedom to its utmost limit."

Another reason to permit more scope for the media was the growing influence of the West as China opened up. If the West produced the computers and machine tools that China needed so badly, why not import its press system, as well? Officials had come to know the Western press over the years through the limited-circulation reference news that they receive. Many commented admiringly on its speed and thorough coverage of difficult stories.

Deng used the media, then turned against them, in two campaigns of escalating harshness, one before Tiananmen Square, the other as a consequence of the democracy movement. The first change took place in the mid-1980s, when the reformers had won the first round against the conservatives and thus no longer needed hard-hitting journalism for their fight. But the main reason was that the journalists had become too hard to control.

Party leaders at the national and particularly the provincial level were worried and angry. Liu and the other investigative journalists were doing their jobs too well, and their editors were standing behind their exposés. Liu's conclusion after an investigation of provincial party corruption became a national slogan: "The Communist Party regulated everything, but it would not regulate the Communist Party." An independent press was turning out to be far more complicated to deal with than a shiny new computer from Wang. Bureaucrats worried about who might be the reporters' next target. Journalists were reined in; some, like Liu, lost their jobs, but no one was imprisoned. It was the quiet before the storm.

In the middle of May 1989, thousands of journalists in all parts of China joined students and other demonstrators in marches supporting the democracy movement. Their posters covered a great many grievances and demands, but those that best described the position of the journalists combined confessions of past wrongs and promises to do better in the future. A succinct summing up, reported from the northeast city of Shenyang, said simply: "We Must Tell the Truth."

China's reporters, editors, and broadcasters were reacting to the democratic revolution taking place on the nation's streets and squares in the way that journalists in many other nations have done since World War II, when authoritarian rule is challenged from below. The fact that freedoms were permitted in some of those nations, crushed, then permitted once more is reason to hope that China's press will be able to speak freely again.

But with many newspapers closed, journalists in jail, and media serving only the state's propaganda needs, China is a good example of how quickly and thoroughly an authoritarian government can reinstitute control. Journalists across the country have returned to reciting propaganda reminiscent of the Cultural Revolution. A month after they demonstrated for the truth, Shenyang's journalists were hailing the repression of the democracy movement as "very brilliant and correct"; similar abject justifications for the Tiananmen Square violence could be found in all the media.

Now, with a Press Guidance Group supplementing the party's already stringent censorship, every word is scrutinized. Approval seems to depend either on complete blandness or on the zeal with which the leadership's statements are reported.

The party has won. But it has also lost, in two important ways. Its own adoption of Western methods and standards in the campaign to enlist the media on the side of reform has created a corps of professional journalists who have not forgotten how to ask sharp questions and check official statements. They constitute a free press in waiting.

The other loss the censors imposed on Chinese society is a diminution of the educational function of the media. As the nation began its transition from a state to free-market economic system, newspapers and broadcast stations educated the public at several levels on how to change work and business habits to take advantage of the new commercial conditions.

The popular press and local television ran lists of current average free-market prices to prevent gouging and help consumers in their bargaining. Newspapers read by the intellectuals carried news of technological advances that had not yet reached China. The best work of all was done by the *World Economic Herald,* the outspoken Shanghai paper that was the leading advocate of reform. The *Herald* carried many columns of translations from Western and Japanese publications on management and marketing. It sent out teams to conduct seminars on pricing and quality control for the hundreds of free-market enterprises that were springing up.

Long before the student protests, the *Herald*'s editors decided that it had to investigate those managers and provincial leaders who were opposing reform or illegally profiting from it through bribes and kickbacks. Eventually its reporters and editors concluded that more than stubbornness or corruption was blocking progress in China. The paper began to speak out more and more on political reform. "The minimum condition for democracy is to allow people to air their views freely," one editorial said.

Seminars for peasant entrepreneurs were fine, but preaching democracy was another matter. *Herald* editor Qin Benli was fired and the paper banned when the first student stirrings began in 1989. He died while under house arrest.

But unless China's leadership decides to repudiate economic as well as political reform, the need for help from papers like the *Herald* is as great as ever.

The ferment leading up to Tiananmen gave China's journalists an opportunity to step outside their expected role as government servants and become, instead, the servants of an information-hungry public. Their coverage of China's democracy confrontation got world attention. Not widely understood, however, was the fact that the journalists' actions were not a sudden turnaround. For more than a decade they had been pushing for freedom to act as professionals, not propagandists.

In the process, a culture of press freedom grew up among journalists, competing and clashing with the culture of team-playing that officials insisted on and some reporters and editors were willing to accept. Both elements could be represented in the same newsroom; arguments over how to handle stories were frequent. Usually caution prevailed, but not always.

Liu Binyan became a national hero for the crusading articles he wrote for the *People's Daily*. Anthony Kane of the Asia Society's China Council calls him the Chinese Bill Moyers, a reporter who looks at things in a more profound way than his colleagues do.

Liu first got into trouble in 1956 as a young reporter for *China Youth News*. Encouraged by the promises of openness in Mao's "Hundred Flowers" campaign, he made his first attacks on bureaucratic abuses. When Mao decreed that the flowers of diversity could no longer bloom, Liu was sentenced to three years as a farm laborer. Later there were more years of forced labor during the Cultural Revolution.

Twenty-one years of silence ended with Liu's rehabilitation when the reformers came to power. One of his first public acts was to praise freedom of expression. "True harm to the prestige of the party . . . is done not by literary works that describe problems, but by the problems themselves," he told the first postreform writers' congress in 1979.

Liu's investigative reporting in the years that followed is credited with raising the circulation of the staid *People's Daily* by millions. Such work was encouraged when the reform faction was struggling to hold power. But Liu eventually alienated too many high officials with his relentless reporting. He was silenced again, expelled from the party, and later forced to live abroad. (Although party membership is required only for top editors, those journalists who want to get ahead usually join.)

This Chinese Bill Moyers behaved like a Western reporter but was an entirely home-grown product. Liu became a crusader for the same reason Western journalists do: a fierce commitment to justice. He was able to exert such great influence because conditions were right for exposés like his in the 1980s, just as they had been wrong for them in the '50s. He helped create the culture of press freedom in China and benefited from its growth. But the nation benefited as well, and until the leadership regains the confidence to restore truly independent media, China's competitive position in the world will suffer.

At the beginning of reform, the leaders made it clear that they wanted media that performed better than the propaganda outlets of old. They wanted the Xinhua News Agency and the English-language *China Daily* to be able to compete with the best the West could offer. Xinhua's officials spoke often of their aims of making the agency the equal of the Associated Press or Reuters—world class, as they put it. *China Daily* was to be the link between the foreign investors and businesspeople and China's drive to quadruple production by the year 2000.

Those plans collapsed in the carnage of June 4, 1989. But the journalists taught to be world class, and their colleagues who have learned from working with them, are not going to forget what they know during the current period of repression.

The leaders had agreed to the relative permissiveness not because they admired dissent but because they were pragmatists. They had studied the information societies of the West and Japan and had come to understand their crucial role in a modern economy. Now the leadership, worried about retaining power, has restricted the flow of information. But China's economic development remains an unfinished task, while its Asian neighbors constantly gain in the high-tech industries that depend on the free flow of ideas and communications.

Ideas and communications will have to resume flowing in China if it is not to lose more ground. When they do, the new leaders will find a populace greatly changed by the democracy movement of the Beijing Spring.

"China will never ever be the same," a Chinese writer told his colleagues abroad in the aftermath of the massacre. "The crux of the matter is that after forty years of autocracy, the country cries for an opposition, even if a mild one."

In his view, people will look to the journalists to lead the way: "Never before in Chinese history have the people felt such an acute need for a free press. Never before has it become so painfully clear to people that a freer press is essential if they are to enjoy a reasonable measure of democracy."

SMALL-PATH NEWS

In the meantime, China's citizens will have to depend on reading between the lines of the official papers and on the lively mixture of gossip, information, news from foreign broadcasts, and rumor passed along by word of mouth called small-path news.

"*People's Daily* can be a chore to read, but it does get read, because it contains the official information we need, either openly or between the lines," a social scientist in Guangzhou said of the organ of the Party Central Committee.

Other readers have turned to the lively urban tabloids, which devote up to 90 percent of their space to local news, people's grievances, human interest stories, and some mild investigative reporting. A Shanghai tabloid exposed the People's Liberation Army's secret participation in some unsavory local business enterprises. The authorities were incensed, but the paper had its facts right and the editors escaped punishment.

The small-path network is at work every day to fill in the gaps left in the official media, but at times of crisis it becomes the country's main source of reliable news. During 1989's student democracy campaign, it was working at full speed. Chinese students at American universities gathered reports filed by U.S. foreign correspondents in China, then relayed them home by fax or telephone on the clear trans-Pacific telephone lines. This international link supplemented domestic loops of telephoned and mailed information that connected Chinese campuses.

Xinhua, the state television, and the mainstream papers tried to ignore or play down the growing demonstrations, until finally many of their journalists joined them. But the news agency's huge staff kept busy with its other task of supplying the private information services to party and government officials, what one employee calls "reporting to the leaders, not the readers."

The leaders get a more interesting file. Xinhua dispatches supplied to Chinese newspapers and television are usually stilted, dull, and lacking in much concrete information. Political and ideological considerations come before reader interest when officials are addressing the masses. The journalists who produce these stories seem like untalented and uninspired people.

When the same journalists write for the in-house information services, providing confidential accounts of events at home and abroad, they can be quite lively. Reporters are encouraged to offer their own interpretations, analysis, and comments.

These internal services are called Reference News, and they come in four editions. The largest circulation service can be read by any official, party or nonparty, from village organizations and high schools to the Central Committee. It contains news that ordinary readers in a free society would expect to see in their papers, but that China considers too critical or revealing for its ordinary readers to have. The other three services have an ascending order of frankness and a descending number of privileged readers. According to Amos Gelb, an American communications researcher, the most closely guarded Reference News deals with errors and shortcomings in the party. The journalists who work for it are given their material by the party's own inspection committee. They are forbidden to meet with foreigners or to discuss their work with friends.

When the leaders make a decision or pronouncement, Xinhua performs another function. It carries the text and a carefully formulated story based on the text, with ministries, propaganda department, and the agency's own politically sensitive editors making sure that every implication and nuance is correct. As a world agency, Xinhua must translate all this carefully selected prose into English, Arabic, and four other languages. Foreign staff members sometimes resist the clumsy formulations they are asked to use, arguing with the political editors that no one outside China would want to print or broadcast such a jargon-filled account. But the story that goes out on the wire is invariably the politically correct one.

TELEVISION

The phenomenal growth of television has brought the world to the millions of villages of rural China, presenting scenes and tales far more vividly than could the previous village information outlets, the party loudspeaker or local paper. But Chinese TV has fallen short in its proclaimed mission of helping modernization by providing information. Now, with viewers turning more and more to television offerings from abroad, the authorities are trying to pull the plug on the foreign broadcasts rather than make the domestic product more interesting.

With few exceptions, Chinese TV news is the same flat, dry, and not very informative product as that carried in the press, which is not surprising, since Xinhua provides most of the copy for both TV and the newspapers. The news is read with little animation by the pretty-faced men and women announcers. Cameras focus on rows of officials attending meetings, or zoom in on blast furnaces and crop harvests. More interesting, if more chilling, are the direct broadcasts from courtrooms that show ashen-faced defendants being sentenced to death and taken away for execution. But then it's back to the meeting, the factory, the farm.

Why, then, do peasants spend a year's pay for a television set, and why do antennae sprout from the remotest villages in the poorer provinces?

"The news isn't the only way people get information from television," a sociologist in Gansu Province, one of China's poorest, said of a study he had conducted. "If you've never been beyond the next big town on the Yellow River, *everything* you see on TV is new and informative. Many people recognize the news as the same sort of thing they're fed from their local officials, and they may dismiss much of it. But they trust their own senses and consider themselves well informed about the things they *see,* whether it's the skyscrapers of San Francisco or the urban backgrounds and expressways of Tokyo, seen on one of the many foreign feature programs, or the crowds at the soccer matches in Beijing."

Even before the advent of direct broadcast satellites, a well-developed system of exchanges enlarged China's video window on the world. American networks were able to sell a few commercials, along with sports, nature programs, and excerpts from *60 Minutes.* Asian nations contribute features on development through a regional cooperative arrangement.

A clothing merchant in Guangzhou recalled that television was the only bright spot in the dour years of the Cultural Revolution, even though the fare was mostly the proletarian operas of Mao's wife, Jiang Qing. "The streets were dead in those days," the merchant said. "Shops were shuttered, nothing was being sold. About all we could do is gather in public places—few people had their own sets—and watch the TV films." Now, she says, her neighbors all have two color sets, one in their shops and one at home, and complain when the reception from Hong Kong is bad.

China's domestic television does better when it entertains than when it tries to inform. The Gansu sociologist said party propagandists are sometimes quite successful in their entertainment efforts, citing a popular variety program that features uniformed men and women from the People's Liberation Army performing as singers, dancers, and comedians. Such programs build goodwill for the huge army, which is a severe budget drain and has a considerable image problem after Tiananmen Square. Other entertainment programs have no particular political message. They feature Ed Sullivan–era vaudeville or ice sculpture in Manchuria.

China has no Nielsen rating system and publishes no results of viewer preference. One poll taken by the Beijing Broadcasting Institute for internal consumption, however, showed that Chinese viewers take the same action those in the rest of the world do when their interest flags: They switch off the set. Only 6 percent of an institute sampling of viewers in the capital said they watched the long domestic news segments of political meetings and tree plantings. Since that poll was taken, there is now another switch in many homes—to the satellite, and the lively and interesting world of StarTV and the other images on the heavenly thread.

THE WRITERS

China's writers and filmmakers have fared better than the journalists in holding on to the freedoms brought by the reforms of the 1980s. "If you want to find out what's going on in China today, look at the films and literature, not the papers," a Beijing writer said.

China may have a 16 percent rate of illiteracy, but in the cities and towns, at least, it is a nation of readers. Men and women in Shanghai's ninety-five-degree summers read by streetlight on their straw sidewalk beds. Peasants travel to Ürümqi, the capital of the Xinjiang region, to buy English texts so that they can learn to read technical books about irrigation and horticulture. Beijing's New China bookshops are as crowded as its produce markets, and across the nation, sidewalk lending libraries provide low wooden stools where customers read comic books and paperbacks on the spot.

As with everything else in China, these mass acts of consumption have a political dimension. What the hundreds of millions of readers are reading is of prime concern to the party, whether it is a lurid tale of prostitution in Hong Kong or a young poet's troubled thoughts about the class struggle. The concern is not only domestic. Officials worry that Western influences are creeping into the works of Chinese authors.

Literature has great power in Communist China, as it did in Imperial China. Mao, himself a poet of modest accomplishments who was later suspected of having had a ghostwriter, thought that literature and art ought to be weapons for "destroying the enemy." Party opponents used literature against Mao in 1966, when Wu Han, Beijing's deputy mayor, attacked him through a play about the abuse of power. It was the opening shot of the Cultural Revolution, which later claimed Wu as one of its victims. The party has continued to punish writers who oppose it and reward those who write favorably about it or might be influenced to do so in the future.

But writers are harder to control than journalists. To use the daily press as a platform to criticize society or push for change, journalists usually have to attack individuals or identifiable institutions. Their disclosures have to be current and fresh; otherwise they're not news.

Novelists and playwrights can choose the characters and periods for their exposés. Occasionally, as with Wu Han, they get caught, but usually they can count on history and invention to cover their tracks. Their imagined dialogue can be pithier than the actual quotes of a beleaguered official, and yet they can use their characters and plots as a screen to retreat behind.

Despite all the campaigns to control writers and their work, the writers have the last word, and the party knows it. If officials crack down too hard, only the hacks will be writing, and few will want to read what they write, particularly with the growing availability of good Chinese-language books from Taiwan and other countries. The writers, for their part, know that they cannot stretch the limits too far. For most, the state is not only their censor but their employer.

This relationship brings about cycles of relaxation and repression. Students of Chinese literature say it is the reason Communist China has yet to produce works of world standard, the contemporary equals of *A Dream of Red Mansions,* the sixteenth-century classic, or early twentieth-century works such as Mao Dun's novel *Midnight* or "The True Story of Ah Q," Lu Xun's powerfully satirical short story.

Many intellectuals have given up on works of native writers and turned to works from the West. A private bookseller in Wuhan, the industrial city on the Yangtze, says that seven out of ten of her best-sellers are translations of foreign authors. Technical and medical works go fast, but there is also a brisk market for contemporary fiction, political science, history, and economics. Translations of Western sex manuals also sell well, since China provides little guidance in this area, except to ban Freud. Booksellers don't worry about getting into trouble with the authorities when works by Freud, Sartre, or Nietzsche are condemned. Censoring is done at the publishing houses or at customs controls; anything released is safe to have on your shelves.

Writers have complained that the sudden changes in party literature policy are too much for them to keep up with, and even if there are no crackdowns to silence them, they waste a good deal of time gossiping and speculating about what might be acceptable and what might be banned. In one five-year period in the 1980s, they recall, the line changed abruptly four times.

At the end of 1984, Hu Qili, a member of the party secretariat, called for "free rein to individual creativity, powers of observation, and imagination." By 1987, after the first round of student protests, writers were reminded by a leading literary editor, Chen Danchen, that they had "forgotten their social responsibilities, producing bad and even vulgar works, spreading corrupt ideas, and blindly worshiping foreign culture." Later that same year they were exhorted by Zhao Ziyang, the party's general secretary, to "liberate ideas." But in 1989 Zhao and the literary freedom he had espoused were both victims of the crushing of the democracy movement.

Some writers manage to follow the dips and turns of the line, producing leftist, rightist, or centrist works that earn them a comfortable living. Some write for the drawer, as their counterparts in other authoritarian societies and their predecessors in Imperial China have done.

From a reading of the well-crafted contemporary novels, essays, and short stories available in translation, three safe topics for writers who want to be critical seem to emerge:

The Cultural Revolution: Writing critical accounts of the ideological warfare that consumed China for a decade is a good way of getting in some disguised jabs at current abuses of power.

Reform and modernization: Plots whose villains or weak characters are opposed to the new ideas Deng introduced have clear sailing with the censors and a ready readership.

China's backwardness: Domineering and ill-educated officials who take advantage of their subordinates, men who mistreat their wives and daughters, and corrupt bureaucrats can all be targets, as long as the basic cause, the lack of any real democracy, isn't addressed.

Zhang Jie, who has been called the nation's first feminist writer, deals with the third strategy in her short stories. "Women's liberation is not only a matter of economic and political rights, but includes the recognition that we have our own value and significance," one of her heroines in *Love Must Not Be Forgotten* says to her male boss.

Gu Hua's *A Small Town Called Hibiscus* makes effective use of the first two strategies. His satire of officialdom gone wild was so biting that a film based on the novel was held up by the censors for weeks before being released. Gu depicts party zealots turning a thriving village into a desolate place, justifying the ruin they cause by asking: "If everyone had money and lived better than the landlords before the liberation, with plenty to eat every day, who would make revolution?"

This kind of literature is thoughtful, provocative, and lively, but it does not confront the crimes and mistakes of Maoism the way Solzhenitsyn and other Soviet writers took on Stalin and his Gulags.

China had its thaw after Mao's death, when the "literature of the wounded," accounts of the crimes of the Cultural Revolution, began to emerge. After a period of toleration, the party told the writers, in effect, to put the past behind them and concentrate on the bright future opened by the reforms.

Lucien Pye, the Massachusetts Institute of Technology China specialist, thinks that factors other than party directives explain why Chinese writers have not come to terms with Mao's misrule. "There is a lack of much introspection, as seen in centuries of Chinese literature," he says, "and also the nationalism and patriotism traditional with China's intellectuals. They're generally opposed to the self-criticism of Western intellectuals and see their role more as team players."

The late poet Ding Ling told Pye after the Cultural Revolution that she had spent a number of years in exile in Heilongjiang Province, on the Russian border, under cold and primitive conditions, but had not been able to write about it because she had been too busy with her assigned job of caring for chickens.

When she was moved to Beijing to serve three years' solitary confinement, she could have written about her bitter experiences in the countryside, she told him, but instead wrote about the power of the thought of Mao.

When they met after the thaw, when she was freed and most of the restrictions on writers were finally lifted, Pye asked her what she was writing. About bourgeois decadence in Shanghai in the 1920s, she replied.

It isn't censorship alone that keeps China's writers from seriously coming to terms with Maoism, Pye concludes.

THE FILMMAKERS

Only thirty films were made in all of China during the ten years of the Cultural Revolution. The nation's studios were in disarray and many directors and actors were purged. Most films were worker-hero documentaries, political posters put on film, such as the 1970 *Red Flag Canal.* The plot was simple. Water was needed for better crops, so a lot of Chinese worked very hard to blast through mountains and move a lot of stone and earth around. The high point is when water flows through the canal.

Now China produces 150 films a year. Some are of such brilliance that they achieve international acclaim; some are devoted to gaudily costumed historical drama and martial arts; and many, never exported, are well-made, realistic accounts of contemporary society, largely free of propaganda and unafraid to address controversial issues.

At Beijing's Friendship Hotel compound in the mid-1980's, where hundreds of foreign teachers, editors, translators, and technicians live, the Friday night movie was a highlight of the week. Earphones linked to interpreters with prepared scripts helped those whose Chinese was not up to following the plot. From our experience in the Soviet Union and Eastern Europe, we had expected heroic war movies and their peacetime counterparts, the struggle to get the harvest in or build the steel mill. Villains, we thought, would be Taiwanese or American agents.

The first week brought a surprise: a film about corruption in the countryside, with a local Communist Party leader taking bribes. As the plot unfolded, the leader turned out to be only a man who had made a mistake, not a propaganda figure. He was portrayed sympathetically as a minor official who succumbed to temptation after he saw his neighbors getting rich while his small state salary stayed about the same. The movie ends with the village elders persuading him to change his ways.

Week after week, the problems of urban and rural China were addressed in these ordinary films with simple plots and unaffected acting. Family planning, health, rich peasants besieged by poorer relatives, crime, youth problems, official favoritism, and nepo-tism—all were depicted with a minimum of preaching.

Most of the actors were salaried employees of the government film studios in Beijing, Xian, or Shanghai, a director in Shanghai said. They earn about as much as a teacher or accountant. Only a few attain star status, but if state actors are recognized in a shop, they're likely to get a better piece of fish than the next customer, he said.

The authorities watch films as closely as the other forms of com-munication, the director said, but the medium doesn't lend itself as easily to censorship. It is one thing to argue an issue in an editorial and another to develop the same argument in an hour and a half in a drama with many other elements.

"The approval process is one of give and take rather than direc-tives from above," he said. "Much of it takes place in the screening rooms of the motion picture production centers. A lot of party mem-bers get to see a lot of free films and express their opinions. Some bring along their families. Those whose opinions count pass them on to the film censors, and then we learn what they don't like. But since there are no rules, we have to make the changes ourselves and hope that they will satisfy them."

These controls have been tightening because of the impression the "Fifth Generation" of young Chinese filmmakers were making abroad. As they harvested awards in Europe and the United States, the party called their plots politically uncommitted and artistically pessimistic. The first of the big Fifth Generation films was Chen Kaige's *Yellow Earth,* which was very nearly banned in 1984 but went on to win more international awards than any previous Chi-nese film.

Yellow Earth tells of the sudden impact of the modern world, in the shape of a visiting soldier from Mao's wartime guerrilla head-quarters, on an impoverished family in a Yellow River village. The soldier tells fourteen-year-old Ciuqioa about equality for women and literacy. Forced into a marriage that is the family's only hope to survive poverty, Ciuqioa shuns her old husband and tries to find her way to the guerrillas, dying in the attempt.

Although the period was 1939, Chen's stark film managed to get across the idea that not much has changed for Yellow River peasants in the intervening decades. This, the party determined, constituted "depiction of the remnants of the primitive past."

Chen used the past as a screen again in his *Farewell to My Concubine,* which won the Palme d'Or award at Cannes in 1993. But the film, which depicted the lives of two Beijing opera performers, covered more recent history than *Yellow Earth* did. Its critical passages on the Cultural Revolution, as well as its theme of homosexual love, got it banned after an initial party screening. Cuts were made, and the film was passed and prepared for a Shanghai premiere, the largest in the city's history. All the tickets had been sold when the word came that the film could not be shown after all. The censors reversed themselves again when Shanghai authorities warned that rioting would probably erupt if the ticketholders couldn't see the film.

Farewell has done better than other controversial films because it has been widely seen in China. Like Chen, many Fifth Generation directors work abroad and get financing as well as an audience in Taiwan, Hong Kong, and other countries outside China. But they want Chinese mainland audiences to see their work—uncensored, under ideal conditions, with as few cuts as possible.

In the meantime, Chinese movie audiences are reacting in the same way that viewers of the official television news have. Annual attendance at the nation's theaters has dropped from 21 billion in 1983 to less than 3 billion.

THE CLASSROOM

It should not be surprising that a regime that devotes so much time and energy to telling its citizens what they may read or watch starts very early in their lives to tell them what they may think.

China's educational achievements are impressive. There were only a million middle-school students when the Communist state was founded, and now there are 50 million. One hundred twenty thousand college students grew to the current 2 million.

But when these accomplishments are measured against the needs of a vast nation trying to catch up with its Asian neighbors and the rest of the world, outside specialists, school authorities, and even the Communist Party say they fall short.

China's educational system faces three main problems. First, the level of literacy and basic schooling must be improved, so that the nation can have the skilled labor and clerical workers needed to run an advancing economy. Second, these better-educated children must have greater access to universities, to fill the thin ranks of adequately prepared managers, engineers, researchers, and teachers. Third, the thinking patterns that education helps develop must be broadened, so that home-grown ideas, not borrowing from the West and Japan, will shape society and drive the economy of the next century.

From the party standpoint, the first two aims are incontestable, but the third poses dangers. Teaching students that there is more than a single answer to a problem is a departure for much of Chinese education and political discourse. Party officials—and not only the Old Guard—worry that habits of questioning authority would not remain in the classrooms, but also could be directed at the government. In 1989, a shaken party and a worldwide television audience witnessed the power of student protest at Tiananmen Square. Everything the party has done since then has been aimed at preventing another such outbreak. But the task isn't easy.

Beijing University and its surroundings nicely illustrate the dilemma the party faces in permitting the free exchange of ideas, on the one hand, and maintaining control of its population, on the other. A gaudy strip of electronics companies lining Haidian Road, along the campus boundaries, is proudly referred to as China's Silicon Valley. This is the place that combines the research strengths of the university and the entrepreneurial skills of the private sector. The Chinese-language software and other innovations help power not only the mainland economy and information systems but those of Hong Kong and Singapore.

But on the campus itself, the gates are closely watched by blue-uniformed guards with orders to check identity papers and confirm appointments. In 1989 student, and some faculty, protesters streamed out of these gates to demand democracy. The university guards and heavy political indoctrination are some of the methods the authorities now feel are necessary to keep the campus quiet.

Separating the kind of ideas that produce a profitable software industry from those that question the need for authoritarian government, is a formidable task for a government. However, Chinese rulers, before and since the Communists, always have tried to enforce standards of behavior on their intellectuals.

According to Chinese dissidents, since 1949 fourteen national campaigns have disrupted the nation's advancement. Intellectuals were the targets in ten of them. Past mistakes have not prevented the party from making more. The reformers recognized the folly of Mao's anti-intellectual campaigns, when examinations were scrapped and unprepared workers and peasants were transformed into university students. But they have been slow to give up the idea of using or denying access to education as a reward or punishment.

Higher education has remained a scarce commodity, under Deng as well as Mao, whether from political considerations or underfunding. No longer must every student have a worker/peasant background, but neither does he or she gain acceptance to the top universities and graduate schools by examination scores alone. The background checks carried out on students who have passed these entrance exams weed out an undisclosed number of qualified candidates every year. Officials say they make the checks so that troublemakers are not given the scarce places in higher education. But the system also has a dampening effect on young people's political activism.

The screening that follows the examinations is designed to test the applicant's "political, moral, and ideological qualities." An education official in Beijing described her part in the process: "We are given the names of those who did the best in the examinations. We travel to the applicants' home cities and villages to see what kind of students they are likely to become. We talk to teachers and to local officials. We want to know if the prospective student has been in trouble with the law or has been a discipline problem." Does class background or parents have any bearing? The official said it doesn't, but students say otherwise, and can cite many examples of friends who didn't make it into the university because of their families.

Troublemaking is a broad term that can include independent ideas in politics, too open a fondness for Western music or books, or even extreme clothing and hairstyles.

Party connections are very helpful. Parents who are party officials or have friends who are use this *guanxi,* or influence, as their children move through the educational system. An American agricultural researcher in the Yangtze delta says families he knows consider banquets and bribes to officials a normal part of succeeding at business, including access to higher education.

As long as there are more students than university places, the party will be able to use the shortage as a means of ensuring compliance and control. But other national goals have entered the equation, and China must decide whether it is better to continue to limit access to higher education or catch up with the rest of the world.

As is common in developing countries, most Chinese don't go very far in school. One hundred thirty million enter the educational system; only 2 million stay in it through college. The government says 95 percent of school-age children begin elementary school, but before junior high, half drop out, and only 8 percent complete high school. From 1.5 to 2.8 percent make it through higher education, depending on whether the vast system of correspondence, television, and night school is included with the regular colleges and universities.

More than lack of money is behind these figures. Most of China is still rural, and more than 100 million of the primary-school children are sons and daughters of peasants, who tend to keep them on the land and out of the classroom.

A Beijing teacher who had been assigned to a hill village near Inner Mongolia said that the peasants are beginning to value education more, now that they are in business for themselves, and want at least one family member able to read the agricultural extension bulletins. But for that, a grade-school education suffices. She enjoyed her work but finally left because of the isolation of the village. Getting to Beijing on her one day off meant a six-mile walk to the next town and a two-hour bus ride each way. Now the villagers are trying to get her back, offering bonuses above the low state wage scale.

"Much remains to be done in remote villages, where there are often no schools at all," another teacher who has been to the United States said. "Young teachers simply won't go there. There's no running water, no decent housing, certainly no films or plays. It's nothing like the United States; there are such huge gaps between city and country. You can't jump on a Greyhound bus and get out of there."

Statistics on how many peasant children complete high school and college are sketchy. Two provinces, Hunan and Gansu, report that about half their college students are of peasant origin. Although that is a high proportion, it also shows that the other 50 percent of university places go to the urban population, which is only 20 percent of the total.

Urban and rural pupils alike are affected by inadequate teaching. Seventy percent of the nation's middle-school teachers are considered not up to standard. Many are the products of the "worker-peasant-soldier" education of the 1960s. Higher pay and better opportunities elsewhere attract bright graduates. A Guangdong Province language teacher said few of his students want to become teachers, since they can earn more than his $60 monthly pay by working in tourist hotels and restaurants.

Poorly paid and educated, the teachers cannot be expected to be innovators in the classroom. During a visit we made to a model primary school, a researcher at a Chinese educational institute remarked on the absence of any indication that the pupils were being encouraged to think for themselves. They copied what the teacher wrote and repeated what she said in unison. "Memorizing isn't really learning," the researcher said. "The children have become part of what we Chinese call the stuffed duck cycle. They're stuffed with information. Those who give it back with the least change get the best marks."

A computer specialist from the Netherlands said the stuffed duck teaching reaches to the graduate level and made it difficult for him to work with a group of young engineers in Guangzhou despite their impressive-sounding qualifications. "When a system would go down, none of them would try to figure out what the trouble was, although they should have been able to do so," he said. "They simply waited for the IBM man to come from Hong Kong."

An American teaching in a Shanghai engineering school said he had difficulty getting his students to form teams to solve problems. They would always wait for instructions from him, he said, "which is okay if you're going to be an engineer in a big factory, fixing things that go wrong, but not okay if you want to invent a new process or machine."

Chinese students themselves recognize the limitations of their educations once they get into another academic environment. "I tend to ask why now," a graduate student in political science at Princeton said. In China, he would find a theoretical premise and write a paper to expand on it, without ever questioning it.

"I used to look at the world as either black or white," a Columbia law student said. "Now the color may turn to gray."

China spends a little more than 3 percent of its gross national product (GNP) on education. The median for developing countries is 4 percent; for industrialized countries, 5.7 percent. Only about 20 per 10,000 Chinese attend university. In India, the figure is 60. College graduates make up about 1 percent of China's workforce; the mean for developing countries is 4 percent.

When Japan, Western Europe, and the United States are brought in for comparison, China's task of catching up looks difficult indeed. The U.S. ratio of college students is 500 per 10,000 population. Chinese officials say such figures have no meaning for their nation. But He Zuoxiu, of the Chinese Academy of Sciences, has called for a doubling of current spending on education as the only way to attain the scientific and industrial level of Japan and the West.

Although China lags behind most of its neighbors in total spending, it has launched some innovative programs to catch up with their educational levels. One is the *Dianda,* the radio-television universities. China leads the world in broadcast instruction, providing a way into the educational system for those who missed or were deprived of their chance the first time around.

A quarter-million Chinese sign up each year for these courses, most of them broadcast on television rather than radio. They receive textbooks and written teaching materials and join discussion groups. The *Dianda* programs are broadcast during daytime working hours, making it difficult to hold a job and study, but enterprises release promising workers for a three-year period so that they can earn a degree. There is also a widespread system of self-study and night courses. More students are enrolled in these nonconventional approaches to education than are registered in the regular universities.

When China opened its doors to Western trade, it also opened up thousands of school posts for foreign teachers and professors, in languages, science, liberal arts, and the professions. During the 1984–1985 academic year, one of the authors taught in Beijing at the school of journalism of the Chinese Academy of Social Sciences. The twenty-two journalism students were marvelous examples of what is right with the Chinese educational system or, in some cases, how to overcome the obstacles it may present. Some had learned English by listening to shortwave radio during years spent in exile in the countryside. Others had scored high enough on examinations to overcome unfavorable class background.

Students worked out their own schedule for chores such as sweeping the concrete floor of the classroom, with their duties posted on a paper wheel on the wall. The school was in the *People's Daily* compound, where soldiers armed with rifles guarded the main gate, and political slogans and chalked announcements greeted visitors in the entranceway. But the school administration tacitly agreed that the slogans would stop at the classroom door. No attempt was made to control what was taught, although administrators knew that ideas about Western press freedoms were being discussed if not necessarily advocated.

Daily deadlines and small-group discussions were a shock to students used to more distance and leisure in the classroom. They also played havoc with the necessities of Chinese student life, which centered around a morning breakfast break, noonday naps, and an early enough lunch hour to beat others to the canteen. But the students were up to the challenge. Some had never used a typewriter before their first meeting in the class newsroom with its mixture of Yugoslav portables, Chinese office machines, and antique models borrowed or brought from home. Their writing moved from simple exercises to interviews with peasants in a nearby free market. At year's end, they were putting out newsmagazines.

Their exposure to Western teaching did not seem to make the students yearn for or copy the ideas of the West, as party officials were always warning they would. It is hard to generalize about such a disparate group, but the influence of the West seemed to be most strongly felt when the students discussed China's backwardness and what they could do as journalists to help it catch up. They identified strongly with reform and modernization, but wanted them on Chinese terms, not simply as a copying of the West.

This connection of personal careers with the nation's needs is a theme that has run through conversations with students in all parts of China, in that year early in the reform period or a decade later, whether with literature majors or MBAs. It is brought up frequently in discussions with their teachers and other professionals. China's intellectuals want to be trusted and want to serve their country. But if they are to be of genuine service, they cannot be expected to operate under the restrictive terms of the party, carrying out orders, not thinking for themselves. They don't want to look to the party for leadership but to provide their own, as their counterparts do all over the world. On their own, they can develop software, resurrect the *World Economic Herald,* and perhaps create literature and films that honestly address the past and current problems.

A conversation with a history professor at a South China university summed up many others: China's intellectuals, he said, have been mistrusted, underpaid, and subjected to the abuse of recurring propaganda campaigns. Nevertheless, they have the power to bring about changes of enormous import. History shows that every time Chinese rulers face a real crisis, they relax their restrictions on the intellectuals and call on them for help. Despite the horror of Tiananmen and the repressions that followed it, many intellectuals think that the time for such action is now.

EIGHT

GREATER CHINA: THE QUESTIONS

OF TAIWAN AND HONG KONG

The Russian embassy in Beijing, the largest diplomatic complex in the capital, is set in a quarter-mile-square compound, a legacy of czarist days. A drive past its walls one wintry day got a Chinese legislator to thinking aloud about the most important event, as he called it, in China's postwar foreign relations, the rupture of the alliance with the Soviet Union.

"They helped the Chinese revolution and undid much of the damage done by the czarist regimes," he said. "Then they tried to direct the Chinese revolution. We could not accept that."

The Chinese once looked on the Russians as benefactors, then as enemies, he said. That has been replaced by "a period of equality—someone with whom we want to have tranquil relations, friendly borders, and normal trade."

The break with Russia, however, had a far greater effect than the ending of an alliance, he stressed. It was the impetus for China's opening to the world.

AN INDEPENDENT FOREIGN POLICY

China lost many years in its self-imposed isolation from the West and Japan. It fell behind in technology, education, and trade. But when it decided to resume its contacts in the 1970s, it did so with a foreign policy striking in its boldness and imagination. It received a succession of American presidents and the leaders of Japan and Western Europe, and eventually even the last president of the Soviet Union, Mikhail Gorbachev. But it avoided any new bilateral alliance, building instead a multisided structure of relations with the major powers of the world.

China, in the process, became acknowledged and respected as one of those major powers, emerging from more than a century of dependency: first to the colonizing Europeans and Americans, then to the Russians.

Under China's newly independent foreign policy, each nation entered these relations with its own advantage in mind, but it was clear that the Chinese, able to pick and choose, emerged with the most advantages of all. The world's governments and businesses began to look on China not as a threat but as an opportunity for trade and mutually advantageous relations. The Russians were offering to modernize the factories they had left uncompleted when the alliance broke down in 1960. The Americans found that their open-door policy for foreign university students was attracting thousands of young Chinese who had previously been barred from applying. The U.S. military was starting to share previously restricted weapons knowledge with China's army. The Japanese were vying with the Germans, Swedes, and French to equip steel mills and exploit mineral resources.

Taiwan, Hong Kong, and the overseas Chinese communities of Southeast Asia were providing investment, advice, and marketing for the special economic zones and booming city economies. Analysts began using the term "Greater China" to refer to the mainland and these Chinese economic partners in the region.

The ties with these Chinese abroad were, in fact, the most notable characteristic of China's recent foreign as well as trade policy. They overshadowed the two older and once-dominating relationships with China's two powerful neighbors, Russia and Japan. Russia was too busy with its own political and economic crisis to pay much attention to China. And Japan's influence was limited by the conservatism of its business leaders, who were afraid of taking too many risks in China, as well as the conservatism of its political establishment, which was reluctant to make amends for the savagery of the Japanese World War II occupation of China.

China made sure that the investors and entrepreneurs from all parts of the world would be arriving at its invitation, not as colonists or occupiers. They came to make money for themselves and their companies, but in the process they helped their Chinese employees, their Chinese customers, and their Chinese suppliers. In addition, their business activity and the technology they introduced helped the nation as a whole make up for the lost years of isolation.

Visitors to China arrive on jets made in both Chinese and American plants. They stay in hotels designed by Hong Kong architects and run by Swiss managers. They watch Chinese families snapping pictures with Japanese cameras on Kodak film made in the ancient Chinese port of Xiamen. They drink Chinese-bottled Coke or Pepsi, and they go to shiny boutiques to buy French- or Italian-designed clothing skillfully made in China.

Some of the other changes from the previous isolation are less visible: the active role played by Chinese diplomats at the United Nations; China's decision to accept foreign Peace Corps workers, the first Communist nation to do so; the contributions made by visiting Chinese scholars in the West, once long-dormant ties were restored, on topics from ancient literary texts to mathematical theory.

Chinese officials and ordinary citizens are discovering Europe, Japan, and the United States. Disneyland is such a popular stop that replicas are being built in South China. More than 30,000 Chinese study abroad, most in the United States, and thousands more line up at visa offices in China every day to plead for a chance to join them.

Rarely have the foreign relations of a nation undergone such rapid change. In little more than two decades, China has been transformed from a country so cut off from the world that it had only a single ambassador abroad to one in which hotels cannot be built fast enough in popular tourist cities to accommodate all who want to come.

All these nations vie for business or diplomatic advantage, but none has managed to dominate. China's economy is still subject to enough state control to keep the business activity spread among many nations. Its foreign policy establishment steers away from alliances and commitments. Often the two have worked hand in hand, as when France lost a subway construction contract to Germany because of Chinese displeasure over French Mirage jet sales to Taiwan.

The costs of previous treaties play a role in China's cautious alliance policy. Czarist Russia, Britain, France, Portugal, Germany, Japan, and the United States had all taken turns carving up China's territory by force or exploiting its resources and workers. The Soviet Union had tried to dictate China's foreign and domestic policy and had fought a bitter border war with it. Japan defeated and occupied China in a long and costly war. America's wars in Korea and Vietnam were widely seen as threats to China. Maoist China's isolation was partly a response to these unwelcome experiences with the world. The Japanese occupation left the deepest scars; Japan's postwar prosperity only increased the resentment.

"When the first Japanese trade fair after the war opened in Shanghai, we boycotted it," a filmmaker recalled. "I would make a detour of several blocks because I couldn't stand to go past that terrible flag." Eventually she and her colleagues were ordered to attend the fair by their superiors.

Although younger Chinese have less strong feelings about Japan, there are constant reminders of the occupation on television, in magazines, and in films. The footage of the Japanese army's Rape of Nanking originally included in *The Last Emperor* was so violent that Japan successfully pressured China to cut some of the scenes out of the Chinese version. But the chilling depiction of the cruelty of Japanese occupation troops in the Chinese-made *Red Sorghum* may have been one of the reasons it won international prizes.

The United States became an enemy for its help to the Nationalists in the civil war and its two wars on China's borders, in Korea and Vietnam. And only ten years after Chinese Communist rule began, the Soviet Union was thrust into this group of former friends who had become adversaries. Differences in interpreting Communist ideology turned out to be as important as the vast ones separating communism and capitalism.

China had received so much Soviet help in winning the civil war and starting up a Communist society that Western nations were astonished when it turned against its benefactor. But Chinese scholars question not why the split between Beijing and Moscow happened at the end of the 1950s, but why it took so long.

There were bitter divisions from the start, some nationalist, some ideological. There were clashes of personality, conflicts of interests, and differences in party strategy, notes one Chinese scholar of the period who has had access to party documents.

Party veteran Bo Yibo says in his memoirs that Soviet advisors made key decisions about many aspects of domestic policy in China, from grain to steel production. He said Stalin himself set the industrial growth rates for China's first Five-Year Plan.

The 1950 treaty of friendship and alliance, concluded by Mao and Stalin after ten weeks of negotiation, brought tens of thousands of advisors, steel plants, railways, weapons, and some Soviet Gothic architecture that still mars downtown Beijing. In its peak year, 1954, it brought China $2 billion in aid and $2 billion in trade—huge sums for the period.

Two years later, the scholar said, the alliance was in such trouble that its breakup was a foregone conclusion, although Western analysts did not detect the split until 1959. The Chinese trace the trouble to Nikita Khrushchev's denunciation of Stalin in 1956. Criticisms of Stalin's crimes, anti-Western stance, and dictatorial methods could be applied as easily to Mao, the Chinese reasoned. Khrushchev, in his memoirs, agreed: "Mao Tse-tung was following in Stalin's footsteps."

Despite these party differences, China continued to look to Moscow as a model of industrial development. The Soviets promised technical help in building China's first nuclear bomb; Soviet-designed jets served the Chinese airline and air force, and factories turned out Chinese copies of Soviet copies of World War II American army trucks.

When Khrushchev boasted that the Soviet Union would surpass the United States in industrial production in the next fifteen years, Mao took on the task of pledging that China would catch up with Britain in some key sectors, including coal and steel production, over the same period.

"Go smelt iron in a big way," Mao told the nation, announcing a Great Leap Forward to overtake the capitalist world. In response, the country and village party officials herded millions of peasants from their ripening fields to makeshift iron furnaces hastily built for the purpose. The peasants were ordered to melt down their iron woks and other utensils and to work long shifts, day and night, to produce iron.

"What they turned out was a kind of reddish brown clot, utterly useless to the steel mills," a Chinese academic recalls. "Meanwhile, tens of millions of tons of high-quality coal was wasted and millions of acres of rice, cotton, and other crops were left to rot in the fields.

"Soon famine stalked the land, and 1959 was followed by what every Chinese calls the 'two worst lean years.' In the three 'Great Leap Forward' years meant to catch up with Britain's steel production, an official estimate never made public said at least 20 million people died of starvation and millions of others were crippled by epidemics of hepatitis and other diseases."

But to the outside world, the Great Leap was hailed as a success, so much so that it became another part of the dispute with Moscow—the idea that China was working directly toward pure communism. Moscow called this ultraleftist. China replied that the Soviets were hopelessly bourgeois.

After the break, polemics like these gave way to armed conflict. Fighting in two areas of the Sino-Soviet border in 1969 killed thirty-five Soviet soldiers and hundreds of Chinese, according to Soviet accounts. Chinese sources say Mao and other leaders were convinced that the border fighting was only the beginning of a Soviet plan to encircle China. The Soviet Union was equally adamant that the Chinese provoked the clashes.

Whatever the truth, the perceived Soviet threat was the reason Chinese officials gave to explain Mao's sudden lurch toward relations with the United States. In briefings for Chinese diplomats and journalists at the time of the Nixon visit in 1972, officials said Mao had sketched out a "global ring of counter-encirclement," patching up affairs with the United States, Japan, and Western Europe as a defense against the encirclement he saw Moscow planning.

Moscow responded with charges that a "NATO in the Pacific" was in the making. But the Chinese, during Mao's time and since, have been careful never to conclude such an alliance with the United States. Chinese officials say their nation values its independence too highly to enter into any arrangement in which it would inevitably be the junior partner. It manages to get most of the weapons technology that it needs, and all it can pay for, from the United States and Western Europe without joining any treaty arrangement.

With a weakened Russia, there is even less incentive for a NATO in the Pacific. China's foreign policy officials worry, as does the rest of the world, about instability in Russia and the former republics. But China also benefits somewhat from the economic chaos there. Its most apparent contact with Russia now is not the Moscow-dispatched advisor and planner but the thousands of street traders who buy and sell at China's markets, using a limited Mandarin vocabulary and lots of energy. Larger trades are taking place in the ministries and private enterprises of both countries, as Russian steel is shipped to China to help in the building boom and cheap Chinese consumer goods go to Russia's markets.

Chinese students can spend two years studying the language at a Russian university for $1,500, then get good jobs in the cross-border businesses, which are doing $4 billion a year in two-way trade, according to Russian estimates.

Government-to-government relations are better than they have been in decades. With the decline of Soviet communism, China announced that the capital of world communism had moved east, to Beijing, but the once-dominant ideological issues play no part in

Beijing's dealings with Moscow. Instead, there are arms sales, agreements on joint space exploration and nuclear power development, and what amounts to a nonaggression pact.

A short time after the collapse of the Soviet Union, Chinese workmen took down the fifteen large porcelain enamel disks that had displayed the coats of arms of the former Soviet republics from the spired Exhibition Building in northwest Beijing. Local rumor had always said that a sixteenth spot, left blank in the display, had been reserved for China. Now all the signs lie rusting in a courtyard.

JAPAN

The Export-Import Bank of Japan lists China as its most favorable prospect for future investment. Investment in China has been doubling in recent years, with the current annual rate more than $1 billion. Major projects are in the works, such as a 540-acre industrial park in the special economic zone in Dalian, where twenty Japanese companies are embarking on a fifty-year project of investment and development, and plans by the Suzuki automotive company to build the first Japanese car plant in China. Japan is still far behind its American and overseas Chinese competitors in investment in China, but its stake is growing rapidly, and now it ranks behind only the United States as China's biggest trading partner.

These developments do not seem surprising, given Japan's aggressive foreign investment policy, the close links between Japanese government aid and industry, and Japan's proximity to China. Shanghai is only 285 sea miles from Nagasaki; Liaoning Province, where Japan's investment is the largest, is a day's sail farther. The new economic zone where the Russian, Korean, and Chinese borders converge in Manchuria is closest of all—250 miles—to Japan's Hokkaido island.

What is surprising is that it has taken the Japanese so long to engage more actively in trade and investment with their giant neighbor. Political, cultural, and historical barriers have stood in the way. But current changes under way in Japan, both economic and political, will increase its involvement in China and pose a challenge to the dominant partners from past years, the overseas Chinese, the United States, and Europe.

When Japanese politicians ended the domination of the Liberal Democratic Party and replaced its conservative leaders with men like former Prime Minister Morihiro Hosakawa, they did more than affect domestic policy. Hosakawa wasted no time in facing up to the difficult issue of guilt for Japanese war actions in China fifty and more years ago. In contrast to his predecessors, he apologized.

At the same time, Japan's longest postwar recession and high industrial wages caused its business leaders to look more favorably on both production facilities and markets in China.

Both changes were welcomed by China, but other problems remain. Many Chinese want Japan to pay reparations for China's material and human losses of World War II. Japan, for its part, charges that the Chinese treat Japanese investors as wealthy cousins and want handouts, not equal partnerships. "We say give and take, but they say take and give," a Japanese banker told Henny Sender of the *Far Eastern Economic Review.*

Japan has long been more hesitant than China's distant American and European partners in entering into joint ventures with Chinese partners. The Japanese automobile industry is worldwide, but in the largest potential market in the world, it is represented only by a few small plants where imported parts are combined with Chinese-produced ones. The most popular product of these Japanese-Chinese ventures is the ubiquitous loaf-of-bread utility vehicles, tiny vans that get their name from their shape and can crowd in five or more passengers and their luggage. They are not years but decades from the aerodynamic glass-and-steel shapes Japan sells in the United States and Europe. Japan also supplies most of China's taxis and the legions of black sedans used by its officials. But they are made in Japan and exported, not built in Chinese factories.

"The Japanese don't want to provide high technology," an American engineer at the Beijing Jeep plant said. "They would rather sell the completed cars, even at a loss or a low profit, because they know they'll be the sole supplier of parts and be able to make it up."

The Americans who helped build the joint-venture Jeep plant in

Beijing and the Germans who train Chinese workers to turn out made-in-China versions of an old Volkswagen sedan model are providing what China needs as well as making money, the engineer said: "We and the Europeans are perceived by the Chinese as willing to share our technology. There is also a residue of resentment against the Japanese for World War II and a surprising residue of appreciation for the American role in the war and in the years since modernization began."

Despite a history of labor and distribution troubles, both VW and Jeep plants are now producing record numbers of vehicles, and the four-wheel Cherokee and chunky black VW sedans are familiar sights on city and country roads. At 100,000 cars a year, Shanghai Volkswagen provides a tenth of the nation's automotive production.

Japanese businesspeople readily supply reasons for not entering into joint ventures with the Chinese. China has a reputation in Japan for volatility in trade deals, dating from the collapse of a vast 1978 agreement for Japan to reequip Chinese industry, mines, and oil fields. The $10 billion cost was to have been repaid through Chinese shipments of coal and oil to Japan. China overextended its foreign currency resources in the arrangement because of what the Japanese call emotional judgments, and the projects came to a halt. More than $2 billion worth of equipment lay in warehouses, and Japanese companies were forced to accept the cancellation of billions of dollars' worth of other orders. Japan's plant and equipment exports to China fell from $4 billion in 1978 to little more than $1 million four years later.

Other factors, the Japanese say, are the low standard of skills in the Chinese workforce, the difficulty of obtaining reliable components from Chinese manufacturers, and the problem of dealing with state and party bureaucracies, which range from delays of months or years in approving plans to demands for bribes and favors.

Japanese entrepreneurs say that the reforms are beginning to upgrade both the work skills of the Chinese and the reaction speed of the bureaucracies, but at the same time, the corruption is getting worse. The Japan-China Investment Promotion Organization told Sender that most of its disputes arise from what it delicately labels "the Chinese partner making use of what the Japanese consider private property or diverting materials and funds for its own use."

Nevertheless, many Japanese businesspeople are rethinking their earlier resistance to manufacturing in China because of recession at home and the rising costs of paying workers, not only at home but elsewhere in Asia. With wages increasing in South Korea, Taiwan, and Southeast Asia, China's workers are still the cheapest around, they say, and Chinese corruption is no worse than what they encounter elsewhere.

The legacy of World War II is an obstacle to better relations less easy to deal with. Japan's invasion and occupation in fourteen years of war cost China 20 million in dead and wounded, and the memories they left are slow to go away. They are expressed in concerns about Japanese militarism and the related issue of Japan's failure to tell the truth about the war to the generations that did not experience it.

Former Prime Minister Yasuhiro Nakasone and members of his conservative cabinet outraged China by joining the annual pilgrimages to the Yasakuni shrine, where war criminals as well as military heroes are buried. On his first visit to China, former Prime Minister Hosokawa took a strong stand against militarism and said he "deeply deplores the intolerable suffering" caused by Japan's warfare against its Asian neighbors.

The issue of how the war is portrayed in textbooks is harder to come to terms with for Japanese politicians fearful of alienating conservatives. Liberals and right-wing nationalists have been arguing for years about how history books should portray Japan during the long war with China: as a nation following accepted battlefield practices or as perpetrator of mass crimes. The controversy centered on Nanking (Nanjing), the Yangtze city that was one of China's wartime capitals. Three hundred thousand Chinese, both civilians and soldiers, were killed in a rampage of the virtually unopposed Japanese army in 1937.

The Rape of Nanking was a myth, the right wing maintained, or at least was exaggerated out of all proportion. Killings occurred, but that was part of war, and it was time that younger Japanese learned the truth. In 1986, as the fiftieth anniversary of the Rape of Nanking approached, the education ministry approved a revised textbook that described Nanking as a "fierce battle." "China," it added, "is calling on Japan to reflect on the casualties suffered by Chinese military personnel and civilians during this battle (the so-called Nanking Incident)."

Chinese protests forced the dismissal of the Japanese minister of education and another revision of the text to say: "The incident in which the Japanese army murdered many Chinese military personnel and civilians (the so-called Nanking massacre) was severely censured internationally."

But until 1992, Japan's conquests throughout Asia were excused in other history books used as class texts with this explanation: "We must never forget that Japan caused inconvenience to neighboring Asian countries in the past." More Chinese protests brought yet another revision: "We must not forget that Japan caused unbearable suffering in neighboring nations in the past."

When Emperor Akihito made the first visit of a Japanese head of state to China in 1992, he created a rare groundswell of Chinese public opinion against the official Beijing line. Party officials in three provinces called on the government to bring up the issue of reparations again, quoting figures in the billions. Opinion polls showed that 90 percent of the citizens questioned thought an apology was in order, and 300,000 signatories of a petition called on the emperor to apologize. Chinese officials decided not to ask for a formal apology from him. Instead, he expressed deep sorrow for China's wartime suffering, and no one publicly discussed reparations.

On Hosokawa's second visit two years later, elderly Chinese war victims turned out to demand reparations payments; 100 of them were detained by security police until the Japanese delegation left. The detention set off another protest: a 500-signature petition to the National People's Congress.

The fact that the differences of opinion were allowed to emerge in public showed that there are similar differences in the Beijing leadership on how far to push Japan to atone for its wartime behavior in China.

Now that Japan has finally expressed regret for the war in China, the issues of some form of monetary compensation remains. China's Communist leadership proudly—and unrealistically, in view of the war's enormous cost to its people—renounced war reparations from Japan, not once but twice. The first opportunity was at the end of the war, when the Communists proclaimed that "the Chinese people make a strict distinction between the very few militarists and the broad masses of the Japanese people" and chose not to exact reparations from the people. The second, with similar pronouncements, was in 1972, when the two nations took up relations again.

"It was a mistake, both times," a Chinese Central Bank official said. "World opinion would back China in gaining some reparations from Japan, particularly now that it has so much wealth."

The Japanese, for their part, say they are doing all they can to keep from irritating China. But they point out that there is a danger of a conservative backlash if too many demands are made about war guilt. China would lose far more than Japan if the relationship were to worsen. Japan has the world as its market, but China needs the technology and the markets for coal, oil, and raw material that Japan can supply.

Below the surface of this propaganda war is the change in China's relations with its two most important neighbors. Japan has changed, throwing off single-party government and daring to question some of the shibboleths of the conservatives and far right about the war and the military. Russia has changed, too, from an imperial threat to a chastened trading partner. When China feared Russia, it wanted a strong Japan without worrying about militarism. But now the concerns about Russia have subsided and China can afford to be a more active and critical partner with Japan.

GREATER CHINA

Fifty-five million Chinese live outside the People's Republic, from Sydney to San Francisco and Hong Kong to Taiwan. Many of them or their families left because of oppression or lack of economic opportunity in this century or the last one, but now their combined wealth and talents are one of Mainland China's great strengths.

This Chinese diaspora includes families long integrated into their new homelands and those with fresh passports or green cards. Some have forgotten their language and have changed their names; others return so frequently that they have homes in China as well as abroad. Their ranks include laborers and millionaires, taxi drivers and publishers, cooks and Nobel prize winners.

Politically and economically, there are three separate Chinese entities outside China: Hong Kong and Macau, the first still British-ruled until 1997, the second, still Portuguese-ruled until 1999, with more than 6 million citizens; Taiwan, more than 21 million; and a further 28 million spread among the nations of Southeast Asia, the United States, and Europe.

This other China has a population twice that of Canada and combined exports larger than those of the mainland. Its economic drive has created three of the four little tigers of Asia: Singapore, Hong Kong, and Taiwan. With these strengths, the other China has begun to play an increasingly important role in the political and business interests of the first China. The trade, investment, and technology of the Chinese abroad are vital to the mainland's reform programs. Their contacts in the world, higher level of education, and technical and financial knowledge are of great value to China. Beijing, recognizing this, has reversed its policies and welcomed the new relationship with the Chinese abroad after decades of hostility or neglect.

But Greater China remains an economic idea, not a political one. Hong Kong is resisting political integration into the mainland system when it returns to Communist control in 1997. Taiwan was once a right-wing version of the authoritarian People's Republic, but since lifting martial law in 1987 and permitting the first of a series of free elections two years later has made great strides toward pluralism and shows no inclination to turn back. And the other disparate elements of Greater China long ago chose other political systems in their adopted countries.

Southeast Asia has had Chinese colonies for centuries. A third of

Malaysia's population is Chinese, as is 80 percent of Singapore's. Thailand has more than 6 million ethnic Chinese, 15 percent of its population, and there are millions more in Indonesia and the Philippines.

When these Chinese return home to the mainland, most of them go to a 500-mile strip of the China coast from the Pearl River delta near Hong Kong to Fujian Province. Eight of every ten overseas Chinese trace their origins to this region. It is not coincidental that all four of China's original special economic zones were located in the area. Reformers on the mainland paid attention to the growing economic power of the Chinese diaspora. They watched as Singapore and Taiwan caught up with Spain and Ireland in per capita gross national product and Hong Kong overtook Great Britain.

Now this overseas Chinese power is being plugged into mainland China's economy. Hong Kong and Taiwanese investors were largely responsible for the successful launching of the special economic zones early in the reform period. Overseas Chinese were the principal partners in the $15 billion spurt of investment in hotels, apartment buildings, food processing plants, light industry, and restaurants in the old emigré areas of Guangdong and Fujian provinces. That infusion prepared the way for the region's continuing growth. Chinese businesspeople and officials are careful to point out that the Japanese deemed both the SEZ and the infrastructure investments too risky to participate in.

Shantou is one of the special economic zones to benefit from overseas Chinese participation. Smaller and less prominent than Shenzhen, the skyscraper SEZ on Hong Kong's borders, Shantou nevertheless has quadrupled incomes in a sleepy South China port and the surrounding farming country. Its connection to the Chinese world abroad is through the thousands of local Chinese who moved to Thailand but maintained close contact with their relatives. Now the Thai Chinese are back with investments, processes, and managerial skills. Shantou provides the workforce and the real estate. Some of the profits go back to Thailand and some stay in China; the products, similarly, are sold in China and abroad.

The Thailand-born grandson of Shantou emigrants manages a

livestock feed plant near the harbor. As the manager drives up in his Peugeot station wagon, a peasant from an outlying village leaves from the other gate, his wagon heaped with feed bags. The wagon merges into lanes of other traffic: bicyclists, some riding singly, some gaily chatting in groups five abreast; pedicab drivers in cone-shaped hats; and a few Japanese-made taxis.

The peasant has paid about $15 a bag for his feed, five times the going rate for feed in the village market. "But this feed is going to produce fatter chickens, pigs, and eels, and it's going to do it a lot quicker," the manager explains. Few would buy from the Thai-Chinese joint venture when it first opened, but word of the benefits of the feed got around quickly, and now more feed plants are under construction. Feed supplements arrive by ship from Thailand and are mixed with local grain. The manager acknowledges that the ingredients that make the feed so much better are the result of his company's long association with American grain companies and their nutrition experts.

American market access is what another Thai enterprise in the zone can offer the Chinese. Nursery rugs, with the man in the moon woven in soft wool pile, have nothing to do with either traditional Thai or Chinese motifs, but they sell well at J.C. Penney. The Chinese and Thai co-managers run a factory high on pay scales and short on social services, the reverse of the Chinese state-managed enterprises, but they have a list of 200 waiting for jobs.

The 200 on the payroll, most of them women under twenty-five, have one-year contracts and no protection from dismissal. About twenty are fired in an average year. The company provides neither day care nor housing, but there is some medical care and a free lunch. The women earn double the money they would in the state enterprises and have working conditions far better than those in the noisy and dirty local garment shops. The Shantou municipality, which benefits from the joint venture through tax revenues and jobs for its citizens, picks up the welfare burden that state enterprises normally undertake.

An overseas Chinese connection isn't necessary for a modern, efficient factory, but the presence of Chinese with experience outside the constrictions of the state economy is very helpful. The overseas Chinese can deal with local authorities as equals. If they are faced with too much red tape or corruption, they can threaten to take their project elsewhere. They are valued for the knowledge and experience in the huge world market economy that China is just beginning to tap. Their commitment to joint ventures benefits both partners. It was particularly welcome in the bleak days after the massacre at Tiananmen Square, when the United States and much of the rest of the world were ostracizing China and the hard-liners in the leadership seemed poised to roll back the economic reforms. The Chinese abroad poured $30 billion into the mainland economy in the crucial five years after Tiananmen, at a time when embargoes were cutting U.S. and Japanese investment back. It is possible that China would have kept its doors open to the world without their help, but many Chinese credit them with saving the reform program at the time of its most critical test.

TAIWAN

When the remnants of Chiang Kai-shek's Nationalist army fled to Taiwan in the wake of the Communist victory in 1949, their chances of surviving for more than a few years were considered slight. It was thought to be only a matter of time before the People's Liberation Army would cross the Formosa Strait to complete the rout that had begun on the mainland.

Taiwan not only survived but also prospered. The Communist invasion fleet never crossed the strait, but, in recent years, a more powerful force has been crossing in the other direction: Taiwan-managed trade, technology, and investment.

Mainland propagandists had extended a welcome to Taiwanese for decades, providing them with tours of the achievements of communism and promising them no telltale stamps on their passports, since consorting with the enemy in this way was considered a serious crime in Taiwan.

Chiang's son, Chiang Ching-kuo, who succeeded to the Nationalist presidency in 1978, a decade later lifted martial law and relaxed the travel ban, which everyone knew had been broken many thousands of times. The stage was set for a commercial and financial rapprochement between Taiwan and China that sidesteps political issues and has brought two-way trade to multibillion-dollar figures in the less than ten years since it has been legal.

Travel and trade across the strait are the impetus for a gradual coming together of these two regimes long in conflict over their claims to be the sole legitimate government of China. Both sides say the end of the process will be reunification, and each says the reunited country will adopt its government and economic system.

Communist China counts Taiwan as a province temporarily detached, as it has been at various other times in history. It will be returned to Beijing's rule peacefully, at an unspecified time, but the use of force in regaining it has never been ruled out.

Taiwan sees the process of return differently. Its Nationalist government will return to the mainland, also at an unspecified time, to restore democracy.

Can the 21 million Taiwanese persuade the 1.2 billion mainlanders to renounce Communist rule, or defeat them in battle? Can the Communists persuade Chiang's successors to adopt the one-country/two-systems model being offered Hong Kong and come back under mainland rule? Neither course of events seems any likelier than it did four decades ago.

Beijing, which knows Taiwan is in a vastly better bargaining position than Hong Kong was, has offered improvements on the one-country/two-systems plan. Taiwan can keep its own army after the mainland takeover, the Communists say, and even the Nationalist flag.

"Two systems, one country," a Taiwanese opposition leader mused in an interview in Taipei. "Eventually it would have to be one system and one country. Why should we pick the system that's failed? Why don't they pick ours?"

Short of war, it is difficult to image the circumstances under which the Nationalists in Taipei or the Communists in Beijing would yield gracefully to their old enemies in choice of political system. But economics is another matter, and many signs point to a new kind of relationship based on the compatability of trade and investment, not political systems. The mainland has the raw materials, the labor, and the undeveloped market. The Taiwanese have the skills, manufacturing and entrepreneurial; huge reserves for investment; and the well-established links to Western markets.

"Taiwan and China can make economic cooperation work now that the legal situation has changed," an opposition legislator in Taipei said. "It used to be that making contacts with mainland businessmen could get you arrested for sedition."

When trade was banned, it was conducted through Hong Kong and overseas Chinese conduits. Since the thaw across the strait, it's possible to be more open. Now annual trade figures are between $7 and $10 billion.

Both nations want the trade to go smoothly, for their mutual benefit, but since neither is willing to concede the legitimacy of the other's government, their business relations are filled with obstructions. Each has set up "unofficial" bodies, the Straits Exchange Foundation of Taiwan and the mainland's Association for Relations Across the Taiwan Strait, which meet infrequently.

Taiwan businesspeople have complaints against both governments. Their own, they say, prevents them from making certain investments in China, such as petrochemicals, because of its concern that such industrial development would be helpful to the mainland's military capability. When Taiwanese do invest in China, they complain that there is little legal protection for them on the mainland. In order for such laws to be developed, China would have to negotiate directly with Taiwan, not through the unofficial foundations. That it will not do, since such negotiations would constitute recognition that Taiwan is a separate state, not a temporarily detached province.

Other topics for the two foundations' talks include the rash of airliner hijackings across the strait. Disaffected mainlanders regularly seize planes on domestic flights and direct them to Taiwan. They know they will be jailed but not be repatriated. Taiwan also worries about the growing numbers of mainlanders who cross the strait to work illegally as laborers and household help. Like the United

States, it says the mainland should do more to regulate illegal emigration.

The most important dispute between the two Chinese governments, however, cannot be solved at the semi- or unofficial level. At issue is Taiwan's renewed diplomatic drive for recognition as an independent nation, at the United Nations and in the region. China has criticized neighboring governments that do not recognize Taiwan diplomatically but nevertheless have met with Nationalist President Lee Teng-Hui on his "vacation" trips to the region. It also applies constant pressure on other nations not to consider resuming diplomatic relations, making arms sales, or supporting UN membership for Taiwan.

Taiwan counters these campaigns mostly with money, creating trade and investment links where diplomatic ones are not possible in Southeast Asia and above all in China. Sinologist George Brick found in a study that at least 75 percent of the 28,000 enterprises in China with significant foreign equity are financed by Chinese from outside the mainland, two-thirds of them from Taiwan and Hong Kong. Total investment from Taiwan alone has reached $11 billion.

An American diplomat in Taiwan said trade began in earnest in the early 1980s, as China's economy began to modernize. Both governments looked the other way, although Taiwan would secretly give permission to deals it thought benefited the island. Taiwanese experts who had left their Nationalist passports in Hong Kong soon were working in Guangdong and Fujian provinces, introducing better technology, maintaining quality control, and sharing export market information.

Much of the production of these thousands of enterprises is sold to the United States, creating the huge Chinese trade surplus that has troubled relations in recent years. At the same time, Taiwan's and Hong Kong's trade surpluses with their American partners have all but vanished—evidence that their production is simply moving to the mainland.

The reason is the growing cost of labor outside China and the continuing low wages paid mainland workers. Taiwan's per capita incomes are now on the threshold of $10,000 a year, enough to qualify the island for developed nation status. Its foreign trade rivals that of the United States and Japan. As contacts with the mainland proliferate, Chinese officials have switched from denouncing Taiwan as a threat to finding out how to copy it as a model for its economy.

Unfortunately for China, the model cannot be replicated easily. Taiwan's compact, export-driven economy can be copied by some regions of coastal China, but it has little relevance for the largely rural remainder of the country. And no one could count on the unique combination of historical chance that put Taiwan on the road to prosperity.

When Chiang's 2 million dispirited soldiers, officials, and families reached the island in 1949, at the end of the civil war, the question was when rather than whether the Communists would launch their invasion. The United States had withdrawn its backing; Beijing needed only the time to gather its forces.

But the next year the Korean war broke out, and Beijing's soldiers went there instead to fight American troops. Washington immediately resumed military and political support to the Nationalists. The most important aid it provided, however, was for the Taiwanese economy.

Taiwan's infrastructure was already more advanced than that of many mainland provinces because of the long years of Japanese occupation. Japan, which acquired Taiwan in 1895, had sought to make the island a model colony, to show other Asian nations the advantages of imperialism. It had built railroads and ports, established factories, and modernized agriculture.

The Nationalists used this base to build up industrial and military strength, after some difficult early years when they brutally suppressed the local opposition. Chiang's government wanted the industrial base as part of its preparation for attacking and occupying the mainland, not for Taiwan's entry into world markets, but the effect was the same. Chiang's policies, coupled with land reform and generous American aid, eventually revitalized the economy across the board.

Ying-jeow Ma, an American-educated Nationalist official, says land reform played a big part in the Taiwanese economic miracle.

When the government divided up large landholdings, he said, "The landowners and their money had nowhere to go in rural Taiwan, so this gentry class went to the cities and started small capitalist ventures."

Industry boomed and agriculture's share in the economy dropped from 70 to 7 percent. Taipei grew from a small town with a single traffic light to a city of 2 million.

U.S. aid was targeted to small businesses, in the hope that helping to establish some economic democracy might compensate the Taiwanese for the lack of political freedom under Chiang's leadership. Taiwanese denied participation in politics were thus given large decision-making roles in the economy. The children of the founding generation took over and expanded their companies. Many were educated abroad and saw the opportunities in the United States and Europe for cheap electronic and plastic products. These entrepreneurs built apartment buildings and beach houses, and traveled and lived abroad.

Chinatowns in New York and San Francisco began to see a new kind of Chinese immigrant—sales managers and computer specialists, there to eat and shop, not to work and live. More than 300,000 Taiwanese moved to the United States, permanently or temporarily. It is notable that these overseas connections flowed eastward from Taiwan, to Hawaii, California, and New York, 6,000 to 10,000 miles, and not the 100 miles westward across the Formosa Strait.

As an unexpected result of domestic liberalization in both countries, the barriers between Taiwan and the mainland began to crumble in the mid 1980s. China, reforming its economy, needed the experience and skills of the Taiwanese. Taiwan, gaining confidence from its success in the rest of the world, ended martial law, permitted opposition political parties, and relaxed press censorship and the ban on visiting China.

Antonio Chiang, who took advantage of the changes to found an opposition newspaper, thinks the reforms in China were the main influence on Taiwan: "Deng changed China's international image," he said. A Taiwanese political scientist credits the aging and deaths in the ranks of Chiang's original leadership circle. Their successors could look on relations with the mainland without the bitterness of defeat in war. Leaders of the Democratic People's Party, the first legal opposition to Chiang's ruling Kuomintang, take some of the credit for themselves, saying that there is now more than one authoritative voice helping decide policy, including how to deal with China.

As the contacts across the strait continue, and thousands of Taiwanese visit their relatives or ancestral homes on the mainland, there is new confidence on the island that Taiwan's system, free-enterprise capitalism, and growing political liberalization are not only preferable to that of the mainland but are also what the mainland should choose.

As this conviction takes hold in Taiwan, there is less and less support for China's appeals for a one-nation/two-systems solution to reunification. More and more personal observation is backing up the official viewpoint that Taiwan would have everything to lose by such an arrangement.

"Beijing fails to tell ordinary Taiwanese how unification would be good for them," Chiang, the opposition newspaper publisher, says. "But that's not surprising. They're afraid of democracy on Taiwan. We have a more active parliament and a student movement. That's against their interests."

Chiang, like other Taiwanese, sees what happens to Hong Kong after 1997 as the real test of what Taiwan might experience if it accepts unification on mainland terms. He is not very optimistic: "They don't know how to keep their promise. Hong Kong would be a good experiment for Beijing, if they could take care of it successfully. But that seems a mission impossible."

HONG KONG

Hong Kong, an island and part of a peninsula a little larger than New York City, will be returned to China at midnight June 30, 1997, at the expiration of the ninety-nine-year treaty Britain forced on a weak Chinese imperial government to gain the New Territories, the island's hinterlands, in 1898. The world is watching the fate of the colony and of nearby Macau, which is under Portuguese rule, not only for what happens to their more than 6 million population and free-enterprise systems, but for what that portends for the two other unsettled legacies of Chinese history—Tibet and Taiwan.

China's treatment of Hong Kong is also a test for its own political strength and stability. The first question is whether the mainland's rulers will keep the promises they made to the territory in the 1984 Joint Declaration concluded between China and Britain. The second is whether the party will be able to control the temptations to corruption and abuse of power that Hong Kong will offer to the Chinese officials moving there in increasing numbers.

Hong Kong does not behave like a colony that is about to be swallowed up by the Communists. Its airport and railway station are crowded, as always, with Hong Kong travelers, but they're leaving on business or as tourists, not refugees. After a number of years of population loss, people are again going to Hong Kong, not leaving it. Many of those who do move abroad come back as soon as they can manage with American or other nation's passports—insurance against Communist rule. More than 117,000 new or returned Hong Kongers raised the population past the 6 million mark in 1993 and set off worries about whether housing, schools, and health care facilities could accommodate them all. The classified employment advertisements in the *South China Morning Post* bulge to 150 pages many weekends, and the jobs they seek to fill include well-paying executive and engineering positions as well as secretarial.

Hong Kong citizens bet more than $8 billion on the horses every season, and now they seem to be betting that they will survive and prosper from the Communist takeover. The basis of this gamble is their conviction that China will become more like Hong Kong after 1997 rather than the reverse. Three million Chinese work for Hong Kong companies on the mainland, equal to the number employed in Hong Kong. Guangdong Province, on Hong Kong's borders, accounts for 725,000 of this workforce. It will soon be linked with the colony by a Hong Kong–built expressway with Western-style shopping centers at every interchange. Guangdong and Hong Kong are already a single economic region. There is no reason the expressway system and economic integration with Hong Kong could not be extended, province by province, to encompass all of South China.

Hong Kong has equally strong links in the region outside China. In the 150 years of Hong Kong's existence as a British colony, it has been transformed from a busy but old-fashioned port surrounded by farmland to Asia's leading financial and shipping center. It has the largest container port in the world and so much demand for office space that its rents are second only to Tokyo's. The Chinese, British, and American millionaires who descend from their hillside villas every morning in Rolls-Royces and Mercedeses, already telephoning about market conditions, help raise the per capita gross domestic product (GDP) of the territory to $18,520 a year, higher than that of France or Sweden.

Many of those Chinese entrepreneurs, and most of Hong Kong's clerical and blue-collar workers, have had experience, either personal or in their families, under Communist rule. Not a few watched Shanghai's decline in the 1950s when, in sweeping away the exploitation of foreign companies, the Communists substituted a cumbersome state bureaucracy that smothered the city's entrepreneurial spirit. Shanghai exiles and old Shanghai shipping firms and department stores prospered in Hong Kong. Now there are concerns that history will repeat itself. Killing the goose that laid the golden egg is a saying often used in conversations about Hong Kong's future.

No nation has ever attempted a political undertaking as delicate as that of absorbing this lively capitalist enclave into the backward and bureaucratic mainland. But neither has any other nation taken on the other task that China has: changing its economy from state control to the free market without a change of political power. Hong Kong has been a powerful factor in this change to date; after its absorption by China its role will be crucial in the success or failure of the Chinese experiment.

Freedom has been the key to Hong Kong's success, and that means more than the freedom to accumulate wealth. Despite the many deficiencies of British colonial rule, Hong Kong's citizens enjoy a range of freedoms far out of reach of people on the mainland. They can worship freely; choose religious or secular or foreign schools; read a free press and write dissenting letters to the editor; complain through local representatives about the way their territory is ruled; go abroad for education, business, or pleasure without passport or visa controls; and rely on the protection of a well-established system of laws if anyone tries to take away or diminish these freedoms.

These are the freedoms that Hong Kong fears will be endangered under Communist rule. But they are also the freedoms that all of China must have eventually if it is to compete with the world's democracies in the marketplace. It is clearly Hong Kong's hope that freedom will follow the Hong Kong dollar northward into the mainland. Such a development would not only benefit the mainland people but provide a shield for Hong Kong against Beijing's authoritarian tendencies.

In the negotiations to date, China has shown no desire to broaden democracy in the territory. Indeed, there is every sign that the method of negotiation is a vivid preview of the way the Chinese intend to govern Hong Kong: with arbitrary decisions from party leaders and a disregard for legalities. The attitude is best summed up in the comment of an official of Xinhua, the official New China News Agency, which has acted as China's embassy in Hong Kong. Asked by the *South China Morning Post* why China planned to dismantle the legislative structure being put in place by Britain, he replied: "The boss has changed."

British governor Christopher Patten created a diplomatic crisis with China with a plan to broaden democracy in Hong Kong's final years of colonial rule. With more authority for Legco, the legislative council, and fairer electoral processes, Britain hoped that Hong Kong would complete the transition to Chinese sovereignty with a solid institutional base of self-rule and thus make it harder for the Communists simply to put their own leaders in.

China responded with threats to dismantle any political institution put in place without its consent. It also threatened not to honor any contracts concluded by the Hong Kong government when it takes control of the territory, but when the stock market plunged on this news, it withdrew the threat.

Legco ignored China and backed Patten in voting for the reforms, approving one-person, one-vote elections and ending the system of appointed members to district boards and municipal councils. But the territory remained divided on the issue of how best to prepare for Chinese rule.

One faction—the realists—includes many civil servants and members of the business community. They are well represented on the Preliminary Working Committee, the group China has established in Hong Kong to discuss the transition to mainland rule or, as their opponents charge, to form a shadow government in preparation for 1997. The realists say China should not be tested with political reform attempts so late in the day. When views like these are criticized as giving in to China, British diplomats respond that they are only recognizing the reality of the territory's situation. "China has been able to dictate Hong Kong's future since the 1950s," a diplomat involved in the original negotiations said. "It is an achievement of British diplomacy that she waited until the 1980s and made so many concessions." For these same reasons of China's disproportionate political power in the region, he added, there was never any question of turning Hong Kong into a Singapore or other independent entity. China, he said, considered Hong Kong its territory, temporarily detached. Its return was never in question—only the mechanism.

The other side of the argument is espoused by the democrats, Hong Kong citizens who say the determining factor in the kind of future Hong Kong will have is how much self-rule it will be able to achieve by 1997. Locally elected instead of British-appointed officials would give the territory the institutional structure it would need to survive in the middle of the huge governmental apparatus of the People's Republic. Some of the democrats want to go far beyond Patten's proposals and have all sixty Legco seats filled by election, instead of the one-third approved by Britain and China.

The democrats label the realists "yacht people" who have enough money to live anywhere if conditions under the Communists aren't to their liking. The realists respond that the democrats are interested only in getting elected and gaining power themselves. Some Hong Kong citizens of more modest means have been joining the ranks of the mobile, using ingenuity rather than yachts. Newspaper advertisements offer citizenship elsewhere. Enterprising little nations such as Belize advertise for capital investment, with a passport in exchange. Without such arrangements, the majority of Hong Kong residents will have a choice of People's Republic passports or documents issued by the British that do not give them the right to reside permanently in Britain.

If local democracy is the key to Hong Kong's future under the Communists, it was paid little attention to in the territory's century and a half of British rule. The Hong Kong success story has been a combination of good civil servants sent from London to govern and good location.

Hong Kong harbor is so well placed that it was handling a third of China's overseas trade as early as 1880. With location came a pragmatic system of colonial rule. Although Hong Kong's early governments were tainted with the opium trade, their successors have been largely free of the corruption endemic to the mainland. Sun Yat-sen, founder of Republican China, called Hong Kong his intellectual birthplace. "How was it that foreigners could do so much . . . with the barren rock of Hong Kong within seventy or eighty years, while in 4,000 years China had no place like Hong Kong?" he asked. Sun's answer was good government. "Why can't we do the same thing in China?"

Hong Kong's good government manages to keep taxes low—a tax rate that averages only 11 percent of GDP, compared to 27 percent for the United States—and yet provide exemplary social services. It has built millions of housing units to accommodate the streams of refugees from the mainland. Health services, although criticized as crowded, are among the best and cheapest in Asia. Socialism, many have argued, works far better in capitalist Hong Kong than it does in Communist China.

Chinese officials in Beijing say they do not understand all the fuss about democracy. The Joint Declaration, they say, contains ample guarantees for Hong Kong, and the Basic Law that becomes Hong Kong's constitution in 1997 repeats these guarantees.

China has made two kinds of promises: the first that the status quo will be maintained for Hong Kong's citizens and businesses after 1997, and the second that institutions will be set up to guarantee that this happens. The promises have been listed in considerable detail, but the Chinese have been far less specific on the means of guaranteeing them. And yet, if the first set of policies is to work, the second must, too.

"The government of the Hong Kong Special Administrative Region will be composed of local inhabitants," China has promised. Hong Kong will "enjoy a high degree of autonomy, except in foreign and defense affairs," in which Beijing's power will replace London's. It will have "executive, legislative, and independent judicial power."

China cannot be expected to permit free elections in Hong Kong before it permits them on the mainland, a Hong Kong journalist aligned to the realists says. "But it is well aware of Hong Kong's commercial value, and this will keep it from killing the goose that's laying the golden eggs," she adds. The journalist said she and her friends have mixed feelings about 1997. They are glad to see the end of British colonial rule, something they have profited from in their educations and living standards, but still resent. They have strong attachments to China, for all its shortcomings. "We may enjoy foreign rule, but we don't like it," she says.

A teacher who fled to Hong Kong from Shanghai in the 1950s said that she'll stay put this time, although she could easily move to California and be with relatives. "This is my home," she said. "My friends and I agree—we'll stay." She said they're proud of what they and other refugees have created in Hong Kong, not only its skyline and great wealth but its public side as a city that really works, a place where no one is really poor.

"As for the Communists, they've changed, too," she adds. "The rough and primitive people who didn't know how to handle Shanghai in 1949 are gone. Now they've got new policies, new leaders.

There's no reason to think they would kill Hong Kong's enterprise the way they killed Shanghai's."

China has been sending its officials on visits to Hong Kong in great numbers since the agreement with Britain in 1984. An American diplomat used to travel regularly on the same train some of them used from the mainland. He would watch their wide-eyed reaction as they crossed the border into the New Territories and began to see the expressways, harborfront towers of glass and steel, and newly built housing projects and schools. Institutions that westerners take for granted, such as a complaint hot line for the customers of Hong Kong's suburban railway, were the subject of animated commentary among the mainlanders.

These middle-level party men and women are given a crash course in how Hong Kong works and how valuable it is to their country. With specialists from the Xinhua News Agency, they tour the city and talk to its people, gaping, at first, at the British double-decker buses, the shops and restaurants, and the swift, clean subways. "And then they go back to their cities on the mainland and tell the conservatives and doubters what they have seen of capitalism and how important it is to everyone in China that Hong Kong stays the way it is," the diplomat said.

A more sustained experiment on how to mix communism with capitalism has been conducted since 1967 in Macau, Hong Kong's smaller Portuguese-ruled neighbor. That was the year Red Guards occupied Macau's government offices and demanded a voice in running the colony. Macau, in effect, has had a shadow mainland government since then. The governors sent from Lisbon in a succession that started in 1456 are now advised by an unofficial alliance between left-wing trade unionists and wealthy Chinese-Macauns.

Portuguese officials in the pleasant six-square-mile territory an hour's ferry ride from Hong Kong say that they have had little trouble with this tacit sharing of power with China, although they deny that the Chinese role is as strong as it has been described. As in Hong Kong, people think more about money than about politics. Macauns say they are more interested in keeping their gaudy bayfront casinos and hotels flourishing than they are in a role in governing the territory. They point to the high wages earned both in the tourist industry and the garment sweatshops in Macau's attractive old downtown, where day and night shifts work to add finishing or labels to mainland goods. Macauns earn six times the wages of the Chinese who live on the other side of the baroque stucco arch that has marked the border since 1557.

"After the takeover here and in Hong Kong is complete, will the Communists follow their heads or their hearts?" a Portuguese official in Macau asked. "Thus far, they've followed their heads and have done well in their role in running the territory. But if you destroy the prize through your actions, what good is the prize?"

NINE

CHINA'S MINORITIES: THE

QUESTIONS OF TIBET AND

XINJIANG

---

*Entering Tibet or the Central Asian province of Xinjiang
seems like going to another country from China. The faces,
the dress, the buildings, even the landscapes are different.
There is now a highway from the airport to Lhasa, Tibet's
capital, but until a few years ago, it was a six-hour trip on
paved and unpaved roads, through high mountain valleys,
past stone fortresslike farmsteads with bright yellow, blue,
and red Buddhist pennants flying. The rusty old Chinese
army buses had to ford dozens of rivers and streams, their
tires crunching on the gravel bottoms as the water level
approached the passenger compartment. Downriver, passengers could see Tibetan fishermen in frail boats of animal
hides stretched over wooden frames. Now there is a Holiday
Inn in Lhasa, but pilgrims still prostrate themselves before
the Jokhang Temple in the middle of the city. Many of them
have walked or moved painfully in repeated prayer prostra-
tions from their distant villages.*

*Religion is also a powerful presence in Xinjiang, the
autonomous region in the Northwest that borders the former
Soviet Central Asian republics. Two-thirds of Xinjiang's 16*

million population is Muslim, and the domes of mosques and spires of minarets rise above the low buildings of cities and villages. But arid Xinjiang's first impressions are the dust clouds. Trucks, farm tractors, and buses raise the clouds behind and above them as they traverse the desert roads to oases where muddy brown rivers water the farm fields. Inside the adobe walls of the Uighur peasant homes, there are cool courtyard gardens, platforms draped with the locally woven rugs in brilliant reds and yellows, and grapes and melons to eat. Kashgar, on Xinjiang's western edge, is like a small Samarkand, the Uzbek city farther west on the Silk Road. Little horses pull passengers and freight in bumpy carts; camels do the long-distance freight hauling. A mosque has dominated the center of town for centuries, through Turkish tribal, Russian, and Chinese rule, and brief periods of independence. Even in cosmopolitan Ürümqi, Xinjiang's capital, the mosques, the sprawling bazaars, and the Turkic signs that overshadow those in Chinese make it hard to believe that the region is a part of China.

Whether Tibet and Xinjiang are dependent Chinese regions ruled from Beijing or nations with long histories that deserve to be independent is an ancient dispute that goes back centuries to the tribal and national conflicts on Imperial China's periphery. As central strength and influence grew and the Han Chinese pushed out in all directions from the coastal and central regions, peoples such as the Zhuang (currently 40 million), in the South, and the Mongols (19 million), in the Northwest, came under Chinese rule. But neither these large minorities nor the more than fifty smaller groups have the cohesion and relatively recent history of nationhood that inspires nationalists in Tibet and Xinjiang.

With the very large exception of these two territories, since the 1980s Han China has had as acceptable a record as any multicultural nation in dealing with its minorities. Traditions and customs are no longer derided as superstition; the government, in fact, makes a big business out of dance troupes and tours to ethnic areas. Tourists can sleep in a yurt in Mongolia or dine in a village in Yunnan that seems more like one in Burma or Thailand. Muslims, who were once forced to eat pork by the Red Guards, have grown rich serving their ethnic food in tourist restaurants. Schools and houses of worship have been reopened or rebuilt; local works of literature and art are encouraged.

Dance troupes and restaurants are promoted but dissent is not. The Chinese draw the line at any political act not in accord with the policies set locally or in Beijing on how the minorities must behave. Under these rules, nationalism becomes "splittism," and opposition to the rulers, whether in action or only speech, becomes counterrevolution, a crime punishable by prison.

This policy is a return to the practice of the Chinese emperors, who, although certainly no democrats, left local customs, religions, and traditions in the minority areas they absorbed in place, as long as the vassals obeyed the laws handed down from the capital. After centuries of expansion, the Chinese empire came to include fifty-five minorities.

By the nineteenth century, foreign powers entered minority politics. The skirmishes among Britain, Russia, and China for territory or influence in Central Asia was called the Great Game. Britain wanted to protect India, and Russia wanted to safeguard its eastern conquests by dominating the weak territories on the edge of China. Both worked by encouraging local separatists.

To Beijing, the Great Game has long been over, with its final results, almost all of them favorable to China, sealed once and for all in the history books. China's central government tells the minorities that despite their different faces, costumes, and religions, they live within China's borders, and those borders are inviolable.

To tens of thousands of dissidents in Tibet and Xinjiang, the Great Game still remains to be decided. Britain is gone from the region, but its successor, India, fought a border war with China in the 1960s that left a large bump of disputed territory on their borders. India shelters about 100,000 Tibetan refugees and their leader, the Dalai Lama, in Dharamsala, on the other side of the Himalayan border with Tibet.

Russia has been weakened and its empire truncated, but it is still a major power in Central Asia, with remnants of the Soviet Army intervening in civil wars and local political disputes, and politicians in Moscow clamoring for more such interventions.

Central Asia itself has entered this modern version of the Great Game. Its independent states on China's border offer both a model of self-rule for the Muslim minorities in China and sanctuary for exiles and others demanding independence from Beijing.

But these influences from abroad are slight compared to the inner strengths of the movements. Independence advocates in both Tibet and Xinjiang oppose the Chinese with tactics as peaceful as prayer or as violent as car and building bombings. There are similar differences in their level of organization, their support from abroad, their realistic chances of success, and their aims. Some would be content with greater self-rule under the Chinese; others seek nothing short of independent nationhood.

Predominantly agricultural societies, both Tibet and Xinjiang are disadvantaged under current central government economic policies that give an edge to industry at the expense of farmers. It is hard to measure how much this economic dissatisfaction has fueled political unrest, but throughout most of the 1980s, when peasants across China made great gains in living standards, political protest in both Tibet and Xinjiang was muted.

TIBET

The Tibetan plateau, at an average 16,000 feet the highest part of China, has a recorded history of independence that began in the seventh century, when King Songtsen Gampo pushed his state's borders deep into the interior of present-day China. The king married a Chinese princess; the Chinese say this put Tibet under Chinese suzerainty. The Tibetans, in turn, point to a treaty signed with the Chinese in 821 explicitly recognizing Tibet's independence. That treaty is commemorated in a stone monument outside the Jokhang Temple in Lhasa, but Chinese authorities have built a wall around it.

The Tibetans say that these two conflicting ancient claims aside, what matters now is recent history. There have been long periods in this century when China was too weak or too occupied with civil war and invasion to pay much attention to Tibet. There was a high degree of independence in the final years of the last imperial house, the Qings, and Beijing's authority practically ceased to exist under the Chinese Republic, between 1912 and 1949. The Communists restored control in 1951, then cracked down in the 1959 uprising that forced the Dalai Lama to flee.

Tibet, which now has a population of about 3 million, became one of China's five autonomous regions, a political device copied by the Chinese Communists from the Soviets to make it easier to rule minority peoples. In the case of Tibet, this means that Han Chinese hold the key posts and Tibetans mostly the ceremonial ones. The top job in Tibet, as it is in interior China, is the Communist Party leadership; it is held by a Han, Chen Kuiyuan, who came from another troubled minority area, Inner Mongolia. Although ethnic Tibetans are appointed to many government and local posts, the Communist Party keeps control by making sure that its Han Chinese representatives are well placed within the system.

Chinese officials say such controls are necessary to help progressive Tibetans modernize their country. Before its liberation, they say, Tibet was a feudal society, practicing serfdom, that had to be brought into the twentieth century. China tried cooperative approaches first, working with the Dalai Lama and other leaders, but eventually had to use firmer tactics. Serfs were freed, ignorance and superstition overcome.

Both sides agree that Tibet was an oddity in the modern world: a place where religion played a more dominant role in personal and societal life than any other. One in every six Tibetans was a Buddhist monk or nun; there were 10,000 monks in the Drepung Monastery alone. As much as a third of the national income was spent on religion. The monasteries, not surprisingly, supported the status quo and opposed attempts at domestic reforms and opening to the outside world.

But to the Tibetans, the cure imposed by the Chinese was worse than the disease. Modernization carried a high price: In its first phase in the 1950s, the monasteries were stripped of their centuries-old power, for good or ill, and leaders were arrested and executed. After a brief respite, the Cultural Revolution burst upon Tibet, with young Red Guards, both Han Chinese and Tibetan, in a frenzy of "Smashing the Four Olds"—old ideas, culture, customs, and habits.

Tibet had nearly 2,500 monasteries when the Dalai Lama fled in 1959, but only 10 were left functioning after two decades of war, occupation, and the Cultural Revolution. One of them was the Drepung. The world's largest monastery, it was simply too vast for the Red Guards to destroy, but it was badly damaged.

Deng's reformers brought peace and concessions to Tibet for a time, but in 1989 Tibet once again became a serious stain on China's record of minority rule. In Lhasa, panicked Chinese soldiers fired on nonviolent demonstrators and killed 200 people. That violence, and the repression that has followed, has damaged China's reputation abroad, particularly in the United States. Despite China's overwhelming armed and police power, Tibet's cause remains an issue that will not go away, for these reasons.

- China is fighting battles in Tibet that were won centuries ago against other groups, when it overcame the armies of strong nationalities such as the Dai in Yunnan Province or assimilated the Manchus, who had succeeded in occupying the imperial throne.

- Tibetans are unified, ethnically and religiously, and live inside well-defined borders.

- Tibetans are further united behind a temporal and spiritual leader, the Dalai Lama, who is based abroad and free to work for independence in meetings with the world's leaders and interest groups. He has widespread support in the United States and Western Europe. The U.S. government uses the level of religious freedom in Tibet as one of its measures of China's human rights performance.

The world has learned little of China's cautious reforms in Tibet, but it has seen or read about rioting, burning, shooting of demonstrators and of police, executions, and torture. The reaction abroad has been a steady stream of commission reports, human rights charges, and condemnations by the U.S. Congress and other legislatures.

China has responded by citing its efforts to modernize Tibet and by denying human rights violations, two tactics that find little acceptance in the West. At the same time, it has continued strengthening controls to stifle dissent. Columbia University specialist James Seymour says the county government used to be the lowest level of Communist Party penetration, but now even at the township level a Han Chinese or trusted ethnic Tibetan party official is in charge.

Occupation rule of any kind is difficult. Han Chinese functionaries face the double difficulty of ruling a very poor populace and being blamed that the poverty continues. In interior China, the economic reforms of the 1980s have produced measurable rises in living standards, along with increases in inflation and official corruption. Tibet seems to get the bad side effects but not enough of the benefits. Its economic growth has lagged, and despite the tax concessions minorities receive, many peasants are being forced off the land by the soaring costs of fertilizer and other needs and the reduced prices the state now pays for their crops. Besides inflation, Tibet shares with China the cheat-or-get-cheated mentality Seymour has found in the government as well as the marketplace. Aware that corruption is further sapping their authority, party leaders are campaigning against it in the press and posters, setting forth the plausible argument that it helps the independence movement: "If we let corruption go further, it will allow the splittists to benefit," one newspaper warned.

Economic as well as religious grievances seem to fuel the demonstrations and arrests that have been a recurring cycle in Tibet since Lhasa's first major outbreak in 1987. Human rights activists say there have been at least 150 demonstrations since then, in Lhasa and in the provinces, with 200 people killed, 3,000 arrested, and at least 367 still being held as political prisoners. The average age of those arrested is twenty-five; the average prisoner's term is six and one-half years. Three-fourths of the political prisoners are Buddhist nuns and monks; most of the rest are students and peasants.

Dissidents have found allies in the foreigners who make their way to Tibet despite Chinese government restrictions. Rules that require tourists to be in groups or stay in the few luxury hotels are easily skirted by young backpackers, and this group is likely to be sympathetic with the dissidents or even serve as couriers for material banned by the government, such as political statements by Tibetans in exile or even pictures of the Dalai Lama. The official press warns Tibetans against contacts with foreigners, who are accused of spying and carrying out "splittism." Despite this, other branches of the Chinese government are trying to get more foreign tourists to go to Tibet to help pay for the hotels built after the territory was opened to the outside world in the mid-1980s but under-utilized since the political resistance movement gained strength.

Since tourists are reluctant to visit monasteries guarded by the military checkpoints set up after the 1987 disturbances, the Chinese have removed them and concentrated control through the Democratic Management Committees (DMCs), groups of cooperative monks chosen to circumvent the traditional hierarchies. The DMCs not only administer the monasteries but also inform Chinese security about dissidents. Not all are willing tools of the Communists, dissidents report. Some DMC members have protected monks threatened with arrest and do their best to keep the monasteries independent.

Visitors have found that some monasteries are coming back to life, with Cultural Revolution damage repaired and large and lively classes of students. There are no longer thousands of monks, as in the old days, but hundreds or dozens, and many of them are young. Talking to students at a monastery outside Lhasa, we found them eager to take up their positions as monks and nuns, tolerant of the Han Chinese, open to the world and eager to find out more about it. But they know their future is limited. Their monastery, which had more than a thousand monks in 1950, was cut down to about 300 by 1987 and will be allowed only half that number under current government plans—not enough, in the view of the monks we talked to, to carry out all the functions of a monastery. Not only are the monks supposed to grow all their food and maintain and repair their ancient structures, but they must provide a combination of church and university to the religious population, counseling, holding services, and educating future monks in seminary studies that last as long as twenty years.

The structures these reduced numbers of monks will have to work in, however, are slowly being rebuilt, in part with local contributions, despite government efforts to discourage donations, in part with government aid that may be dispensed with an eye to tourism. In 1980 Hu Yaobang, the reformist general secretary of the Communist Party, visited Tibet and was shocked by the Red Guards' destruction. He announced the economic liberalization that has since ended the extremes of poverty in Tibet and also proclaimed a policy of more toleration for religious and nationalist sentiment. By 1985, 50 monasteries had been restored; we saw many others in various states of rebuilding. In 1989 China's delegation to the United Nations reported there were 234 functioning temples and monasteries, along with nearly 2,000 other religious centers.

China defends its seven centuries of rule in Tibet and says that the trouble there is caused by a handful of splittists. Foreign correspondents are not permitted into the territory to check firsthand, although some informative reports have come out of visits of academics and others who have gone to Tibet as tourists.

The authors were able to conduct extensive interviews with officials in Tibet, both Han Chinese and Tibetan, during a window of opportunity in 1985, when free travel was permitted and the protest movement was only beginning to gather its forces. Violence in those days was limited to a rock or two through the window of our Chinese government guest house. But in conversations with ordinary Tibetans, the extent of the discontent was palpable. The concessions granted by the liberals in Beijing were having the salutary effect of rebuilding monasteries and permitting more religious education. But as soon as they were reopening, the monasteries were resuming their traditional positions as political as well as religious centers.

The talk among the younger monks, nuns, and students was openly scornful of the Han officials, who reciprocated with racist stories about the backward Tibetans.

Above all, we found that the Cultural Revolution had left a legacy of distrust and suspicion far deeper than that in any other minority area we visited, and vastly different from the effects we were able to measure in the Han majority parts of the country. When Cultural Revolution stories are told in Interior China, they are about disgraced officials and humiliated intellectuals, and the occasional suicide at worst. In Tibet, the tales are of war waged on a largely defenseless population by an army of Red Guard invaders more ferocious than the PLA troops who preceded them, and fought on racial and religious grounds.

The aim of the campaign was to eradicate Buddhism and all its manifestations. Tibetan dress and hairstyles were banned. In rampages in the monasteries, scriptures were burned and precious stones stolen from statues. Thousands of monks and nuns were rounded up and sent to concentration camps; hundreds died through executions and suicides.

Tibetan monks we talked to spoke bitterly of these deaths and the destruction of religious property. In one poignant encounter in Lhasa, an elderly monk pointed to the scores of robes draped on the prayer cushions before a monastery altar. A small gathering of monks, mostly old but a few newly ordained, sat cross-legged in prayer. The robes, the old monk said, belonged to the monks killed during the Cultural Revolution.

Tibetans who had cooperated with the Chinese administration were mostly nonreligious and thus less affected by the Cultural Revolution. But they were open in their advocacy of more self-rule, along the lines of the proposal the Dalai Lama was to introduce in 1988 as a way out of his country's cycle of protest and repression.

Charges and countercharges about Tibet are so wildly at odds that it is hard to find the truth. A U.S. congressional resolution said in 1987 that "over one million Tibetans have perished since 1949" from repression and famine. The Chinese government says that, on the contrary, Tibet has *gained* a million in population since the

Dalai Lama left in 1959. Congress responds that the gain has been in Han Chinese in a plan to make the Tibetans a minority in their own country. Beijing says 95 percent of Tibet's population remains Tibetan, with only a few thousand Hans working there temporarily.

Tibetan nationalists say the Chinese have gutted the centuries-old monastery school system as a means of crippling Buddhism. Chinese officials say they have created a whole new school system. There were practically no schools before they came, and now there are 2,500. Nationalists say Tibetans got good religious education in the monasteries before 1950 and that the new schools are aimed at reducing the influence of the monasteries, which are now forbidden to accept children before their teens. Because of all the restrictions the Chinese impose, Tibetan nationalists say, a monastery education now is like a school "where there is no classroom, no teacher, and no books."

The final and most critical dispute is about sovereignty. The Chinese say their social engineering is the best hope for Tibet's modernization, and in any case it is their right to carry out—Tibet is a part of China, and has been so for centuries. Chinese officials say that in the modern era, there has never been an independent Tibet, and that to try to create one is like removing California or Alaska from the United States because it once belonged to other rulers. They do concede that an independence movement succeeded for a time after the 1911 collapse of Imperial China, but it was defeated, as was the Dalai Lama's 1959 uprising.

Tibet, the Chinese repeat, has been an unalienable part of China for more than 700 years, and is recognized as such by the United States, the United Nations, Britain, and even India, the headquarters of the 100,000 Tibetan exiles.

China stressed this claim in brusquely rejecting the 1988 plan of the Dalai Lama, who offered for the first time to renounce hopes for total independence in exchange for Tibetan self-government on all matters except defense and foreign policy. Acceptance of the plan would not have satisfied the extremists on either side—the Tibetans who want to see the last Han soldier go home, or the party officials in Beijing who fear that any concession to one minority group will open the way to demands by the other fifty-four.

But the Dalai Lama's plan would have given Tibet a large and welcome measure of internal autonomy without endangering ultimate Chinese sovereignty or reopening the Himalayan power game with India, Russia, or any other nation. It would, in short, have been the application of the one-country/two-systems plan to a third region after Hong Kong and Taiwan. If carried out successfully, it might have constituted an encouraging example to Taiwanese weighing the risks of reuniting with the mainland but keeping their distinct society.

China now seems set on a course of limited religious freedoms for Tibet and tight security controls to keep religion from spilling into politics. From a distance, it seems a reasonable centrist policy, one that favors neither the party zealots who want to root out Buddhism nor the independence advocates. But up close, it must be seen as a failure. The thousands of protesters in Tibet who brave some of the toughest security measures in the world to take to the streets are a sign as reliable as that of Tiananmen Square: If all were well in Tibet, there would be no reason for so many people to risk liberty and life.

XINJIANG

Parts of present-day Xinjiang were conquered by China as early as 76 B.C. as outposts on the Silk Road to Persia and Europe. Its majority population is made up of Uighurs, a Turkic people whose language is distantly related to modern Turkish and whose religion is Sunni Muslim. Independent Central Asian kingdoms, some allied to Imperial China and some in opposition, rose and fell until the Chinese captured the region in 1759. After that, Xinjiang remained under Chinese rule, although like Tibet, it frequently used the turbulence in interior China for its own ends. A Muslim warlord ruled briefly in the 1930s; a Republic of East Turkestan was proclaimed in the 1940s and subdued by the Communists in the 1950s. Older Xinjiang residents still recall the republic. Those not very old can recall the Chinese military occupation that crushed the republic and then the ravages of the Cultural Revolution, when the two mainstays of the Xinjiang way of life, religion and trade, were targeted as counterrevolutionary.

As in Tibet, Deng Xiaoping's reformers tried to make amends, permitting the construction and repair of mosques in Xinjiang's villages and cities. Religion was not promoted by the state but certainly not hindered; mullahs became respected leaders again, and it was again possible to follow the dietary and other strictures of Islam. The most popular part of the reforms of the 1980s in Xinjiang was the economic. The bazaars, centers of both social and business life in Central Asia, were allowed to flourish again. Beijing seemed to have found a workable formula for governing Xinjiang: giving the local population the freedom to make money, and getting in exchange its acquiescence to Communist Party rule, whether the leaders were Han Chinese or Uighur.

But since 1989 the formula has failed to keep the peace. The territory has been convulsed by nationalist protest demonstrations and bombings with considerable loss of life. China's response—stronger security and a series of warnings that might seem to strengthen nationalist resolve—has been ineffective. Song Hanliang, the Communist Party secretary of the Xinjiang Uighur Autonomous Region, has warned that "nationalist separatism poses a threat to Xinjiang's stability," which is exactly what the nationalists are aiming for. Ismail Amat, Beijing's minister for nationalities affairs, said on a tour of Xinjiang that "stability is a central task that overrides everything else." He rejected nationalists' attacks and demonstrations as "the attempt by a handful of bad elements to split the mainland and undermine political stability and unity."

Domestic and foreign factors combined to change Xinjiang from a placid outpost of Chinese rule to another Tibet. Officials may blame outside agitators for the trouble, but they stress in their statements that Xinjiang's economy needs to be brought up to the levels of the rest of the country, too. Xinjiang, like Tibet, shares the economic malaise of the rest of China's rural regions, where incomes, after a sharp rise when Deng's reforms took hold in the 1980s, have failed to keep up with the industry-driven economies of the coast and river valleys.

Resentment is directed against those in power. Often incidents are set off by a publication considered offensive to Islam; since China controls all media, its officials must take the blame. But sometimes the protests are more direct. A Uighur scientist described three bombings aimed at the same Chinese official, a man blamed for encouraging immigration of Han Chinese to Xinjiang and thus diluting the Central Asian proportion of the population. "It's simply terrorism," he said, condemning the violence but not the motive.

Columbia's Seymour, who regularly visits both Xinjiang and Tibet, says anti-Chinese protests in Xinjiang have become more violent because the Uighurs have no leader abroad like the Dalai Lama to restrain them. But Xinjiang is also influenced by many developments abroad that affect its nationalists more than those of Tibet.

Tibet's ties abroad are easy to diagram: in its favor, a large emigré population and a revered leader, effective and widespread public relations and lobbying in the West; against it, the fact that no foreign government, no matter how sympathetic, questions the legality of Chinese rule over Tibet.

Xinjiang's situation is far more complex. Its cause gets little attention outside its borders, with the important exception of the Central Asian states that broke away from Russian rule in 1991. Three of these states, Tajikistan, Kazhakstan, and Kyrgyzstan, border China, and the latter two have seen remarkable growth of trade and contacts between ordinary citizens as well as Chinese diplomats and officials. This has changed the static situation in Xinjiang in several ways.

The Central Asian republics serve as a model of what an independent Muslim republic carved out of a larger empire could be— for good and ill. On the one hand, there are the 6,000 mosques built in the Central Asian republics (those bordering China plus Uzbekistan) since the collapse of the Soviet Union and the image of governments that have achieved a greater or lesser degree of independence from the distant imperial capital. On the other hand, they are part of the chaos that followed imperial rule, with 20,000 dead in Tajikistan's civil war and the victorious faction again dependent on Moscow. The new republics also share the economic misery that has befallen Moscow and its former dependencies. Independence thus both attracts and discourages the Xinjiang nationalists.

The Central Asian republics have connections across the Chinese frontier that can help or hinder independence moves in Xinjiang. In the first category are the Uighur separatist movements, which hold independence rallies in Kyrgyzstan and Kazhakstan and are suspected of aiding the protests inside Xinjiang. Chinese diplomats moved quickly to put pressure on the Central Asian governments to restrict these independence movements after rallies in Biskek and Almaty demanding a "free Uighuristan" on Xinjiang territory, according to a Western analyst.

But an equally strong movement is the desire of the Central Asian governments to seek the support and friendship of China—as a counterweight against Russia, or simply for furtherance of national interests in trade and diplomacy. There was little trade in the Soviet era, but now entrepreneurs from Xinjiang are a common sight in Central Asia's bazaars, and more ambitious deals for Chinese industrial products and Central Asia's minerals are being discussed.

"Our countries are small and can do little to influence China," a Central Asian diplomat said. "But we can benefit greatly from friendly relations with China."

The Central Asian states are far more worried about a resurgent Russia than they are about supporting Uighur nationalists inside and across their borders. Uighurs represent a small part of their population, so they are under no real pressure to risk provoking China to come to their aid. They are also not very sanguine about the chances of the movement's succeeding in Xinjiang because of the overwhelming force China can summon to contain it.

In conversations with Central Asian diplomats and Western specialists on the region, a far greater concern about Russia emerges. The threats of nationalists such as Vladimir Zhirinovsky and the use of former Soviet troops to turn the tide in the Tajik civil war have made it clear to Central Asian leaders that their continued independence cannot be taken for granted. Although there would be little prospect of China's coming to their aid against the Russians, they think that friendly ties with a neighbor that has 3 million men under arms is not a bad idea. If Uighur nationalists have to be abandoned to maintain Chinese friendship, this might seem like an easy choice.

A new round of the Great Game might be in prospect, with China protecting its status in Xinjiang by supporting Central Asian states' independence against a Russian threat. The United States' role in such a game would be unclear. Although both the administration and Congress have opposed China for years on its repressions in Tibet, they have said little about Xinjiang. U.S. Uighur-language broadcasts to the region were stopped after the rapprochement between the United States and China in the 1970s. Nationalists listen instead to the Uzbek-language broadcasts beamed to the former Soviet side of the border, most of which Uighur speakers can understand.

Three possibilities seem likely for Tibet and Xinjiang in the years ahead, unless there is a sudden surge in independence demands, perhaps brought on by some unexpected incident in either territory.

The first is continuance of the present policy of limited religious freedom and a strong security presence. Under this policy, officials would permit enough monasteries to be rebuilt in Tibet and mosques to be constructed in Xinjiang to satisfy local critics and keep their complaints about restrictions on religion from intruding into politics. The security apparatus provides backup for this policy, censoring speeches and written independence appeals, containing or breaking up demonstrations, and arresting and imprisoning dissidents.

This policy can work, however, only if there is continued stability at the center in the succession process after Deng's death. Russia's Central Asian colonies took advantage of factional fighting in Moscow to declare their independence; officials of those nations are frank in admitting it never could have happened otherwise. The nationalists in Xinjiang and Tibet are waiting for a similar situation to arise in Beijing. In this, the second possibility for the future, the two territories would simply leave China and be secure in the knowledge that Beijing's leaders and troops would be too divided and preoccupied to prevent their secession.

Many would rather push along the process of disintegration, the third possible course. If independence movements in Tibet and Xinjiang grow strong enough, this in itself might cause the dissension in the leadership ranks in the capital, and Beijing might find it easier to grant the dissidents their wishes for greater autonomy, or even independence.

TEN

CHINA AFTER DENG

Private plots are no longer regarded as tails [of capitalism]
The news now tells the truth
We can travel the whole country without grain coupons
Ownership enterprises support more than 100 million
Intellectuals don't worry about making self-criticism
The special economic zones have become China's new models
How are you, Xiaoping? Good?
I know that history will tell us the same thing.

— Rock-and-roll song "Xiaoping, How Are
You?" popular in South China

DENG XIAOPING'S LEGACY

Deng Xiaoping did more for China than any other modern leader.
Mao Zedong united the country, at great cost, but Deng brought it
into the modern world by freeing the individual talents and ambitions that Mao had stifled and by creating a thriving economy.

But Deng failed to provide the political freedoms China expected
with economic modernization. After initial encouragement of
democracy, he became one of its greatest adversaries.

By combining relative prosperity with authoritarian rule, however, Deng accomplished something the Communist leaders of Russia and Eastern Europe failed to do: He saved communism in the last important nation under party rule.

Many Chinese don't see this as an accomplishment. They think a modern economy needs a modern political system. But, as the song that blasts from compact disc players in boomtowns in Guangdong Province shows, Deng's reforms are enormously popular among ordinary working people and peasants.

Many millions of them have been freed from poverty in the twenty years between 1970 and 1990, almost all because of the reforms introduced by the Deng team. In that period, China's poverty rate fell from 33 to 10 percent of the population, the World Bank says, raising the possibility for the first time that such a large developing country will be able to emerge from poverty largely through its own resources.

If Deng saved communism in the process, many Chinese accept that as a lesser evil. After all, they had a communism based on poverty for the first thirty years of the People's Republic, and they certainly see the advantages of a communism shored up by relative prosperity. Is it now time for the next step, a system not only without poverty, but without Communists? No one is able to take opinion polls to see how many Chinese agree with the dissidents who advocate this further step. But in conversations with the authors, some Chinese have echoed the warnings of their government that demands for democracy will lead to chaos.

Democracy advocates respond that China's recent history shows that chaos has been caused by a Communist Party resistant to democratic pressure or control, not from the pressure or control itself. They are referring to the Cultural Revolution, when Mao's leading lieutenants "committed many crimes behind his back, bringing disaster to the country and the people."

These words are not those of the dissidents but of a party commission convened in 1981 to assess the damage of the Cultural Revolution. The commission found it to be "the most severe setback and the heaviest losses suffered by the party, the state, and the people since the founding of the People's Republic."

Such a political disaster gave the new or rehabilitated party leaders, Deng's forces, unparalleled strength against those factions that could be blamed for Cultural Revolution. But to their credit, the reformers used their advantage not only to win internal party struggles, but also to launch the bold and unprecedented plan of economic reform that began to unfold in the 1980s. The misery and chaos of the previous decade was such a weight on the party's standing in society that they thought only dramatic improvements in ordinary people's lives could save communism, even if they had to borrow from capitalism to do it.

The role of Deng and his key leaders, along with the thousands of other liberal officials at the national, local, and provincial levels who wanted to break with the past, was to lift the restrictions communism had wrapped around the economy at every level, from the farmer's roadside stand to the international trading companies. Once that was done, China's workforce—peasants, workers, and intellectuals—stepped out of the party propaganda posters and began to transform the economy through their individual efforts. The sum of these efforts gave China a level of prosperity unheard of under previous regimes.

The pragmatists of Beijing borrowed only part of the Western system, the features that reward the hard work and individual enterprise of their people. They did their best to ignore the other part of the system, the political freedoms, not trusting their constituents with such power. Deng dismissed his two closest lieutenants, Hu Yaobang and Zhou Ziyang, after the political liberalization they had encouraged appeared to be threatening the party's grip. Their replacements, Jiang Zemin and Li Peng, are rigid and dull, but safe. The most attractive leader in the post-Deng lineup is Deputy Prime Minister Zhu Rongji, who has managed the remarkable economic surge of the 1990s. Zhu's brain trust of young Chinese university economics graduates reminds Chinese of the teams Zhao and Hu assembled to extend the reforms into the political sphere. But no such talk emerges now from Zhu's two domains, the Bank of China and the State Council. His teams keep their focus on the economy.

Since Tiananmen Square, "liberal" has become an economic rather than a political term when used to describe factions in the Communist Party of China. Despite the party's professed belief in the virtues of struggle, it has never provided for struggle within the political sphere or approved any public process to accommodate genuine conflicts of views. The reform-minded members of the Chinese Communist Party are bent on pursuing more liberal economic policies than the conservative group that wants to retain central planning and vigorously opposes modernization. The liberals, however, have never suggested sharing power with another political party, any more than have the party stalwarts.

Can this selective approach to modernization work? History shows that it can, for a while, as it had been doing in Taiwan, and did in Spain and other dictatorships that managed to silence dissent while keeping living standards rising.

But people in Taiwan, Spain, and other countries got tired of selective freedoms in their own lives. They were able to exercise complete decision-making powers in their investment companies or computer research laboratories, but then were told which slate of party mediocrities they had to vote for. Worse, they knew that trying to use the same pragmatism in politics that had made them successful in business or the professions could land them in prison.

When these contradictions between their economic freedoms and their lack of political ones got to be too great, they changed the system, helped by the diminished authority of regimes that had weakened their control by the very economic progress they had promoted.

Deng's successors, too, must face the likelihood that the more successful the economic reforms in China, the more inevitable the political changes. "By initiating economic reform . . . Deng Xiaoping unleashed powerful centrifugal forces that threaten to overwhelm the Communist party-state he sought to preserve," David Shambaugh, editor of *The China Quarterly* of London, has written. "Deng studied the East Asian developmental model carefully, but learned incomplete lessons. He did not, or refused to, recognize the inevitable political pressures that well up from below as a result of economic growth and wealth accumulation."

What is not certain is the form change will take—whether it will come from above or below, and whether it will be violent or peaceful.

Part of the Chinese nation, Taiwan, has already begun to broaden democracy, under a combination of increased pressure from the citizenry and concessions from the leadership. Mainland Chinese have ringside seats to this political metamorphosis through their television sets.

China halted all attempts at political reform after its tanks crushed the democracy movement of 1989, but it cannot stop the process forever. Will change in the People's Republic come from the rulers or the ruled?

POLITICAL REFORM

In the first years of reform, talk of political democracy was so much in the air that it seemed only a matter of time before changes in the political sphere would follow the economic ones. Democracy walls, where citizens could set out their ideas in hand-lettered posters, bloomed in China's cities, and Deng himself extolled democracy in 1980 as a way to "promote the smooth development of our modernization drive" and solve the problem of leadership succession.

But that same year Deng also banned democracy walls and imprisoned the leading advocates of democracy. Wei Jingsheng was given a fifteen-year sentence for using the temporary right to free speech to call Deng a dictator. Wei was lectured at his trial that he was free to believe or not believe in the Communist system, but by *opposing* it, he had broken the law. From that point on, Deng made it clear that democracy was fine, as long as it did not question Communist Party authority.

Nevertheless, the voices for democracy, more muted, continued up until their final tragic crescendo at Tiananmen Square. They were not from the democracy walls or the streets but from the think tanks and government departments set up by the reformers themselves, including the Chinese Academy of Social Sciences and the young academic associates of Bao Tong, a leading aide to Zhao Ziyang.

Terms such as "pluralism" and "grassroots involvement" rolled out of those shops regularly. "How can a party in power be prevented from committing mistakes and shortcomings in the policies it adopts?" a political scientist at the social sciences academy wrote in a typical contribution. "It is also necessary to have some kind of supervision of the ruling party itself. As long as there is no democracy in government we may scream and struggle as much as we want to but it will all be to no avail."

In our conversations in China in 1984–1985 and 1987, academics, officials, and businesspeople spoke freely of the coming political liberalization. It was considered as normal as any other aspects of reform in the 1980s that democratic change would accompany the modernization of the economy.

Tiananmen stopped that. Talk of and hopes for democracy died. Zhao's lieutenant Bao Tong was sentenced to seven years in prison, becoming the highest former official caught in the crackdown against student activists and others in the democracy movement. Everything that the leaders, whether hard-liners or moderates, have said since then shows their great worries about chaos, brought on by "a rebellious clique," as Deng called the democracy movement, one that wants "to establish a totally Western-dependent bourgeois republic." This change shows the impact of the student uprising on party thinking. Hu and Zhou, although products of the communist system, could see the benefits of modernization in both political and economic spheres. But instead of a distant goal, democracy became a threat.

Deng's bold reforms have been confined to the economy. Even when pushing for market forces and pragmatism toward foreign investment, he has warned consistently about the pernicious influence of democratic ideas.

THE IMPERIAL PAST

"When we speak of democracy, we can adopt neither bourgeois democracy nor the tripartite division of governmental power," Deng has said. "I have repeatedly criticized the rulers in the U.S.A., telling them that in reality they had three governments."

China has never had these three governments, and its lack of experience in the checks and balances of a legislature and independent judiciary is as good an explanation as any for its backwardness. Most nations had to wait longer than the United States for democratic institutions, but by the early twentieth century, even the Russian czar was sharing rule with a parliament. In England, liberals were setting up health insurance and old-age pensions; in America, monopolies were being restricted; in France, church and state separated—all by parliaments.

In China, until the last dynasty sank of its own ineptitude in 1912, the country was ruled by a small boy with nine titles, the least of which was Lord of Ten Thousand Years. Instead of a parliament, the emperor had hundreds of courtiers and priests so tangled in ancient superstitions and traditions that their ranks included "miracle workers," men whose job it was to make offerings to ward off floods or drought.

Dr. Frank Goodnow of Columbia University, who had been brought to China to help draft a new republican constitution after the collapse of imperial rule, was disappointed when early moves toward democracy faltered, but he could understand how a nation just emerging from feudalism could be overwhelmed when suddenly confronted with the modern world.

"No wonder the Chinese were dazed," he wrote after his return from China. "For a time they stood stupefied like men awakened from a sound sleep. Accustomed during their millenniums of existence to autocracy, they were expected in a few years to organize a republic. With no experience in popular elections, or indeed in any kind of elections, they were obliged to [elect] a legislature [to] legislate for a people with little knowledge of and no respect for the written law.

"Is it to be wondered at that under these conditions they have become the prey of a military despotism?"

Military and party despotism, it turned out, was to be China's future. While most of the rest of the world is turning anew to democracy, China has many of the same conditions Goodnow criticized in 1913: a parliament with no real power, an executive unresponsive to the will of the people, a constitution that gets changed every time there is a new policy line from the Communist Party.

Goodnow's advice was rejected by both Nationalists and Communists. But his basic ideas—that China needs a firm foundation of democracy and the rule of law if it is to take its rightful place among modern nations—are discussed more and more among intellectuals. Wei Jingsheng's demand that China needs a Fifth Modernization, democracy, to accompany the reforms in the economy can now be heard, in less strident form, in university seminars and among some legislators. Many Chinese intellectuals would agree with Goodnow's conclusion: "The choice must be made between what is in the long run probably the worst form of government which a country can have, namely a military dictatorship with no fixed rule of succession except that of force, and on the other hand some sort of parliamentary government."

But isn't this forcing Western ideas on ancient China? Not if one goes back far enough in ancient China, more than 2,000 years, and reads what Han Fei, the leading philosopher of the Legalist movement, the modernizers of their day, wrote. Without "public or just law," nations cannot be ruled equitably, Han Fei wrote, acknowledging that although people cannot be expected to be good, laws could make it impossible for them to be bad. There must be "an inviolable law which should apply to both the ruler and the ruled alike," he wrote. "Wherever the law applies, the clever will submit and the powerful will not protest; the nobility will not be exempted from punishment and rewards will not go over the heads of the humble."

For those who say China isn't ready for democracy, or that Asians can't be expected to behave like Westerners, Columbia political scientist Andrew Nathan cites "the relative success of pluralism in other countries with approximately China's level of development, such as India; or . . . the apparent compatibility of robust political rights and freedoms with political stability and economic growth in other settings with Confucian cultural traditions, such as twentieth-century Japan and even, to some extent, contemporary Taiwan."

A PARTY DIVIDED

Deng also leaves a legacy of a party divided, as did Mao and other rulers back to imperial times. China's internal struggles used to be just that, domestic quarrels, but now they involve the world—when a hard-line faction provokes the United States over human rights or a new round of repression causes a new round of emigration.

China's neighbors must reckon with a militarily powerful China, with its core the 3-million member People's Liberation Army (PLA), the largest in the world. Although recent budgets have recognized the great need for more spending on education and agriculture, the PLA has always been given precedence in the allocation of tax money, at great cost to the country's progress. Officials defended the last 20 percent increase in PLA spending as only keeping pace with inflation. A few cautious critics have pointed out that much of the nation's infrastructure—railways, irrigation projects, and power plants—is woefully inadequate, and ought to get some of the funding reserved for the military. Every nation, from the Soviet Union to the United States, has sacrificed much-needed national programs to buy military weapons, to their regret. China is no exception. The difference is that with a strong military and a vulnerable leadership, critics of military spending have little chance to be heard.

As the Soviet Union also discovered, having a huge army doesn't guarantee superpower status. China, with a fifth of the world's population, qualifies as a superpower in sheer size. Because of changes in World Bank accounting, allowing for the buying power of a nation's wealth rather than its value converted to dollars, China has leaped to third place, behind the United States and Japan, in reckonings of economic strength. Outside the military and economic spheres, it has much to offer its smaller neighbors in Asia as well as the rest of the world in science and culture.

But there are many obstacles to superpower status, even for the world's most populous nation. All have been examined in this book—population pressures, inflation and corruption and the protests against them in cities and rural areas, lack of legal and regulatory institutions, and, above all, the absence of checks on the absolute power of the party. Outsiders, impressed with China's growing economic power, its potential consumer markets, and its sheer size, may be overenthusiastic about its future. They may be overlooking domestic problems that could slow progress or dissolve into political conflict and chaos.

THE SUCCESSION

China after Deng will be an important nation worthy of the world's concern no matter what policies his successors follow. Several divergent paths seem possible in the succession process.

A Chinese analyst said that the military is certain to play a role in the succession, probably not in taking power directly, but in deciding who does. No one in power can match the military stature of Deng Xiaoping, a veteran of the Long March and countless civil war campaigns, but Jiang Zemin has spent the last few years courting the military, visiting remote bases, and congratulating border guards, apparently to make up for his lack of military background. Zhu Rongji, with a background in the economy and government (he, like Jiang, is a former mayor of Shanghai) is not thought to have links with military people powerful enough to be of any help to him in a power struggle.

The Communist Party apparatus is still considered very powerful, even though there is talk of its having lost its grip compared to what it was a decade or fifteen years ago. The new freedom in society as a whole brought on by the economic reforms has weakened the party's day-to-day controls over ordinary people. But as a jailed dissident noted bitterly, when the party is challenged, as it was in the wake of Tiananmen Square, its fear of losing power pushes aside its normal torpor and sloppiness and turns it into an efficient political weapon.

Party and military jockeying for power in Beijing and other parts of interior China could weaken controls on the periphery, on the model of the Soviet Union and Eastern Europe. "Tibet, certainly; Xinjiang, probably" is how the analyst puts the chances of an attempted breakaway. The governors of China's wealthy coastal provinces have repeatedly performed like economic warlords, steering their own way to prosperity, ignoring the central government's attempts to make them pay a greater share of taxes or control inflationary investment. They might welcome the opportunity to break away from the poor inland provinces that are a drag on the national budget and resources and escape the new tax laws designed to redistribute money from rich provinces to the poorer regions. But the analyst doubts that a crisis would lead to a clear rich-poor division in China, with prosperous provinces allying themselves to Hong Kong. The well-off areas, he said, have already achieved enough autonomy from Beijing's fiscal controls to content them for some time.

What kind of a future regime would satisfy the militarists and the party hierarchy, hold down dissent, but allow breathing room for ideas? China's detached province across the Formosa Strait provides a working model. Taiwanese-style democracy, not Western, seems the likeliest next step in China's liberalization.

Intellectuals on the mainland describe a path to democracy that may take as long as forty years and be economy-driven, not human rights–, pluralist-, or civic society–driven. In a sense, they are saying that the mainland is in the stage Taiwan was forty years ago and may have to go through the same kind of tug-of-war between authoritarian rule and democratic hopes. As such, there will be many disappointing stages for those who want more direct steps to democracy. But Taiwan could point the direction.

If the mainland is to follow the Taiwanese recipe, the first ingredient, a growing economy, is already in place, but the second, a viable opposition party, will be difficult to manage. Taiwan's Democratic Progressive Party emerged only after martial law on the island was relaxed, then lifted. But that took three decades. Mainland China's equivalent of martial law is the constitutional guarantee of the dominant role of the Communist Party. But as the ruling Kuomintang Party on Taiwan demonstrated, internal factions inevitably form, split, and, if conditions are right, turn into an opposition.

Beijing's economic policies have had the same effect as Taiwan's did decades ago: They have created a growing middle class of merchants, entrepreneurs, and self-employed who work, plan, and think for themselves and are less apt to accept meekly party dogma and edicts. Television from satellites and the economic opening to the world have reacquainted them with Western ideas, culture, and democracy.

The pragmatism and flexibility Beijing has shown in the past to further economic reforms might be stretched to encompass limited political liberalization. If the pressure from below or within the party is strong enough, the post-Deng leaders may see the writing on the wall and find a face-saving but satisfactory way to allow diverse voices to chart the future, using those most Chinese of desired Chinese characteristics—harmony, stability, and unity.

That, at least, is what those intellectuals still willing to give the Communists a chance advocate. Still pained by the bloodshed at Tiananmen Square and the confrontations and demonstrations that led up to it, they say that diversity can best be promoted by patience and compromise.

But courage is also needed. The loyal counselor who dares differ with the leader is as much a part of Chinese tradition as is the striving for harmony, stability, and unity. Such a man is Xu Liangying, a 74-year old historian at the Academy of Sciences in Beijing. Xu and six other intellectuals boldly mailed a petition to President Jiang at a time when the authorities were arresting dissidents to prevent their meeting with U.S. secretary of state Warren Christopher. Xu himself was later detained under house arrest for his actions.

"We appeal to the authorities to bravely end our country's history of punishing people for their ideas, speech and writing, and release all those imprisoned because of their ideas and speech," the petition said.

"People of insight, who are concerned with the fate of the nation and who are dedicated to our country's modernization, feel shocked and at the same time upset and worried. To talk about modernization without mentioning human rights is like climbing a tree to catch a fish."

INDEX